RETRO BALL PARKS

RETRO BALL PARKS

Instant History, Baseball, and the New American City

By Daniel Rosensweig

SPORT AND POPULAR CULTURE

S. W. Pope, *Series Editor*

THE UNIVERSITY OF TENNESSEE PRESS / KNOXVILLE

The Sport and Popular Culture series is designed to promote critical innovative research through a wide spectrum of works—monographs, edited volumes, biographies, and reprints of classics.

Copyright © 2005 by The University of Tennessee Press / Knoxville. All Rights Reserved. Manufactured in the United States of America. First Edition.

This book is printed on acid-free paper.

Library of Congress Cataloging-in-Publication Data

Rosensweig, Daniel, 1966–
Retro ball parks : instant history, baseball, and the new American city / Daniel Rosensweig.— 1st ed.
    p. cm. — (Sport and popular culture)
Includes bibliographical references and index.

ISBN 1-57233-351-0 (hardcover : alk. paper)

1. Baseball fields—Social aspects—United States.
2. Baseball—United States—Psychological aspects.
3. City and town life—United States.
4. Popular culture—United States.
 I. Title.
II. Series.
GV879.5.R69 2005
306.4'83—dc22   2004010584

For my parents,
Marjorie and Charles Rosensweig

CONTENTS

ILLUSTRATIONS

PREFACE

This book examines the cultural and economic role of retro ball parks in the contemporary American city. Since 1992, when the first of these new old stadiums—Baltimore's Oriole Park at Camden Yards—opened its gates, they have come to be seen as vital components of downtown redevelopment. As of 2004, fourteen new downtown major league parks at least partially outfitted with accents of the past have been placed in operation (in Baltimore, Cleveland, Denver, Detroit, Seattle, Pittsburgh, Milwaukee, Arizona, San Francisco, Philadelphia, Cincinnati, Houston, San Diego, and Arlington, Texas). In the early years of the twenty-first century, as a new urbanist ethos has achieved significant traction in American culture, people who fled the city beginning in the middle part of the last century have been looking back nostalgically to urban life as a way to reconstitute the real or the authentic. Retro baseball stadiums have emerged to provide them, their children, and their grandchildren comfortable, convenient, and often controversial access to the old city.

I conducted the majority of my research in Cleveland, where decades of factory closings, race riots, and suburban flight had left its center city in need of a significant reinvention. Out of the rubble, Jacobs Field, the sterling new home of the Cleveland Indians, has surfaced as the anchor of the Gateway Developmental District. The Gateway serves as a fascinating case study in the cultural shifts enacted by the transformation of a city's economic base from local commerce and manufacturing to recreational tourism. As such, the evolution of downtown Cleveland is relevant to many cities contemplating a similar type of spatial reconstitution as the centerpiece of downtown redevelopment.

Thanks are in order to a number of people who contributed to this project. In Cleveland, my friend and colleague John Kunat walked around with me, talking to local officials, sports fans, activists, and others intimately involved with the area's transformation. Bob Dibiasio, the Indians' vice president for public relations, gave of his time generously and was extremely forthcoming about details related to the construction and operation of Jacobs Field. Local journalist Roldo Bartimole, in many ways Dibiasio's foil, was equally candid in expressing his concern about the propriety of the financial deals required to make "the Jake" a reality. At the stadium itself, longtime bleacher fan John Adams and the man often referred to as the "Mayor of Jacobs Field," Craig Mahovlic, introduced me to regulars and shared their fascinating accounts of the past forty years of Cleveland and Indians history.

Eric Lott advised me and inspired me with his own work on race and culture. Steve Arata, Kelly Cresap, David Herman, Jeremy Howell, Frannie Nudelman, Robert Rinehart, Marge Rosensweig, Kenny Marotta, and G. Edward (Ted) White each read the original manuscript at some point in the process and helped me chart a course for further research. Steven Pope, the editor of this book series, revivified the project after it had been languishing on my shelf for a while. He encouraged me to update it for publication after a couple of years of dormancy. In the latter stages of writing, Scot Danforth of the University of Tennessee Press helped immensely with suggestions for photographs and final revisions, and technical wizard David Holton rescued the book's pictures after a formatting glitch threatened to render them unusable. Finally, over the course of several years, my wife Julie Jones has encouraged me to forge ahead even as it meant sacrificing vacation time for days spent conducting interviews or toiling in front of the computer. Without her love, support, intelligence, and creativity, I could not have completed this project.

INTRODUCTION

CHEAP GRACE

As a child, I was a passionate Baltimore Orioles fan. Growing up in the Maryland suburbs, I would punctuate long summer days of front-yard baseball or soccer by flicking on the local station to catch the inevitable late-game heroics of my beloved "Birds." Back then, in the early to mid-1970s, baseball's blue-collar team, lead by crafty manager Earl Weaver and his flock of homespun overachievers (Boog Powell, Paul Blair, Mark Belanger et al.), always seemed to be able to pull a fast one on their more highly paid opponents. Their "Orioles' Way" combined a deep farm system with organizational endurance and managerial moxie. This unique blend routinely enabled the workaday Birds, baseball's model small-market franchise, to find a way to best the free-spending yet undisciplined Yankees and Baltimore's other more glamorous American League East rivals.

But my connection with the underdog Orioles was stronger than simple fandom. As is the case with many children, identification with a sports team helped me shape my own identity. Even though I grew up in an upper-middle-class suburban Washington neighborhood, I believed myself to be spiritually linked to both the Orioles and the blue-collar town they represented. While around me the Maryland suburbs were becoming more upscale—consumer paradises where suddenly one could buy brie cheese and Scandinavian furniture—my notion of Baltimore as a final refuge of authenticity, and thus of myself as authentic and real, remained tied up with the images and sounds on the television screen showing Orioles games. In those days, former Oriole great Brooks Robinson, who had stayed with the organization as a color commentator, would supplement low-budget UHF broadcasts by reading the corny pitches of local sponsors Ball Park Franks ("They plump when you cook 'em") and National Bohemian Beer ("Natty Boh: Oh boy, what a beer"). "Forget Heineken and fancy meals," I reasoned, "cheap beer and dogs are good enough for me." It was as if these consumer choices, like my love of baseball's hardest working team, could somehow endow me with a kind of reverse class status.[1]

My occasional trips to cavernous, concrete Memorial Stadium to see the team play live helped reinforce this status—in my own mind at least. Over time, because the stadium was tucked inside a densely populated neighborhood, with scanty parking and poorly marked streets, I was able to develop an insider's knowledge, helping me make the best of the experience. Even before I was old enough to drive, I gained great pleasure from guiding my father and other older chaperones through the many shortcuts en route to the park. Once in the vicinity of the stadium, I led my entourage to hidden parking spaces, found the cheapest scalped tickets, and uncovered the lowest prices on concessions and baseball paraphernalia from the many unauthorized and renegade local vendors and scalpers who set up shop just off the beaten track.

Within the gate of the park, this sense of being on the inside only intensified. I directed my gang to the sections with the most lax ushers, allowing us to sneak into practically any seats we chose; I exchanged friendly banter with the other regulars; I showed off to my friends by reliably predicting the seemingly eccentric moves of Manager Weaver. I was just like the Orioles, I told myself, just like the ball club, which year after year assembled a collection of journeymen and budget-priced castoffs into a regular contender. Instead of undervalued players, however, I took objects that few coveted (below-face-value resold tickets, etc.) and used them to form a priceless experience.

I have come to see this brand of what John Fiske calls "productive pleasures," or the generation of meanings somehow in opposition to authorized prescriptions for one's experience, as a curious fantasy (49). Thinking myself both on the inside as well as more *Baltimore* than *Washington* to a large degree helped me come to grips with my discomfort over the isolating qualities of an economically privileged life. Although I grew up surrounded by green space, in a safe neighborhood in affluent Montgomery County, Maryland, with big lawns and well-funded public schools, I still had waking fantasies of living in the gritty and real streets of Baltimore row houses. From an early age, I dreamed of moving to the city, where community life unfolded on vibrant street corners, where I could mix with folks from widely disparate backgrounds, where I might be able to share with my neighbors a sense of class, ethnic, or racial solidarity ignored in the upper-middle-class suburbs.

Of course, this fantasy is at least in part a product of a peculiar hegemonic conceit. It involves the tendency to fetishize the experience of poor people, to see a lack of material sustenance as somehow generative of authenticity. I have come to understand that this way of looking at the world both denies someone from the middle class (like myself) the possibility of heightened experience and undermines the rationale for eradicating poverty. If marginal material circumstances indeed stimulate creativity, energy, and connection to community, it does not make sense to work toward the elimination of these conditions. Nonetheless, looking back on those days, I realize how the longing I negotiated through my identification with the Birds and Baltimore motivated me to undertake this project. In large part, I began my research of stadium culture out of a desire to understand some of the implications of the pressure I felt to be simultaneously outside and inside, part of an oppositional community.

I also began this project trying to come to grips with conflicting feelings I experienced after spending a few years watching the Orioles in their new home, Oriole Park at Camden Yards. I still vividly remember the thrill I felt when, on a midseason day in 1988, the ball club announced that it would soon be moving into a venue that seemed to me at the time to fit the organization to a tee. Touted as the first "retro" park in the majors, incorporating architectural elements of the game's and the city's past, Camden Yards promised to bring the urban pastoral sport downtown to a setting that would be just as thrilling as the action on the field. In May of the following year, the club broke ground on a spot situated wittily behind the long-deserted Baltimore and Ohio train warehouse that had served as a border to the renovation of the city's Inner Harbor redevelopment district for the previous two decades. Although I loved Memorial Stadium for its familiarity and memories, I could not wait to see this new old park. It seemed to me that this was one of those rare cases when architects would be able to capture the essence of what was graceful and enduring about both the building's future tenants and its location. The Orioles and Baltimore, a ball club with such a glorious and memorable past and a charming big city of small neighborhoods, were, I believed, highly deserving of a venue with such promise of heart and soul. In short, the new park struck me as the perfect place to rekindle that Orioles magic.[2]

Architectural models of the stadium suggested that it would be everything that Memorial Stadium was not. It was to be cozy and small, seating just forty-five thousand people and putting them close to the action. It was to be constructed of warm materials—brick, wrought iron, and expressed steel left exposed to remind patrons of the girders forming the skeletons of the downtown skyscrapers, themselves constructed during an era of theretofore unprecedented economic prosperity. It was to feature asymmetrical playing dimensions, including a short porch in right field to remind fans of old Ebbets Field in Brooklyn and Fenway Park in Boston, two of the most revered venues in baseball's history. Finally, it would leave the area beyond much of center field open so that the cityscape would become a regular part of the stadium's sight lines. The new ball park promised patrons the ability to renounce the present in favor of an updated rendering of a ball park created in what felt like a richer, distant past, a time when the city really mattered.

Indeed, even before the first brick was laid, Camden Yards was promoted as an antidote to the immediate (commonly described as "inauthentic") past of the previous few decades. It was characterized as a fitting replacement for Memorial Stadium and the other massive multipurpose stadiums in which I had grown up watching games. Praise for the design of Camden Yards brought with it widespread denunciation of the multiple-use venues characteristic of the preceding forty years of ball-park construction. The architects of Memorial Stadium and other multipurpose buildings were made to seem guilty of a type of inexcusable baseball hubris. By designing these leviathans, they were thought to have turned their backs on a century of unique, classic urban parks and instead drawn their ideas from the excessive rationality of postwar America. Monumental, cavernous, and round, these stadiums seemed inevitably to flatten out the experience for baseball fans insofar as each looked (and played) more or less like the others.[3]

From the perspective of most fans enamored with the preciousness of both the older stadiums and the new one being built in homage to them, the multipurpose stadiums seemed to be gaudy monuments to function over form. While they employed many of the engineering advances representative of an era of postwar expansion, they seemed to do so at the expense of character. For instance, they featured massive concourses seating tens of thousands of people while eliminating the distracting columns and other obstructions characteristic of the first generation of American concrete and steel ball parks. In doing so, however, they elevated (undeniably impressive) engineering feats over intimacy, providing for a kind of lowest common denominator of seating options. None of the seats in these parks was outrageously far from the action, yet none was very close either. To many fans, these slights seemed reminiscent of Soviet-style social engineering, producing a bland experience for everyone. Yet even these concerns, though passionately felt, were not the basis for the most vehement aspersions cast against multipurpose parks. Instead, the most grievous offense committed by the designers of these stadiums seemed to have been the sin of suggesting that baseball was just like any other sport or recreational activity. Indifferent homes to baseball, football, tractor pulls, and rock concerts alike, these venues failed to allow for the elevation of baseball to its erstwhile privileged status as a unique American pastime.

Camden Yards was designed to address this mistake and thus help revive something fundamental about the franchise's (and baseball's) history. Home only to baseball, its foul territories were kept to a minimum so that the stands would literally hug the contours of the playing field, bringing fans into close contact with players. It was created to privilege coziness and warmth over the industrial sublime, propinquity over mass access. But just as important, it was to serve as a dramatic symbol of the new urbanism just then coming into vogue. This anchor of downtown redevelopment was going to buck the forty-year trend of American suburbanization. Unlike multipurpose suburban ball parks—which, like cookie-cutter strip shopping centers, failed to promote a sense of regional uniqueness, a specialness of place—this new stadium was to look back reverently to Ebbets

Field or to Fenway, built within existing city grids, part of the fabric of an integrated urban existence. It was to afford patrons the ability to combine a ball game with shopping, dinning, and, above all, a simple city stroll. A tonic to the perceived atomization of the suburbs, Camden Yards, like the thousands of new urbanist developments in the works across the country would be, as Lonnie Wheeler says of Wrigley Field in chapter 4 of this book, "a real place, one that feels different from other places" (2). Renouncing the perceived sterility of monumental and cavernous parks like Memorial Stadium and high-tech ones like SkyDome (in Toronto), this stadium promised the ability to rekindle the fundamental and magical simplicity of an earlier era.

Thus Camden Yards seemed to hold the promise of cheap grace. In the early 1990s, the dawn of virtual reality, when faster microprocessors were allowing for the simulation of so many kinds of previously inaccessible experiences, a simulated world of the past seemed suddenly, imminently within reach. If the engineers at Orlando's Universal Studios could construct a virtual reality ride that made riders feel like they were actually traveling in a flying DeLorean in 1956, the architects of Camden Yards could surely take fans back to a mythical past.[4]

When I visited the park a few days before the grand opening, I found it to be truly a thing of grace. It was at once massive and intimate, able to immediately conjure up the thrill of the urban pastoral. The nascent climbing ivy in center field drew my eyes immediately toward the delightful clutter of the city just beyond— Baltimore's downtown skyscrapers brilliantly framed by the open portion of center field. The park literally drew in the city, incorporating a section of Eutaw Street (one of downtown Baltimore's most important arteries) as a brick walking path within the gates of the park. It thus provided for a nice promenade between the warehouse and the right and center field bleachers and porch, making seamless the visual transition between city and stadium. Its delicate craftsmanship rendered it a lovely organic aria amid the cacophony of downtown verticality. The impossibly elegant outfield seating section down the first-base line rose abruptly then vanished gently as it approached the warehouse. The effect of this ocular magic trick was to make this huge section seem as if it tapered off into thin air. I was indeed impressed.

Yet even through my excitement that day I felt something remotely agitating. Because I'm not wealthy, well connected, or fanatical enough to wait in line overnight, I was not able to procure a ticket to any of the games during the first few weeks of the inaugural season. Already this was a sign that something significant had shifted when the Birds moved downtown. Suddenly my insider's status had vanished. Because tickets were now coveted, they fell into the hands of a more exclusive set. Season ticket holders, renters of corporate luxury boxes, wealthy contributors to campaigns of Maryland politicians, and other important and/or affluent people were the among the few who could gain access to baseball played in this new authentic venue.

Thinking about my impending exclusion indeed gave me pause that day. Nevertheless, I assured myself that, over time, I would again be able to discover the hidden parking spots and cheap concessions which had theretofore endowed me (at the old park) with the psychic capital of an insider. When I did finally manage to get tickets to a game about a month or so into the season, I found the experience not bad, but not exactly transformative either. The amenities were, all in all, pretty decent. I snacked on somewhat authentic but pricey Maryland crab cakes. I drained a couple of pints of handcrafted ale. I walked past the smoking barbeque pit on Eutaw Street and brushed up against the portly and jovial Boog Powell, the former Oriole first baseman, shaking hands with each patron who waited in line to buy one of his special recipe sandwiches. Even though I was still somewhat grumpy about having been excluded from the stadium for several home stands, I had to admit, as I waited in line, that I was absorbed by the presence of one of my childhood idols cooking and serving up his own barbeque. It seemed a cool touch—the ultimate symbol of the old Orioles greeting each customer with a firm handshake and a bellowing, yet folksy, "How ya doin'?"

Yet after proceeding through the line and shaking hands with the old slugger, I realized the experience felt kind of perfunctory and staged, a photo opportunity with cachet derived from the tension between Powell's aura and his ordinariness. In other words, Boog's nightly ritual seemed to me a bit like a ride in an urban theme park. It was as if I had waited in line to experience an elaborate, live-action simulation, a replicated impromptu street-corner chat harking back to an era when professional ballplayers and other celebrities actually lived in the same neighborhoods as the fans who admired them. The casual (but also scripted and production-line) quality of this interaction provided me and other fans with merely "virtual" access to the public city streets that newly privatized Eutaw Street had replaced. Each of us buying a sandwich seemed to be attempting to purchase temporary connection with much of what is often missing in gated communities and urban shopping and entertainment destinations—safe, random, low-stakes encounters with friends and acquaintances.[5]

But at the time I did not get too bogged down by the contradiction between Powell's aw-shucks posture and the postmodern dynamics of the encounter. Instead, I rode a three-story escalator past the ring of luxury boxes toward my seat in the upper deck. When I got there, I looked around and noticed some subtle changes from my favorite perches at Memorial Stadium. The faces, the clothing, and the behavior of my section mates in the upper deck seemed somewhat different from the ones to which I had grown accustomed at the old park. The section in which I now sat was 100 percent white and, judging by conversations I had, composed mostly of members of the middle and upper middle classes. Equally profound for me was that, once the game began, there in the eighteen-dollar *cheap* seats, everyone was so eerily well behaved. There was some cheering, but only at appropriate moments, like when an Oriole reached base or

FORMER ORIOLES SLUGGER BOOG POWELL SIGNS AUTOGRAPHS FOR FANS ON EUTAW STREET IN CAMDEN YARDS. COURTESY OF JERRY WACHTER.

made a nice play in the field. Within a couple of innings, I found myself terrifically nostalgic for the excessive, the inappropriate, the picaresque—the vernacular behavior and comportment of the rowdies blissfully exiled together in the cheap seats at the old park.[6] I longed for foul-mouthed commentary about the umpire's decisions or for someone to "accidentally" spill beer on the patrons in the corporate luxury boxes just below.[7]

So I left my seat and began to navigate the park, hoping the section I had just vacated was an anomaly. I descended the escalator and walked around the main concourse toward the bleacher section in center field, confident that there I would find rowdier fans. Surely, in the bleachers I'd uncover some of the oppositional sentiment of my youth, a community of folks on the outside looking in. Much to my dismay, however, an usher stopped me at the entrance. This seemed borderline blasphemous. The bleacher seats, formerly a place of exile with open admission and bench seating, had now become the most exclusive area in the stadium. In this new old park, the bleachers had been reduced to a mere token, four small sections in the outfield for the lucky fans who could pay to revisit something like an old-time bleacher experience. The area that had for generations allowed those on the margins of stadium life freedom to generate their own forms of pleasure and oppositional sentiment had now been transformed into something akin to a novelty item, a space for a select few to exercise fantasies of being a participant in outsider culture.

I was still not completely dejected, however. Even though I had been forbidden to enter what had always been my favorite part of any ball park, I headed up to the large patio on the stadium's middle concourse to view the brilliant sights of Baltimore's harbor and the surrounding downtown. From there, I was able once again to admire the park's immense architectural achievement. Taking in the full tableau, I found myself appreciating just how cleverly the stadium had been situated in order to pay homage to Baltimore's history as an important industrial city. Its massive steel beams and seemingly endless red brick allowed it to blend harmoniously with the surrounding industrial structures and skyscrapers. Its location, in a former rail yard, gestured back to the locomotive era, when Camden Yards was the epicenter for the movement of goods and raw materials making their way into and out of the city.

From this vantage point, the modern version of Camden Yards seems to stand out an important symbolic intersection of the various modes of transportation linking the different mercantile epochs in the city's history. The harbor in the distance once brought millions of immigrants to work in the factories and populate Baltimore's lively ethnic neighborhoods. It also brought goods from Europe and the Far East and enabled local industries to export their products around the globe. The train line sent the facts of Baltimore's production into the interior of the country, helping other cities expand and construct their own skylines. Meanwhile, the ribbons of highways converging directly outside the park (the primary means of transportation in today's economy) serve as unmistakable harbingers of the changing cultural and economic role of the city. The convergence of these highways at Baltimore's primary recreational destination reveals a crucial truth about Camden Yards, about Baltimore, and about revitalizing American cities in general. Even more important than any of its specific architectural details, Camden Yards and the Inner Harbor redevelopment of which it is an anchor are able to succeed largely because of their proximity to Interstate 95. Unlike Memorial Stadium, which forced visitors from outside the city to negotiate labyrinthine neighborhoods through rush-hour traffic, Camden Yards is located in the most tourist-accessible spot in Baltimore. It is thus much more inviting to the millions of people who live in suburban Baltimore and the more distant Washington, D.C., suburbs.[8] In short, the park functions as a magnet for tourism, a way to bring outsiders into the city, where they will contribute currency to the Baltimore economy. The area around it has evolved (at least to a degree) into a kind of themed environment for tourists, conventioneers, baseball fans, and others interested in experiencing a taste of the urban.

Of course, the stadium is not directly responsible for this shift. The very idea of downtown in Baltimore had been transformed long before the construction of Oriole Park. Harborplace, the brainchild of architect James Rouse, brought development energy back to the city in the late 1970s, using the (by-now much-replicated) festival market formula. Highlighting eating and entertainment in a physical space dominated by historic architectural themes, Harborplace had already been drawing a mostly affluent clientele back downtown for a decade and a half. Oriole Park, then, constitutes part of an essential second phase of downtown festival development, functioning for the Inner Harbor as a "special activity generator" (Hannigan 56). A brick and mortar update of the concerts, boat shows, and mini-festivals organized by the Rouse Company in the early days of Harborplace, the park was developed to a large degree to host events bringing people to the area to shop and eat. Its inclusion in Baltimore's Urban Entertainment Destination (UED) was more or less necessitated by the fact that Harborplace, like other festival marketplaces developed after it, had not yet proved to be the moneymaker it was intended to be.[9] Thus Baltimore, like many cities that had also built urban shopping destinations, felt it needed to follow its initial investment with the fabrication of a contiguous entertainment complex. Around the country, these complexes typically comprise a mixture of convention centers, casinos, stadiums, amusement parks, and themed restaurants in order to attract enough people downtown to validate the initial investment.[10]

In the past decade, many academics have taken aim at economic justifications for large public investments in this kind of development.[11] For example, Marc Levine criticizes the "Rouse-ification" of downtowns, arguing that Harborplace and its spin-offs (Faneuil Hall in Boston and South Street Seaport in Manhattan in particular) create pockets of prosperity surrounded by extreme poverty. These festival market place developments often fail to provide the "trickle-down" effect that, in theory, would help surrounding local merchants and residents by increasing foot traffic and providing jobs. Levine argues that the self-contained nature of Rouse developments limits the amount of new business created for surrounding establishments and thus often worsens their condition. Also, he insists that the jobs created by UEDs tend to be largely of the dead-end, minimum-wage variety, with a few midlevel managerial positions going to suburban commuters.[12]

Similarly, Mark Rosentraub argues against what he considers to be a system of corporate welfare allowing owners of professional sports franchises to effectively hold municipalities hostage by demanding huge subsidies for new stadiums in exchange for their promise not to move to another town. His book, *Major League Losers: The Real Cost of Sports and Who's Paying for It*, undermines most arguments suggesting a substantial and direct economic benefit for cities choosing to invest in sporting arenas. Although he does concede that sports facilities allow cities to benefit from improvements to their image while also allowing them to compete for human capital in an increasingly competitive global market, stadiums themselves create relatively few jobs and bring in small amounts of tax revenue relative to the investment. In fact, several economists have suggested that families spend money at sports arenas in direct proportion to money they do not spend at other leisure venues.[13] In other words, leisure dollars seem to be relatively fixed in a community. If they are not spent at a baseball game, they will be spent at a theater, museum, or arcade.

There is, of course, an opposite camp of politicians, entrepreneurs, and sports enthusiasts who argue just as passionately for the benefits of constructing downtown arenas. Many of their arguments center on a belief that even if these projects fail to satisfy the immediate bottom line, their construction is a visionary endeavor, allowing the host city to position itself competitively against other towns in the new millennium.[14] Most supporters of stadium deals believe cities simply must have professional sports franchises playing in new, user-friendly facilities in order to attract a young, educated, and affluent demographic in an increasingly cutthroat global market. Even most economists who to a large degree criticize these deals acknowledge the existence of a host of side benefits, including the generation of civic pride and an increase in positive perceptions of downtown that often ends up spurring other, more vital types of development (housing, transportation, etc.) nearby.[15]

Regardless of sharp ideological divisions about the validity of public investment in these stadiums, critics and foes alike must acknowledge that these venues are, at the very least, enormously popular. Baltimore's back-to-the-city, back-to-the-past experiment was so immediately successful (allowing the Orioles to sell out practically every home game in the early years) that it became a template for the other stadiums constructed, or now under construction, in the wake of Camden Yards. In the seven years after Oriole Park first opened its gates, retro stadiums, or stadiums at least accented with retro touches, in Cleveland, Denver, and Arlington, allowed those cities' franchises to become among the league's wealthiest and most successful. As of 2004, additional taxpayer-funded or subsidized venues in Phoenix, Seattle, Milwaukee, Philadelphia, San Franscisco, Houston, Cincinnati, Detroit, San Diego, and Pittsburgh also have opened for business.

Meanwhile, small-market clubs, increasingly squeezed between escalating player salaries in an era of free agency and smaller television revenue in proportion to the size of their market, have looked to the construction of these parks as the only way for them to compete with the larger-market clubs. While once thrift, patience, and player development allowed the Orioles to thrive against the Yankees, the club's success in the 1990s was largely a product of creative marketing strategies in the early 1980s convincing taxpayers to foot much of the bill for their private, profitable new venue. Maryland literally set the standard for public entrepreneurial investment in sports complexes with its provision of more than $250 million in subsidies facilitating the construction of Oriole Park (Rosentraub 1997:18). Still reeling from the beloved (National Football League) Colts' 1984 midnight exodus to Indianapolis, Maryland officials became convinced, as many politicians across the country have in recent years, of the necessity of retaining their teams. In the late 1980s, the prospect of a city of Baltimore's size without a major sports franchise frightened state and local politicians into taking drastic measures. Maryland's actions in turn paved the way for a generation of political strategies in cities such as San Francisco and Seattle that have sought to remake sections of downtown as planned twenty-four-hours-a-day working, living, and playing environments. Seattle, just like Baltimore, now has two separate, gleaming stadiums as anchors to its primary urban entertainment district.[16] As a result, the area around these stadiums surges to life on evenings of sporting events, filling restaurants and increasing foot traffic.

Yet these projects remain controversial. Clearly, at some point in the mid-1990s, the practically unadulterated euphoria surrounding the opening of Oriole Park began to wear off as local civic activists, economists, and academics started asking hard questions about the wisdom and fairness of public investment in privately owned arenas. This has fostered a lively debate and (as I chronicle in chapter 1) in many cases empowered civic officials to demand a better deal for their cities than Baltimore negotiated. Nonetheless, although I do spend some time describing the political economy of urban stadium development, my primary interest is in the *cultural* capital of retro stadiums. Boog Powell's performance on Eutaw Street, for example, is highly representative of attempts to reinvent perceptions of the present through large-scale commodification of the past in this important new form of urban space. Powell's banter and handshakes are part of a savvy, coordinated effort by city and club officials to favorably accent the history of the area, in the process perhaps both compensating for a sense of something missing and smoothing over the jagged edges of city life.

Without question, since the time of the earliest discussions about relocating the Orioles downtown, Baltimore political officials, urban planners, and architects have gone to great lengths to reinvent the story of Camden Yards in order to make it more attractive to tourists. In official histories of the area, in archeological reports from preconstruction excavation, on placards hanging in buildings, and in coordinated public relations campaigns, they have highlighted small, relatively insignificant occurrences (such as Babe Ruth's father's brief stint operating a saloon in the area). All the while, they have attempted to elide references to what historians agree is the most significant occurrence on the site, one of the bloodiest strikes in the history of the American railroad in 1877.[17] In the Baltimore of Harborplace and Camden Yards, a genial history has been made available for pleasant consumption by urban tourists, most of whom (judging by late-twentieth-century demographic data) come from newer suburbs, edge cities, and gated communities.[18] Just as the Babe Ruth Museum next door softens and domesticates the history of the area for modern enjoyment, Boog's handshakes encode Eutaw Street as a throwback to a simpler era (real or imagined) of Baltimore neighborhood life.[19]

In and of itself, this transformation is not too disturbing. After all, throughout history the idea of the city has been subject to changes based on trends in transportation, commerce, and aesthetics. Yet the often theme-park-like and anachronistic nature of this new generation of urban space is worthy of serious consideration. It is crucial at the very least to examine how the new urban landscape (around Camden Yards and elsewhere) tends to present a more homogenous culture than the one replaced. As visitors (like me) with memories of Memorial Stadium have surely noticed, the scene outside the new park is dramatically different. For better or for worse, the rows of local, largely unlicensed vendors congregating outside Memorial Stadium are for the most part gone, replaced by official Oriole concessionaires and ushers as well as an army of Baltimore police officers maintaining order and ensuring that pedestrian and vehicular traffic flow only in prescribed directions. Similarly, ticket scalpers, most of whom had been African American teenagers at the old park, are now systematically shooed away by the police, replaced by individuals and families selling tickets at face value under the watchful eye of local authorities in the "scalp-free zone." In short, the nature of this revived, urbanesque space requires that many of the loose ends (the unpredictability and the diversity) of the old city be tied up—consciously kept out of sight or at least contained—so that the downtown ball-park experience can be more comfortably consumed. To many, this transformation is representative of a positive evolution. Families can now attend ball games unworried about harassment. To others, this evolution brings with it a sense of loss.

The retro stadium movement of the 1990s is in many ways a feature of the culture's invocation, common in the waning years of the twentieth century, of the past as a tonic to feelings of belatedness, to a sense of living at the end of history.[20] Like bell bottom jeans, reemergent swing dance societies, wrap-around porches on suburban homes, and a host of popular movies such as *Back to the Future* and *Pleasantville,* retro ball parks at once commemorate and commodify cultural forms from earlier years of the final century of the millennium.[21] They thus create an important juncture between the past and the future. I believe that at this juncture we can learn about cultural desires underlying contemporary urban development through a close examination of how the past comes packaged for consumption. Like my initial desire for Camden Yards to restore the blue-collar shape of my youthful identification with the Orioles, parks accented with old time elements provide perspective on contemporary longings for contact with a vanishing version of the American city.

As the original form of this kind of venue, both in terms of its package of public financing and its specific cultural register, Camden Yards could well have served as the focus of this project. However, after spending some time in Cleveland, Ohio, it became clear to me that that city's Jacobs Field and surrounding Gateway District provided the most fertile ground of all for this type of examination. Cleveland is a potent symbol of the transition from one era to the next. Once the center of national steel production with an awesome skyline dominated by blazing smokestacks, downtown Cleveland had become, by the late 1960s, one of the most recognizable casualties of the end of the great era of American manufacturing. Shrinking Cleveland lost one-third of its downtown population between 1970 and 1990. It endured two race riots (1966 and 1968) then saw its polluted Cuyahoga River literally catch fire in 1969. Its City Center, which used to be the region's primary shopping district, the place where area residents of all incomes and races converged, experienced suburban flight to a greater degree than almost any other major American municipality. A city, which at the beginning of the twentieth century was blossoming into perhaps the most prosperous location of industrial activity in America, found itself at the end of the century in need of a dramatic reinvention.

The particular path Cleveland chose for this reinvention, after thirty years of wrangling over how best to restore downtown, speaks volumes about the collective psychological dimension of ball park–centered revitalization. The same city that rejected Mayor Dennis Kucinich in 1977 (in part because he wanted to divert public money from large-scale tourist and business development initiatives into the city's schools and public infrastructure) has surpassed Baltimore as the national leader in forging partnerships with professional sports franchises. Since 1990, Cleveland has invested more subsidies into private playing facilities than any other community in the United States. One estimate of the public cost for building Jacobs Field, the adjacent Gund Arena, and their surrounding parking garages is $462 million.[22] However, by the time such extras as overtime pay for police patrolling the area and free apartments and furniture for the Indians' management are factored in, the city appears to have contributed more than $1 billion to help augment the profit of two sports clubs that, according to some critics, might be profitable without such public subsidy. More than perhaps any other location, Cleveland, its postindustrial image in utter shambles, felt it needed capacious forms of public largess to assure itself and the rest of the country that it was still of major-league caliber. Yet despite this huge investment in sports-centered redevelopment, tremendous urban problems remain in Cleveland. In fact, by many standards, they have gotten worse since 1990. City schools are still considered among the worst in the country, and welfare reform of 1996 cost many urban neighborhoods upwards of 17 percent of their total yearly income.[23]

Nonetheless, the town that was not long ago considered the "Mistake by the Lake" is now almost universally touted as America's "Comeback City." The ball park, basketball arena, Rock and Roll Hall of Fame, and Flats restaurant area attract millions of visitors each year from neighboring suburban counties and indeed from around the world. Dozens of new restaurants and cafés with outdoor seating have opened up around the ball park, and scores of buildings that sat vacant for years are now being converted to condominiums. Increased foot traffic has brought renewed energy to the Gateway, making the area seem safer and convincing hundreds of businesses to relocate there. So I spent time in Cleveland hoping in part to understand how the city negotiates the contradictions between its new vibrancy and the sense among some that too many people have been left behind.

When I arrived in Cleveland, I immediately noted the widespread optimism of a city in renewal. The first person I met, an enthusiastic clerk at my suburban hotel named Shelly Perkins, told me (unprompted) that she volunteered daily to give tours of the ball park because "it's just so much fun to be a part of all the exciting things happening downtown." At the park before the game that first evening, I witnessed scores of fans arriving early, congregating outside the wrought-iron gate on Ontario Street to watch batting practice and socialize. I saw thousands of others happily passing time between work and the game hanging out in nearby eating and drinking establishments. Walking to the park from the other end of downtown, I dodged a few of the approximately twenty thousand cars full of suburban fans arriving via the bridges spanning the Cuyahoga. In dramatic contrast to how things had been—a predictable dusk-time emptying out of this erstwhile home to drug dealers, prostitutes, and low-end businesses—the revitalized Gateway surrounding the stadium now bristled with energy immediately prior to games.

Along with this palpable liveliness, I also noticed many of the ironies associated with an urban area undergoing this kind of transformation. On a dark, narrow street leading directly to the stadium area, I saw a few of the controversial markers of gentrification. A locally owned store specializing in discount hair care products for African Americans displayed a "going out of business" sign next to a placard proclaiming its space the "future home of Chesapeake Bagels," a national chain. Panhandlers, ignored uncomfortably by passing baseball fans, hid from the watchful eye of club-wielding police behind imitation wrought-iron lampposts. Condemned and boarded-up buildings underwent restoration by speculators eager to provide luxury housing for those with the financial resources and the desire to either move into the city or set up for themselves a convenient pied-à-terre. In short, what I found in the Gateway, like what I had seen at Camden Yards, was simultaneously inspiring and suggestive of some potentially distressing facts about urban revitalization.

ABOVE: LUXURY CONDOMINIUMS ADVERTISED ABOVE ROSE'S NAILS ON PROSPECT AVENUE.

LEFT: A SIGN OF THE GATEWAY IN TRANSITION, LUXURY CONDOMINIUMS REPLACE DISCOUNT RETAIL STORES AND OTHER BUSINESSES THAT, FOR DECADES, CATERED PRIMARILY TO AFRICAN AMERICAN CONSUMERS.

Like Oriole Park, Jacobs Field (popularly called the Jake) is a unique aesthetic marvel. Nestled comfortably between highways and skyscrapers, it nevertheless feels impossibly grand and open. Its concourse combines dazzling views of the southern part of the city beyond the nearby Cuyahoga River, the verdant, manicured baseball field below, and the brilliant downtown skyline to the north. Its design includes a range of witty signature touches helping patrons make an emotional connection with other places and other times. For example, the open gate on Ontario Street reminds fans of the elevated platform outside Yankee Stadium, where, for three-quarters of a century, Bronx commuters waiting for a train have been able to see part of the action for free. Inside the park, a large stand-alone bleacher section allows fans to recall fondly the storied outfield bench seats of Chicago's Wrigley Field. Even more poignantly, the exposed steel structure of the park's upper deck and other similar accenting details invite patrons to recollect Cleveland's own grand past. But perhaps the best examples of this kind of appreciation of ersatz materials and design are the majestic floodlight stanchions rimming the park, connecting visitors to the vertical smokestacks of the closed steel mill directly across the Cuyahoga.

It is important to note (accents of the past notwithstanding) that Indians' management argues passionately against the characterization of Jacobs Field as a retro ball park. They point to the modern glass-encased Terrace Club Restaurant overhanging the third-base-side box seats and the 150-foot JumboTron video screen above left center field as signs of the Jake's inherent, state-of-the-art modernity. Insofar as the designers of the venue rejected an all-out theming of the past (à la Camden Yards with its wrought-iron weathervanes and analog clocks), these officials have a point. Jacobs Field is clearly not simply a knock-off of Oriole Park, not merely the second in a series. It is its own singular achievement, intended as an organic interpolation into its own specific time and place. Nonetheless, it is so thoroughly accoutered with accents of the past, with material icons of nostalgic culture, that refusing to consider it within the evolving retro tradition would be disingenuous. Because so much of its appeal involves a rejection of cold, dank (and now demolished) Cleveland Municipal Stadium across downtown and an attendant promise to patrons that they will be able to enjoy something akin to an old-time, charming baseball experience, Jacobs Field has to be considered, at least partially, a retro stadium.

Ultimately, however, even as the park successfully reminds patrons of the past, the meanings it generates and the pleasure it provides need to be understood within a contemporary context. Chapter 1 of this book situates the building's most profound economic and cultural value within the dynamics of a changing American city. For close to thirty years, major structural changes in the organization of capital have brought about a subtle but steady shift in the very purpose of many of this country's urban areas. Retro ball parks like Jacobs Field have emerged as key components of urban entertainment-based development in

JACOBS FIELD AND DOWNTOWN CLEVELAND FROM THE UPPER DECK. THE PARK IS NESTLED
COMFORTABLY BETWEEN HIGHWAYS AND SKYSCRAPERS YET STILL FEELS IMPOSSIBLY GRAND
AND OPEN.

order to facilitate this shift. As they become progressively more geared toward
servicing recreational tourists, third-millennial urban spaces like Cleveland's
Gateway rely on images of the past to reinvest them with the energy perceived by
many to have been lost along with this shift. Available now in simulated form,
emerging through carnival mascots, nostalgic photos, and other substitutions for
the eroticism of an old urban order, accents of an integrated city life provide baseball fans and others who pursue urban "safaris," a safe way to enjoy this space
(Hannigan 200).

Chapters 2 and 3 theorize historical explanations for why the ball park, as
opposed to other kinds of venues, has emerged as the most celebrated anchor of

nostalgic downtown redevelopment. Since the origins of baseball as a professional enterprise, spectators have come to ball parks looking to satisfy their thirst for temporary access to forms of antiestablishmentarian pleasure within a larger culture that seeks to systematically suppress them. As early as 1861, baseball team owners set up separate bettors' pens enabling middle-class men, most of whom conducted themselves according to Victorian codes of respectability outside the park, to act out against behavioral norms. This saturnalian function was able to persevere even as baseball learned to package itself as a wholesome enterprise, as the national pastime. The resulting tension in turn allowed the ball park throughout the twentieth century to serve an important dual role for the emergent American middle class: it enabled the rehearsal of a variety of oppositional behaviors among the bourgeois sporting community while affording the game's image makers the ability to promote baseball as a symbol of American wholesome "verve and vigor" (Spalding 4). Today this duality still exists, offering many visitors to retro parks the opportunity to think themselves authentic, just as I did as a child attending Orioles games. The retro park invites a kind of psychical class play-acting by connecting the experience of the visitor with those of mythologized patrons of actual old ball parks. Along with this, increased security, improved surveillance technology, and economic stratification have allowed these same patrons to visit the city, to indulge in these fantasies, without actually having to risk too much contact with members of the urban underclasses.

Chapter 4 focuses on the bleacher section, perhaps the most popular site of this kind of rehearsed opposition in retro parks. Once the only option for immigrants, African Americans, "bleacher bums," and others on the margins of stadium life, contemporary bleachers capitalize on feelings of communal solidarity created precisely by the economic and racial stratification of which ball-park segregation has historically been part and parcel. This chapter describes the history of bleacher sections and suggests how, throughout the last century, bleachers have served as important sites of vernacular or unauthorized pleasure for a relatively marginal population. Recent manifestations of the bleachers on the other hand have attempted to commodify the experience for many of the retro stadiums' newer clients eager to purchase, among other things, community, authenticity, and solidarity. These stadiums attempt to enact the *old* and the *urban* for their audience in part by replicating sensations of exile or marginality for new fans, considered derisively by longtime bleacher dwellers to be the "in" crowd. This section examines what happens when the outside becomes in.

Chapter 5 extends this discussion of longing for outsider status to include race. Part of this examination involves describing how, over the course of the last quarter century, baseball has been subject to re-segregation. On every level, from little league to the major leagues, African American participation as players and spectators has been dropping precipitously. However, along with this re-segregation has come a notable geographical reemergence of the game in sections of town that are, or used to be, majority black. Across America, just like in Cleveland's Gateway, whole sections of cities have been razed in order to build ball parks catering to a relatively homogenous suburban population eager to experience the urban. This chapter demonstrates how images of, and sounds from, African American culture have been carefully articulated in and around these parks in order to code these new spaces as different from suburbia. Simply put, in places like the Gateway, "blackness" has come to replace blacks. Yet ultimately, this replacement seems to articulate utopian longings for racial solidarity even as the renewed infrastructure of baseball, and indeed of the city, helps reestablish a color line.

Chapter 6 describes the limitation of the American city when experienced primarily as simulacrum. It begins with a close examination of Don DeLillo's *Underworld,* a haunting novel about baseball and the American city in the twentieth century. Nick Shay, DeLillo's main character, functions as a stand-in for the millions of pilgrims who flock to retro stadiums in search of an experience helping them close the chasm between the present and the past. Nick, who as a young man witnessed ball games at Ebbets Field, attempts throughout the novel to employ the logic of commemoration to help him regain emotional connection with the gritty and "real streets" of his youth in Brooklyn (810). Nonetheless, as his attempt is thwarted at every turn, he becomes increasingly aware of the primacy of mediation in a world gone "hyperreal."[24] Nick's search for a famous baseball, the authenticating object of one of his darkest moments—when the Dodgers lost the 1951 pennant on the last pitch of the last game of the year—like the quest of many retro stadium patrons, remains vexed because, as Benjamin writes, "even the most perfect reproduction . . . is lacking in one element: its presence in time and space" (220). Ultimately this section attempts to contextualize these quests in relationship to sensations of late-millennial belatedness, to the psychological limitations of both suburbanization and the postindustrial, postmodern city. This chapter takes the project full circle by helping theorize my own undifferentiated sensations of longing when I first visited Camden Yards in 1992. To a large degree, the gap between my expectations and my experience links me to the fictional Nick Shay, who, having lived a life of hyperreality, looks to baseball and its preponderance of commemorative items for a way out.

Like many scholars within the field of cultural criticism, I draw my methodology from a variety of disciplines and styles. In part, this project is a peripatetic analysis. Many of my ideas resulted simply from walking around downtown Cleveland, talking with fans, local shop owners, police officers, ball club executives, homeless people, community activists, and others in and around the Gateway. Sitting in the bleacher section, taking a tour of the Jake, interviewing members of the Indians' front office staff as well as behind-the-scenes workers, I was able to get a sense of both the pride Clevelanders have in their new park and some of the theoretical and practical questions arising from this particular form of urban renewal.

In part, too, this project functions as an interrogation of my own subject position. As a child, I needed to identify with the blue-collar Orioles as a reaction to my belief about what was lacking from my own identity. In comparison to popular cultural images of working people, African Americans and others, I grew up feeling distinctly uncool. Baltimore, its darkened streets of row houses and porches of people congregating to watch the visiting baseball fans flock toward the stadium, seemed to me (raised as I was on the wide streets and endless lawns of the suburbs) more authentic, more gritty and true. Ironically, it was not just the brick-and-mortar distant city but even televisual or cinematic representations of it that seemed more real than the actual life I was living in the suburbs.

What is it about reality encoded through urban experience that promises so much recompense? Each chapter of this book attempts in its own way to answer this question through a search for provisional understanding of the *real* as it is expressed and packaged in and around new old urban baseball stadiums.

CHAPTER ONE

UNDERSTANDING THE BIG PICTURE

You gotta understand the big picture.
—Bob Dibiasio, Cleveland Indians'
vice president for public relations

Long before 1969, when a bizarre fire blazed on the Cuyahoga River near Cleveland Municipal Stadium, the old drafty arena had come to be recognized as a calamitous mistake. A massive, dank structure first used for baseball in 1932, during an era of large concrete and steel ball-park construction, the stadium had for years been home to baseball's most notorious losers.[1] At the moment the polluted river burned, the Indians were in the midst of a record-breaking forty-year period without a pennant and were routinely playing in front of minuscule crowds of only the most die-hard fans, virtually lost in the cavernous building. Yet after the Cuyahoga caught fire that day, downtown Cleveland itself, its behemoth stadium, closed steel mills, and boarded-up buildings already serving as dramatic symbols of rust-belt depression, began to share with the stadium a rather infamous nickname: the "Mistake by the Lake."

Three and a half decades later, however, Cleveland is being touted as America's "Renaissance City." Downtown, home by the late sixties and early seventies to a multitude of low-scale enterprises, boarded-up businesses, and open-air drug and prostitution markets, now shimmers with a mixture of restored brick office buildings and newer glass and stone skyscrapers. In the shadows of these buildings, on the site of the now-demolished stadium, the city has built a brand new football-only arena complete with revenue-generating luxury boxes and all the other amenities of the modern sports venue. This glitzy new facility joins the Indians' new park, Jacobs Field, the Gund Arena basketball complex, and the Rock and Roll Hall of Fame as the revived downtown's marquee attractions. Just as in the days when the woebegone ball park symbolized the town's blighted status and decaying infrastructure, Cleveland's state-of-the-art sports facilities and entertainment venues represent the city's rebirth.

Accented with aspects of storied parks built in the first few decades of the twentieth century and constructed as the crowning jewel of the Gateway District—a reinvention of Cleveland's former main market and shopping section which had been withering away in the wake of the 1960s race riots—Jacobs Field stands as perhaps the most dramatic symbol of Cleveland's renaissance. The old-fashioned park, which replaced the decaying structures of the area's most depressed era, emphatically advertises to the nation watching ball games on television and coming to downtown Cleveland as a tourist destination that the city is no longer the Mistake by the Lake.

The success of the new park and the attendant pride and tourist dollars it has brought to Cleveland are a large part of what Indians' vice president Dibiasio refers to as "the big picture." A native of Cleveland and an Indians employee for more than thirty years, Dibiasio has seen the city's and the team's fortunes come full circle. As a child in the early 1950s, he used to accompany his mother to the Italian section of the markets, where the ball park now stands. He still remembers gazing in awe at the massive steel mills ablaze along the banks of the Cuyahoga and cheering wildly as the Indians won what was to become their final division title for a staggering four decades. As young adult, conversely, he watched in disbelief as, one by one, the mills—the heart and soul of industrial Cleveland—shut down operations. For most of his adult life, then, he has been forced to wonder about job security as the perennially second-division Indians struggled to remain financially viable in Cleveland. During that time, he witnessed far more games amid a scattered few thousand freezing fans at Cleveland Stadium than events at sold-out, sterling Jacobs Field. Thus his sense of the "big picture" is informed by the guarded optimism of the renewing rust belt. As a young man, the idea that the indomitable mills might someday stop producing would have seemed absurd. Now, as an executive for a high-profile, successful sports franchise in postindustrial Cleveland, he wants desperately not to repeat the mistakes of the past. Experience has taught him that success can be fleeting. Therefore, the "big picture" describes his charge of keeping the business healthy so that, even better than the manufacturers of Cleveland's past, it can do its part to maintain a strong regional economy. Within his conception of corporate noblesse oblige, the team's value in the community hinges on its long-term ability to create jobs, increase consumption, invoke civic pride, and provide a recreational space suitable for his fellow Clevelanders.

But the big picture is even more complex than job creation and organizational stability. Dibiasio's use of the term provides valuable insight into the convergence of culture and capital in the postindustrial American city. Among other things, it points to a significant reorganization of the Cleveland financial world in the wake of the economic crisis of the late 1960s and early 1970s. The oil cri-sis and subsequent recession of 1973–75 brought about a remarkable break in the arrangement of American capitalism. Signaling an end to the postwar boom, this crisis sparked a prolonged era of restructuring necessitated by low growth rates, high unemployment, and inflation. Profits suffered, requiring American corporations to become much more flexible at the point of production. The era of "Fordism," or an economy based on American mass production, stable tech-nologies, and immobile capital, abruptly came to an end.[3] In its wake, America moved away from large-scale mass production in favor of flexible specialization. Thus, service industries, financial organizations, media-based technologies, and now ball parks and other urban entertainment destinations have begun to claim the American downtown. In many ways, Cleveland's transformation from the "Mistake by the Lake" to the "Renaissance City," serves as a perfect case study in the evolution of a post-Fordist city.[4]

Dibiasio recognizes that American cities must remake themselves in order to compete for both labor and capital in a global market. Producers and service providers are freer than ever before to take their operations elsewhere, so they routinely shop themselves to other municipalities in search of tax incentives and a favorable work force. Dibiasio's pride in the big picture comes from an acknowledgment that the Indians, and in particular Jacobs Field, provide Cleve-land a leg up on many other towns in terms of its ability to attract many of the components of economic vitality. More and more, American urban economic development relies on the creation of large-scale entertainment destinations, not so much for the direct revenue they generate as for the indirect benefits—a positive image, a healthy buzz, fun things to do 24/7—which attract a young, skilled labor force free to choose between competing cities. In short, Dibiasio is extremely cognizant of Jacobs Field's important economic role in renewing Cleveland.

Yet he seems somewhat less focused on the park's cultural role in facilitat-ing the shift as well as the multiple ironies involved when new meets old. As a utopian urban space dedicated to reconstructing an idealized past for contem-porary baseball patrons, the park promises abundant recompense of a variety of mourned-for cultural forms. Ironically, however, many of these same cultural forms have been squeezed out or replaced as part of the area's sports and enter-tainment-centered transformation. Allowing its patrons to experience the city as a big picture, or as a kind of witty tableau vivant, Jacobs Field and its environs offer up for consumption often sanitized forms of traditionally risqué or pica-resque urban behaviors, sights, sounds, and smells. On some level, then, the area serves as a kind of carnival for adults satisfying a widespread desire for the *urban* experience and revealing important characteristics of contemporary American longing for connection to city life.

FROM NOBLESSE OBLIGE TO
ECONOMIC DEVELOPMENT

The seeds of Cleveland's urban renewal were sown well in advance of the actual depression of the early 1970s. A city that was born great, where "iron ore met coal to become steel and rode off by railroad to build America's skyscrapers, railroads and bridges," Cleveland, through the first half of the twentieth century, was home to one of the country's strongest economies as well as some of the richest and most charitable families.[5] The Rockefellers, Mathers, and Boltons became fabulously wealthy and, in turn, created a system of foundations and corporate charities that enabled Cleveland to enjoy a strong social welfare system. As long as the mills remained profitable, Cleveland remained graced with high levels of steady employment, stable communities, and private noblesse oblige—the antecedent of Dibiasio's big picture. Yet after World War II, when the steel industry began to fade, increases in poverty, middle-class flight to suburbia, rapid construction of highways, and the erosion of the privately financed safety net brought about the erosion of the downtown infrastructure. In the wake of this, Cleveland's wealthy and close-knit business community began to look almost uniformly toward large-scale packages of urban renewal to save the city.

For better or for worse, the particular vision of this wealthy circle of businessmen has largely informed the direction of urban renovation to the present day. Faced with widespread racial and economic problems, urban developers and other Cleveland business interests worked closely with the government in the 1960s and early 1970s to plan a city that was to be rebuilt through projects geared toward tourism and corporate service. Gradually, hotels and skyscraping office towers began to crowd out a fabric of local businesses, shops, and manufacturing entities. Because the majority of these corporate towers were propped up by significant tax abatements and because the middle class had long since fled for the suburbs, the tax base which might have paid for needed schools and social services for the remaining (by then predominantly African American) residents of the city was severely eroded. While increasing investment downtown and attracting tenants like British Petroleum (BP), which built the massive BP America building off Public Square, this strategy also seemed to contribute to a descending spiral of poverty and misery hidden in the shadows of urban renewal.

In the wake of the oil crisis in the early 1970s, which brought about a further erosion of the town's manufacturing base, Clevelanders attempted to reverse the trend toward this proliferation of subsidized downtown development by electing populist mayor Dennis Kucinich.[6] Kucinich sparred with increasingly strong banking interests, refusing time and again to sign legislation approving new downtown projects. But his crusade was short-lived and, frankly, doomed from the start. He was humiliated by a united front of business leaders and bankers determined to force him out of office. His administration had inherited $15.5 million in bank loans, which, in the past, had simply been allowed to roll over. Now, spurred on by business interests frustrated by Kucinich's efforts to slow downtown development, Cleveland Trust (now Ameritrust) chose to demand payment.[7] This aggressive action on the part of a corporation destined in a new world order to become a "subject of history," helped send the city belly up.[8] If the fire on the Cuyahoga had not already signaled rock bottom for Cleveland, the fact that the city went into default in December 1978 as a result of Cleveland Trust's actions most certainly did.[9]

More resolute than ever, an influential group of Cleveland businessman both drafted George Voinovich to run for mayor and funded his election bid. In turn, after winning the race, Voinovich, working in conjunction with rather than against corporate interests, pushed forward an ambitious program of rapid downtown development. For his efforts, Voinovich has been seen as a savior; and, in fact, from many perspectives, downtown Cleveland, during his term, did enjoy a remarkable recovery.[10] The new Cleveland skyline, its impressive stone and glass monuments to commerce book-ended by the two voluminous stadiums, has become a symbol of the town's resiliency. This transformation has allowed Cleveland to be touted nationally as a model for revitalizing the rust belt.

But, of course, all that glitters is not necessarily gold, especially during a period of transition. Near these skyscrapers, hotels, and new stadiums stand rows of vacant stores and, farther out, southeast of downtown, a quilt of severely decimated African American communities continues to wait for its own renaissance. Mark Naymik, in an examination of the chain of events occurring after the city went bankrupt on so-called Black Friday, concludes that high-profile projects have not begun to solve what he considers to be Cleveland's core problems. "Cleveland, while ranking number one in amenities (sports, arts, recreation), rank[s] second to last on economic vitality and community prosperity based on median household income, employment growth, and the income gap between city residents and suburbanites. Only Detroit rank[s] worse" (11). The results of the 2000 U.S. Census support Naymik's claims. From 1979 to 1999, the period roughly corresponding with Cleveland's renaissance, the city experienced the smallest gain in median income among the largest fifty American cities. Median income rose from $5,770 in 1979 to $14,291 in 1999. However, adjusted for inflation, that increase amounts to just under $1,000 in real dollars. Prospects for future generations look similarly bleak. Cleveland schools, despite the so-called economic miracle, are among the worst in the nation, even in the wake of a stream of largely unfulfilled promises that taxes generated by new development would go directly toward them.[11] City neighborhoods have continued to decline, crime is still on the increase, and many districts remain largely devoid of capital, especially in the aftermath of welfare reform.[12]

Of course, the two-tiered nature of downtown is not simply endemic to Cleveland but pandemic in post-Fordist urban America. Following the long decay of the

American manufacturing base and the recession of the early 1970s, the urban economy has clearly split into two distinct yet symbiotic growth sectors. On one hand, the high-paying corporate service segment, consisting of bankers, speculators, lawyers, and managers, has boomed in order to facilitate the increasing mobility of capital. On the other hand, the poorly paying sector of lower-level services—janitors, secretaries, couriers, and so on—has needed to grow in order to service these high-end workers. This has created the conditions under which each skyscraper has become, in itself, a microcosm of the new class structure of urban America. Flexible and often temporary labor cleans wastebaskets and answers the phones for members of a mobile corporate class. In this way, Voinovich's economic miracle has indeed produced plenty of new work for an expanded work force. But to critics, it has done so largely by creating a *hamburger* economy of low-wage, expendable, and low-ceilinged jobs.

This part of the big picture is an unintended byproduct of Cleveland's primary brand of urban planning. It is a controversial element of the ideology behind the conviction that the key to economic recovery is a realization of large-scale projects of urban renewal. This renewal, instead of focusing on the immediate needs of current city residents, is geared primarily to the recreation, working patterns, and consuming desires of the both commuters and those visitors who engage in urban leisure safaris. The principal economic benefits to existing residents are believed to trickle down.

SWEETHEART DEALS OR PRUDENT PUBLIC INVESTMENT?

Questions about long-term benefits notwithstanding, this facet of the new economy would be much less controversial were it not for concerns about the political arrangements deemed necessary to accomplish such large-scale urban renewal. The new Cleveland downtown, especially the Gateway, is arguably a product of thirty years of favorable deals given by the government to corporations and investors benefiting from the mobility of capital in a post-Fordist economy. Franchise relocation in baseball, or at least the threat of relocation, is now a routine bargaining chip on the part of shrewd owners. Just like other companies that, for three decades, have been playing one municipality against another in order to earn tax abatements and better labor contracts, baseball clubs (themselves increasingly owned by corporations instead of individuals) have steadily demanded, since the early 1990s, that cities pick up more of the tab for both the construction of their facilities and the operating expenses.

The history of Cleveland's stadium deals is representative of a generation of marketing and political strategies employed nationwide by public-private partnerships looking to sell arena projects to taxpayers. During the years of Jacobs

Field negotiation and construction, arguments in favor of public subsidies for these projects went relatively unchallenged; and when challenges did occur, they were largely unsuccessful. Voinovich's successor, Michael White, was elected in 1989 by promising racial peace, improved neighborhoods, and no new taxes in his first term. However, shortly after the election, he led a campaign to pass a $275 million "sin tax" on liquor, beer, wine, and cigarettes to finance the new arena and stadium. The tax referendum easily passed, winning by a landslide in the affluent suburbs even as it was rejected by those living within the city limits. Campaigning on behalf of the tax, White promised creation of sixteen thousand permanent jobs to the most needy city neighborhoods and said that he would allow no tax abatement to the stadium, which, he reasoned, would provide for $15.6 million to be funneled into Cleveland schools. Just one year later, however, he ended up lobbying the state legislature to grant a tax abatement in perpetuity to the stadium and the arena.

When the cost of this tax abatement is added to the amount of public money spent on stadium construction and operating costs, it appears that the city has contributed more than $1 billion to the project. This includes a city-financed security team of police officers working overtime directing traffic and shooing panhandlers off the streets surrounding the stadium during events. It also includes a loss of city revenue for such items as parking spaces given free to members of the Indians' and Cavaliers' (Cleveland's basketball team) management in civic-owned garages, and tax- and rent-free apartments, suites, and corporate offices built in the complex for the teams' owners and personnel.

Working in concert with the city, the Indians almost overnight became one of baseball's most profitable franchises. The team's relationship with the government allowed it to evolve from sellers to buyers, suddenly able to become among the game's biggest spenders. Management added to a core of home-grown talent by signing a string of high-profile, high-salaried free agents.[13] In turn, this spending spree allowed the Indians to put a team of unusual distinction on the field, much to the delight of local baseball fans long starved for a contender. In this sense, the big picture signifies the network of deals helping the club achieve profitability and success on the diamond, which then provided pleasure and a sense of civic pride to all Clevelanders who supported the baseball team during the tremendous run of the late 1990s.

Was this sense of pride worth an investment of more than $1 billion? It is impossible to say objectively. One cannot begin to quantify the extent to which widespread good feelings about a town contribute to overall community health. Each skilled surgeon, community organizer, or dedicated teacher who chooses to remain in Cleveland (rather than apply his or her skills elsewhere) enriches the city in a small way. Bringing people together to root for the Indians creates a sense of solidarity among citizens, prompting random checkout-line conversations among fans who otherwise might not speak, smoothing over race and class differences, and providing a degree of connection among an increasingly mobile and spread-out community. Additionally, the existence of a popular urban entertainment destination stimulates the investment of private capital in other local projects, bringing jobs, revenue, and in some cases valuable services to an urban area previously in decline. For example, it is unlikely that any of the new restaurants in the Gateway would have opened up without Jacobs Field. Similarly, it is improbable that the nearby restored Theater District around Playhouse Square would have continued to enjoy the comeback it has without the healthy buzz and increased foot traffic generated by the new sports facilities.

Yet as political winds shift, more and more taxpayers are beginning to ask themselves and their elected officials if sizeable public investment in private sports facilities is prudent. Once activists in places like Cleveland and Baltimore began giving their version of the bottom line—that the direct economic benefit of stadium construction to cities is relatively minimal—a political backlash began to emerge in the 1990s and continues to this day.[14] In Cleveland, where most locals have always supported a degree of governmental help for the beloved local franchises, many people became positively outraged when it was revealed that the Indians, during their second year in the new park (a year in which they sold out the stadium every night and made millions from television revenues alone), wrote a rent check to the city for a mere $461,415, or less than the club pays its most inexpensive ballplayer.[15] In the wake of this backlash, initiatives for taxpayer-funded stadiums failed outright in Minnesota, San Francisco, and Montreal. Similarly, in Washington state, where $7.5 million was invested in funding a special statewide referendum and in providing an advertising campaign to secure its passage, voters approved a $425 million publicly financed stadium for the NFL's Seahawks by only a single percentage point.

What has emerged (since the early days of sweetheart deals) is a more complex give and take between private developers and political authorities. Cities have discovered a host of tools at their disposal, making investment on the part of owners more attractive. Local governments can condemn properties or claim eminent domain to make large urban areas available for development. They can offer to improve or add public infrastructure. They can provide some tax relief, and they can waive or relax certain regulatory policies.[16] Meanwhile, they are also beginning to understand the need to drive a hard bargain, to resist rolling over for sports owners who often resort to legal forms of coercion or blackmail. Increasingly, local authorities have learned that it is all right to simply walk away without making a deal. Teams do in fact move, yet their communities remain intact. After all, Los Angeles' economy is still one of the largest in the world even if the (NFL) Rams and Raiders no longer play home games there. Similarly, in San Francisco, after voters refused public financing for a new ball park, team president Peter A. Magowan and a consortium of partners put up their own $360 million to build Pacific Bell Park. This turn of events made

Pac Bell Park one of the first mostly privately financed baseball stadium built since 1962.[17] The successful early years of the park suggest that this will be a long-term profitable venture for the consortium even without hundreds of millions of dollars worth of direct public investment.[18]

The rules for creating the big picture have thus evolved nationally since the Indians first started negotiating with Cleveland. Citizens have begun to take a closer look at the magnitude and relative one-sidedness of deals like the one that ball club management struck with Mayor White. Now, rather than simply embracing or dismissing a possible stadium deal for ideological reasons, they are demanding that politicians limit public investment and exact adequate proffers while still supporting some agreements enabling private sports enterprises to augment their bottom line and spend money on players.

A CONSUMING HISTORY

While it has become clear that a better balance between public investment and economic benefit can be struck in cities looking to replicate Cleveland's program of revitalization, it remains murky how to do so without significantly altering the culture of downtown. Although he takes issue with anyone who argues that Jacobs Field is unfriendly to "the working man," Dibiasio is quick to acknowledge both the changing expectations of a more upscale baseball audience and the fact that consuming patterns at retro stadiums mirror those of other, uniquely late-twentieth-century venues such as festival marketplaces and themed gift shops. Somewhat wistfully, the Indians' VP notes that as the Gateway's signature attraction, Jacobs Field is obliged to present a wide range of customized purchasing alternatives. At the old stadium, vendors simply offered a cuisine that promoted (perhaps unintentionally) a certain democracy of consumption. Working classes joined the middle classes as buyers of standardized mass products— generic hot dogs and brand name beer. "But now," says Dibiasio, "you are not just selling hot dogs." Both inside and outside the stadium, he suggests, having more consumer choices signifies "freedom."

Several years ago, the 7-Eleven convenience store chain came up with a highly representative advertising jingle summing up this particular semiotic relationship: "You're going to like the freedom of 7-Eleven." By equating consuming ease, the ability to purchase 24/7 everything from Ben and Jerry's ice cream to cigarettes and car supplies, with "freedom," a long-cherished American ideal, the 7-Eleven slogan suggests a certain loss Dibiasio seems to sense when describing changing ball-park fare. Not only does the need to provide for the modern consumer compel his organization to cater to a new breed of fan unlike himself as a young man, but it also requires it to service a debased conception of freedom. Freedom as the ability to choose from sixteen types of micro brews, as opposed to such exalted rights as the freedom of religion or speech, suggests a certain profaning of the sacred against which Dibiasio, a patriotic man, seems to recoil.

Nonetheless, even though he personally appears to prefer an idealized version of the baseball consumer of the past, Dibiasio recognizes the need to understand his job within the evolving big picture. He knows he cannot pretend that Jacobs Field exists in an era prior to the disorganization of American capital, a time when mass-market American beer would have been the only thing in stadium concession stands and on store shelves. He recognizes that in contemporary America (apart from some nostalgic middle-class consumers) it is primarily only the poor who now favor Schlitz and Pabst Blue Ribbon, icons of standardized mass-consumption goods, that for a while, suited most beer drinkers. He knows that the modern spectator tends to insist on a more flexible system of product development, marketing, and shipping. In short, he understands that the Indians' new clientele at least partially judges the quality of its experience by the spectrum of consumer choices available at the park and by the ability of management to make these choices interesting and ever-changing.

This demand for accumulative flexibility is dramatically remaking the new American city. Private-public urban spaces such as the one surrounding Jacobs Field attempt to anticipate the desires of nostalgic visitors, leading to the reinvention of downtown according to a set of interesting, yet increasingly standardized and often-problematic, aesthetic idioms. Largely forgotten during the city's "economic miracle," the area now comprising the Gateway had, during the 1960s and 1970s, fallen into considerable disrepute. Literally in the shadow of Cleveland's sterling new downtown, the Gateway had come to embody the collateral damage of urban renewal and suburban flight—a part of town so neglected that even some stores catering to the urban working poor fled from it to distant neighborhoods. As such, it was almost universally believed to be in need of desperate attention. Yet the specific type of economic development stimulated in the Gateway by the construction of the two stadiums suggests the future of this portion of downtown as, in part, a kind of theme park for an increasingly homogenous crowd.

On East Fourth Street, a side street linking Euclid and Prospect Avenues adjacent to the stadium complex, many markers of this type of theming are visible. During the 1940s, 1950s, and into the early 1960s, East Fourth was perhaps the most vibrant street in Cleveland. It was the only open connecting road between Cleveland's two main avenues, and thus served as a turnaround point for the bus line. "It was so crowded on this street that you could barely walk through here," says Irv Zimmer, who bought A. Sisser Jewelers on East Fourth in 1959 and whose son Bob still owns the business. "This whole area used to be the main shopping district for Cleveland. Everyone, white and Negro, used to come down here." But, as Zimmer recounts, in the late 1950s and early 1960s, most of the upscale shops in the area moved to either nearby Tower City or the suburbs, leaving behind boarded-up buildings and a host of small businesses—discount shoe stores, afro-wig suppliers, check-cashing shops, and so on—catering primarily to a poor black clientele. "For a long time now our customers have been mostly Negro," says Zimmer, who now works for his son. "But that's changing. We're trying to go upscale."

This choice, the decision "to go upscale," was clearly rooted in economic reality for the Zimmers. "You know what, these stores around here really haven't been doing much business since the baseball stadium opened up," the elder Zimmer says, referring to their neighbors, U.S. Wigs, Rainbow (discount clothing), and Hair Plus. "They will mostly be gone soon," he continues, replaced by high-end national specialty shops, luxury condominiums, restaurants, and a side entrance to the House of Blues chain nightclub expected to open soon on Euclid.

But, of course, not everyone is thrilled with the street's evolution. "They [landlords] don't want retail stores like ours anymore," says Sue Kim, for fifteen years the manager of Hair Plus, which is being forced to close down. "Now, black folks don't come downtown anymore. The city wants a new kind of business," she adds. "It's kind of sad, but money talks." Kim's plight is not at all unique to the area. In the decade since Jacobs Field opened for business, dozens of recent Korean immigrants who had built businesses selling essential products primarily to local African Americans have been forced to close down their shops. In turn, African Americans, for years relegated to the level of consumption in the Gateway, have been squeezed even further out of sight. No longer even catered to as customers, many of Cleveland's downtown blacks are largely vanishing as a result of gentrification.

As this has happened, as the area has undergone a not-always-smooth transition from black to white, a fascinating gentrification aesthetic has emerged. In 1996, in order to bond with his black customers and attract the attention of baseball fans coming to the area for the Major League Baseball All-Star game, Bob Zimmer placed a photographic exhibit in his store window detailing the exploits of the various Negro League teams that played in nearby parks long before Larry Doby broke the American League color line in the late forties. The display commemorated the five Negro League teams that competed in downtown Cleveland between 1922 and 1948, and particularly celebrated the Buckeyes, who won the Negro World Series at League Park II in 1945. Meanwhile, two doors down from this pictorial commemoration and across the street from a recently boarded-up check-cashing shop, contractors were putting the finishing touches on the "Historic Buckeye" luxury condominiums. This tableau enacts a semiotics of replacement—cultures and people of the past subsumed by appellations and images for consumption. The use of the name "Buckeye," like the aisles of Negro League gear—"X" hats and Jackie Robinson jerseys—filling the Indians' official gift shop on the concourse of the stadium nearby, both pays homage to a disappearing past

POSTERS HANG IN THE WINDOWS OF A EUCLID AVENUE BUILDING UNDERGOING RENOVATION. THESE COMMEMORATIVE IMAGES OF AFRICAN AMERICANS PROMOTE THE HISTORY OF THE AREA'S STREETS AS DIVERSE AND ALIVE AND BRING TO MIND AN OLD RACIAL ORDER.

and recycles some of the leftover energy of the original. It invests the new space with residue of some of the diversity of the old city even as (or perhaps precisely because) it gentrifies.

Zimmer's use of these images is not at all unique. Throughout the transitional Gateway, this kind of juxtaposition has become extremely commonplace. On Euclid Avenue, for example, five old black-and-white photographic images of African Americans—a street saxophone player, female mannequins displaying "relaxed hair" wigs, a parking lot attendant, a photographer, and a group of construction workers—grace the windows of a building being renovated by the Downtown Cleveland Partnership. Much of this impromptu exhibit's symbolism seems clear. All of the images both promote the history of the area's streets as diverse and alive and bring to mind an old racial order. The musician and the photographer performed for passersby, enhancing the sensory experience of being in the city. The wigs represent both a passing period of black commerce and, more troubling, the need for African American women to alter their bodies to fit a homogenized (or perhaps white) conception of beauty. The exhibit, although perhaps an innocent product of noble intentions on the part of the Partnership—attempting to pay tribute to the many African Americans who had been the primary inhabitants of this area for close to forty years—clearly attempts to ease a transition that may someday completely erase the presence of those being commemorated. Fred Brown, panhandling in front of this display, is quick to notice the irony. "They built the stadium for the people in the suburbs," he says. "People like me can't get jobs around here no more."

In the years since Bob Zimmer's first simple act of commemoration, the display of Negro League memorabilia has become a veritable cottage industry for the jeweler on East Fourth Street. His original exhibit created so much interest among passing baseball fans and collectors that it inspired him to create a full-fledged Baseball Heritage Museum on the site. Devoted to preserving and protecting "the history of diversity in baseball," the nascent museum will eventually occupy the entire second floor of the building above his store.[19] Over the course of the past few years, Zimmer has worked tirelessly, collecting artifacts, staging conferences, raising private money, and tracking down grants in order to show his enormous respect for the game's many black pioneers. His work underlines his appreciation of the ability of sport (and baseball in particular) to pave the way for societal acceptance of racial mixing. It also highlights his and his father's dedication to the city. One by one since the early 1960s, other white shop owners downtown moved their businesses to the suburbs, abandoning their clients, white

A. SISSER JEWELERS AND THE BASEBALL HERITAGE MUSEUM STAND NEXT TO STRUGGLING DISCOUNT RETAILERS ON EAST FOURTH STREET.

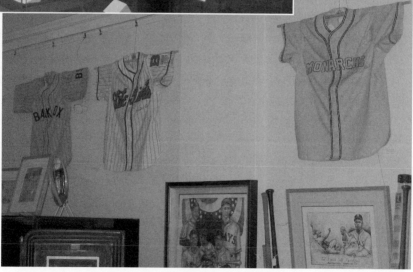

and black, who had been patronizing them for years. The Zimmers, on the other hand, stuck it out and embraced what had become an almost exclusively black clientele.

All of which makes Zimmer's actions as an inspirational force behind the Gateway transformation seem especially complicated. According to Irv Zimmer, his son "got the whole Gateway development moving. He came up with the plans to bring the stadium here and convert all these old buildings to condos. He worked hard to get the city to get behind the idea and to get them to register East Fourth Street as a historic landmark." Converting buildings to condominiums, replacing a run-down market with two sports arenas, and trading in small-scale enterprises for national retail chains and restaurants of course makes sense from a business perspective. The paucity of income among what was left of the Zimmer's clients meant a bleak future for the business unless something drastic happened. Yet setting out in the late 1980s to effect these drastic changes, Zimmer also put in motion a process that perhaps will have as its end point the preservation and presentation of "the history of diversity" in the Gateway largely in commemorative form only.

Zimmer's ability to attain a "historic landmark" designation for East Fourth helped enact a commemorative *historic* aesthetic familiar to most people who have ever walked the streets around Camden Yards in Baltimore, South Street Seaport in Manhattan or Penn's Landing in Philadelphia. During the first few years of redevelopment, architects, designers, and private property owners offered up a range of intriguing decorative details on the street. Perhaps because a dwindling number of commercial and social reasons for locals to walk East Fourth Street on nongame days ensured that the block was often deserted and thus somewhat forbidding, local officials dressed up this erstwhile important artery in order to reassure tourists and baseball fans of its safety and walkability. Interestingly, they did this in ways not unlike how Main Street USA in Disney World was fashioned. They laid brick sidewalks and installed lampposts covered with faux wrought-iron sheathing, materials suggesting the *historic,* but in reality relatively anathema to the area's stone and steel history. The brick and fake iron on East Fourth are signifiers of genial history, the raw goods that code retro urban destinations as somehow historical, whether they are found in Cleveland, Baltimore, New York, or Philadelphia.

These details are clear material manifestations of a psychological transformation intended by the original renaming/reinvention of the area. The appellation "Gateway" at first seems perfectly appropriate for a zone located between two important bodies of water. It suggests that the space was once a significant port of entry for both goods and immigrants. In reality, however, it was never

SIGNIFIERS OF GENIAL HISTORY, IMITATION WROUGHT-IRON LAMPPOSTS WERE INSTALLED ON EAST FOURTH STREET AFTER IT WAS DESIGNATED A HISTORIC LANDMARK.

FAUX GAS LAMPS IN THE FLATS RESTAURANT DISTRICT INVEST THE SPACE WITH AN ANTIQUE FEELING.

much of the sort. It did not feature docks, cargo storage, an immigration office, a railroad terminus, or any other recognizable marker of a maritime port of trade. Instead, it has a somewhat less easily romanticized recent history of high-end and discount shopping, legal and illegal markets, and marginal and illicit local trading. Yet its clever name comforts and reassures contemporary visitors by now accustomed to the pleasant, uncontroversial feel of urban "historical" waterfront reconstructions increasingly popular across America.[20]

The impulse to package the area as nebulously historic is made clear by the marketing rhetoric employed by the owners of the Buckeye and its nearby cousin, the Windsor Building. Speaking about the home of his two renovated buidlings, Ari Maron told *Cleveland* magazine the following: "It's a brick street and the buildings have a wonderfully *historic feel* with all the amenities of 21st century living. It's a nice juxtaposition."[21] This language suggests how seamlessly history itself can become a consumer choice in the new American city. The symbiotic impulses of commemoration and commodification, so central to the logic of contemporary gentrification, flourishes on East Fourth Street in order to ease its transition from the past to the present.

The "big picture" thus transcends simple political economy by describing how countless postmodern cultural forms tend to arrive on the scene as downtown becomes an urban entertainment destination. These forms, many of which are writ large on the stadium stage, promise psychical connection with the past through a series of replacements for many of the desired elements of urban life either missing or perceived to be missing from the post-Fordist city. It thus seems almost a given that retro Jacobs Field, a veritable petri dish for the generation of postmodern symbols and images of the past, would emerge as the centerpiece of the Gateway project.

URBAN NOSTALGIA

The construction of parks that attempt to replicate the past is entirely congruent with a central baseball motif: tying the excitement of the present to feats of yesteryear.[22] Throughout the past century, baseball has continually elevated the exploits of past ballplayers to heroic dimensions, immortalizing players in its pantheon, the Hall of Fame in Cooperstown, New York, and, when expedient, fabricating its own history in order to more thoroughly validate the present. For example, the very foundational myth of baseball—that Civil War hero Abner Doubleday invented the sport behind a barbershop in Cooperstown—is apocryphal. This myth was generated and supported by a bogus commission enlisted by Commissioner A. G. Spalding during a time when the sport's executives were trying to market the game as a symbol of uniquely American "vim" and "vigor" (Spalding 4).[23] Much like Spalding and his cohorts, today's baseball management and fans seem perhaps more eager than ever to worship the past as a way to counteract negative feelings generated by a string of player strikes and lockouts as well as a decade and a half of lagging popular interest in the "national pastime."

The particular epoch chosen for promotion, the era producing models for contemporary replication, is worthy of some consideration. The retro stadium movement leapfrogs the immediate past in order to feature a more idealized history of early-twentieth-century stadium construction and urban space. Just as the Historic Buckeye condominiums were renovated to commemorate East Fourth Street as it was imagined to be at the beginning of the twentieth century, Camden Yards, Jacobs Field, and the retro stadiums built after them are aesthetic reactions against the massive, multipurpose stadiums in vogue during the 1950s, 1960s, and 1970s.

Smaller in scale, located once again downtown, the new old stadiums gesture back toward the first concrete and steel ball parks constructed in the early part of the century.[24] They were inspired by, among other parks, now-demolished Ebbets Field in Brooklyn and the perhaps soon-to-be-renovated Fenway Park in Boston, two venues notable primarily for the way in which they bent to fit into the existing city landscape.[25] Both Fenway and Ebbets feature (or featured) large outfield walls enclosing an extremely short field on one side of the park. In Boston, the existence of a road forced architects to devise the "Green Monster," which serves as a dramatic backdrop to left field. In Brooklyn, Charles Ebbets, after several years of surreptitious land acquisition, was unable to obtain a final parcel of land that would have

ABOVE: IN BALTIMORE, A SECTION OF EUTAW STREET IS INCORPORATED WITHIN THE GATES OF CAMDEN YARDS. COURTESY OF JERRY WACHTER.

LEFT: ONTARIO STREET IS LARGELY DISCONNECTED FROM THE DOWNTOWN CLEVELAND GRID, SERVING PRIMARILY AS A PATHWAY FOR TICKET HOLDERS COMING TOWARD OR LEAVING THE PARK.

allowed for more outfield symmetry. Thus he too was forced to construct a tall wall in right field in order to keep ordinary fly balls in play. In turn, these walls—and the strange, game-turning caroms and massive blasts that cleared them—became the centerpieces of legends.[26]

HOK architects in Cleveland and in Baltimore paid homage to this kind of resourcefulness by situating their parks in such a way to account for a partially faux, or at least a refashioned, urban grid. In Baltimore, designers left standing the old Baltimore and Ohio train warehouse and Eutaw Street in front of it as a backdrop to right-center field. To compensate for the smaller field dimensions this necessitated, they then built a tall right field wall to keep balls in play. Similarly, in Cleveland, stadium designers incorporated adjacent Ontario Street prominently into the plan for the park and created the "mini green monster" in left field.

Both Ontario and Eutaw Streets are central components of the new urbanism so much a part of the attraction. In Baltimore, Eutaw Street, incorporated within the gates of the park, is a privatized walking street for paying customers. It hosts a food court, rest rooms, and Boog Powell's famous barbecue stand just beyond the outfield bleachers. In Cleveland, the large gate on Ontario Street serves as the stadium's main entrance. Gesturing back to Coogan's Bluff outside the Polo Grounds in New York, to the old elevated platform outside Yankee Stadium in the Bronx, and to the apartment roofs outside Chicago's Wrigley Field—sites of urban democracy, where even the poorest fan could see a game—this iron gate affords passersby a free glimpse of the action.

The architects' gestures are witty and creative attempts to integrate the park into the city. Yet to some patrons, they also contribute toward a somewhat contrived feel. "It's not like Wrigley Park, in an actual neighborhood," said John Zajc, executive director of the Society for American Baseball Research (SABR), whose office is two blocks from Jacobs Field. "In order to make it as comfortable as it is and to eliminate obstructed views, the footprint had to be huge." Zajc loves the new stadium but recognizes that, in terms of its relationship to the surrounding city, the Jake is somewhat of a fish out of water: "The suburban ethos [which required the construction of capacious parking decks] doesn't necessarily have a good fit in the downtown space." His ambivalence about the area around the park suggests the extent to which, instead of redesigning Jacobs Field to account for an existing grid, architects actually chose to create spatial conflict. This difference is crucial. The resulting tension gestures back to a time when cities were necessities, not commodities, to an era prior to both suburbanization and the industrialization of recreation, when baseball architecture somehow had to integrate itself into the vibrant city. In the post-Fordist city, by contrast, the structure of downtown is adjusted to accommodate the ball park, even as it creates the illusion that the city's shape came first. This distinction serves as one possible metaphor for the place of the ball park in the city. Recreational and entertainment venues are perceived to be so important to the vibrancy of the new down-

IN CLEVELAND, GATE A ON ONTARIO STREET PROVIDES PASSERSBY A FREE GLIMPSE OF THE ACTION.

town space that the city literally bends in order to accommodate them. Yet a large part of the mission of their architects is to situate and design ball parks so as to mask this fact, to underscore architecturally the belief that baseball is an integral part of the very fabric of American culture. In short, one intended message of stadium designers seems to be that retro parks merely fit into a city's big picture instead of dominating it. Thus the designers cater to a desire for the city to regain the relevance of an earlier epoch.[27]

Of course, as Zajc suggests, diminishing the organic quality of the streets incorporated by the two parks is the fact that both Eutaw and Ontario are privatized and/or isolated. In Cleveland, the road is so far dislocated from natural downtown pedestrian traffic that it serves primarily as a pathway for ticket holders to use after they park in the lots.[28] During a recent four-game series, only two non–ticket holders (a pair of rollerbladers who seemed to have arrived on the scene by accident) approached the Ontario Street gate while a game was going on. Although during marquee events such as the playoffs or the All-Star game, some people actually do come downtown specifically to watch the game from this vantage point, their freedom is somewhat restricted. Because they are watching from a private street, their behaviors are subject to control by the Indians organization.[29]

Nonetheless, in comparison to suburban baseball stadiums, surrounded as they are by acres of parking (explicitly private land flattened and regularized for automobile culture), the ersatz public streets surrounding retro parks are at least pedestrian-friendly. As such, they are genuine attempts to reconstitute a golden age in the history of American cities before car culture threatened their relevancy. They are also laudable efforts to bring back a sense of regional variation to cities and stadiums perceived to be missing since mass construction and culture homogenized the landscape. Yet as with many attempts to proscribe or simulate the lived experience of passed cultures, perceived by many to be more authentic than the present, these gestures have their limitations. As similar architectural idioms have been employed in newer retro stadiums across the country, this sense of uniqueness becomes endangered. Of the fourteen stadiums constructed completely or partially in the retro mode, ten were designed by a single architectural firm, HOK Sport, and most utilize the same materials and forms: brick and steel with repeated archways. Though they all have their unique features—cast stone in Cincinnati, "Uecker" obstructed view seats in Milwaukee—they also have perilously much in common.[30]

SYMBOLS OF STABILITY

In the new economy, as Cleveland's population has become increasingly mobile, gestures of rooting have taken on increased significance. In the days when the city was predominantly organized around a manufacturing economy, it was not uncommon for several generations of men and women in the same family to live in the same neighborhood and to work in the same place.[31] Conversely, many Cleveland workers in the post-Fordist era are simultaneously privileged with and expected to endure geographic and occupational mobility. Many of them require at least a degree of flexibility to change jobs or even cities in order to find professional success. Thus connection to a sports franchise can quickly earn them a degree of psychic rootedness even as their professional lives continue to demand physical rootlessness. Different by degrees from opera houses, parks, and other traditional public works designed for the gathering of large audiences, stadiums are built to create an atmosphere of approximated tribalism. Fans, who more and more lack a common history, join together for a common purpose—cheering on the home team.

Similarly, the world they inhabit, the postmodern physical world, is itself defined by flux and flexibility. Architecture is increasingly more ephemeral in order to meet a consumer aesthetic defined in part by a thirst for novelty. The primary form of suburban public space, the shopping mall, now routinely gets a facelift every decade or so to account for increasingly dynamic popular tastes and in order to avoid looking obsolete. Perhaps largely as a response to these general trends, retro stadiums have arrived to signify something more enduring. Stadiums, with their roots in antiquity, are very good at offering up images of continuity. The exposed steel trusses of new old parks, like the imposing marble arches of the Roman Coliseum, advertise to residents and visitors the potential staying power of the present.

The Ballpark at Arlington, Texas, serves as a good case study for examining the role of retro stadiums in the creation of this sense of longevity and permanence. Much of Arlington's modern history is largely informed by its location about halfway between Dallas and Forth Worth. When the Texas and Pacific Railroad built a line between the two towns in the 1870s, Arlington was chosen as the stop in between. In 1902, when the Interurban trolley line linking the small village with the two larger towns was created, Arlington's role as a convenient home for commuters was established. Although by the 1960s the town's population had reached nearly fifty thousand and some industry as well as a branch of the University of Texas had settled there, Arlington was still best known as the location of the Six Flags Over Texas amusement park. In other words, it was still largely a regional hub for amusement and a bedroom community for those who worked in Dallas or Fort Worth. After 1972, when Turnpike Stadium, a minor-league venue adjacent to the amusement activities, was upgraded to house the Texas Rangers (relocated that year from Washington, D.C., where they had been the Senators), the town grew according to fairly standard 1970s and 1980s idioms—shopping centers, subdivisions, and motels.

Thus, the decision in 1991 to build an *urban* park in this rather non-urban (or newly urban) location was a fascinating one. In order to compensate for its somewhat contextually challenged nature, David M. Schwartz Architectural Services endowed the park with characteristics riffing on those found in Yankee Stadium. The firm designed historicist brick arches anathema to Southwest architecture and built an elaborate Ranger Hall of Fame that pays homage to the famous monuments in center field of the Bronx ball park. In contrast to the Yankees, however, the Rangers are a team without much of a history, having been a recent expansion franchise in Washington before their move and having never reached the World Series. Clearly a large part of the retro park's purpose is to help the now more than a quarter-million-person municipality transition away from an identity as a mere suburban way station or edge city.

In Cleveland, the historical nature of the stadium comes across as a bit more genuine. Jacobs Field is laced with witty postmodern forms accentuating structural or ornamental details helping relate the stadium to the city's actual past. The floodlight poles reminding visitors of the steel mill smokestacks are easily recognizable as relics of Cleveland's great industrial age. At the same time, these white steel structures advertise the significant changes occurring in the postindustrial city. The steel that once supported the massive tresses covering the great furnaces where thousands labored daily now holds up lights illuminating the central recreational pursuit of the new downtown. Once, downtown Cleveland was the site of large-scale feats of production. Now, it caters to thousands of citizens and tourists nightly as the site of recreational consumption.

This contrast underlines the fantasy investing retro stadiums with much of their appeal. Cleveland is no longer a place where the average person breaks his or her back, day after day feeding the infernal furnaces of the steel mills. Instead, it is a place where these same, formerly oppressive, raw materials are now used to provide pleasure. As the status of downtown has changed, from one based on production to one based on recreational consumption, the venue housing its most popular recreational pursuit commemorates this important symbol of the past. In minivans (many of which were assembled in Mexico out of steel products fired in Korea), Jacobs Field patrons crossing the Cuyahoga from the suburbs can consume an experience accented with vestiges of the epoch of production.

This crucial tension between consuming and producing informs a great many of the design and decorating choices inside the new old stadium. The ball park is virtually packed to the rafters with relics of the past, accentuating the primacy of the passing age of Cleveland productivity. This package includes expressed steel beams, analog clocks, and copious displays of black-and-white photographs—objects with obsolete exchange value and/or forms of the anti-technological. The operating logic of this facet of the big picture is a metonymic replacement of experience with commemorative items. Like corsages kept pressed in photo albums, the various relics of an earlier era serve as souvenirs of the original experience. Thus, like so many postmodern mementos, they are invested with the promise of narrowing the gap between the status of contemporary consumers pitched into hyper-speed reality and an imagined pre-commodified self. For example, the momentary struggle involved in reading an analog clock provides nanoseconds of relief and reassurance. A small act of renunciation, it enables sensations of a self that existed prior to the technological present. It also allows for a small-scale psychic subversion of modernity's techno-consumerist ethos and the attendant promise of greater and greater ease. This kind of subversion is made necessary by the changing nature of middle-class work in downtown America. White-collar work, while saving the body from abuse, deprives contemporary Americans of many acts of creation associated with manual labor. Therefore, items such as analog clocks and hand-operated scoreboards, reminiscent of an age when men and women toiled, are seen as essential features of these new parks.

Recognizing the compensatory nature of items like these seems crucial for understanding the role of the ball park in a rapidly changing city. Retro ball parks facilitate the shift from the Fordist to the post-Fordist city by providing a host of meaningful cultural forms. From the creation of a sense of regional variation, to architectural gestures highlighting the uniqueness of a particular location, to simulated urban promenades and the injection of thousands of relics or souvenirs of a previous order, these stadiums offer a link to an increasingly elided past which is nonetheless perceived to be more stable and authentic than the present.

BALANCING RELEASE AND CONTROL

In this new world of the old city, it is crucial that the Indians organization and public officials carefully manage and control the baseball event in order to help patrons negotiate the contradictions associated with a downtown space in the process of transforming itself. The big picture that emerges from this management is not simply a whitewashed superimposition of the suburbs onto downtown but a fascinating world of simultaneous tolerance and control allowing patrons to witness and even act out boisterous city behaviors within a carefully controlled, relatively safe space. Paul Goldberger, in "The Rise of the Private City," calls areas like the Gateway "urbanoid environments," faux city spaces appearing to provide the benefits of the city—proximity, energy, and so forth—while actually sheltering suburban visitors from the problems of city life (140). While Goldberger's description of this kind of total insulation functions accurately when discussing a well-established urban entertainment district or festival marketplace like Harborplace in Baltimore, it is not quite as operational in Cleveland. In the Gateway, the relationship between urban and suburban is a bit more complex. The very transitional nature of the area works against any attempt to completely shelter visitors from city danger. In fact, this transitional status seems to heighten the experience for patrons attending a ball game at Jacobs Field—or at least it has in its early years.

The Gateway, for a whole generation a symbol of urban decay and danger (first the site of race riots, then home to a ramshackle market, drug dealers, prostitutes, and boarded-up buildings), bridges a host of dual worlds. As it undergoes transition, it brings into contact the often-distant realms of the legitimate and illegitimate, the alive and the dead, the decaying and the gentrifying, the black and the white. As such, it simultaneously keeps alive the energy of the vanquished and works to replace it, achieving much of its cultural cachet from the fact that the past remains always partially visible. On game nights, visitors witness rows of Cleveland's police disciplining and chasing away panhandlers and others left behind by gentrification. They watch officers sweep human remnants

BY DAY DURING THE SEASON, HUNDREDS OF PRIMARILY BLACK LABORERS TOIL BEHIND THE SCENES AT THE JAKE, CUTTING GRASS, COOKING MEALS, STANDING GUARD, POLISHING SEATS, AND HOSING DOWN SIDEWALKS.

of the old area back into dark alleys. They see, just off the beaten path, homeless men like Fred Brown sleeping in makeshift shanties built with pirated real estate placards under boarded-up buildings with faded signs advertising liquor and check-cashing services. If they arrive early enough, Indians fans might also pass a crowded bus stop overflowing with Jacobs Fields' mostly black day laborers waiting for transportation back to their neighborhoods. By day during the season, hundreds of laborers toil behind the scenes at the Jake, cutting grass, cooking meals, cleaning windows, and polishing seats. Like the janitorial night shift in office buildings, this crew of mostly African American employees remains just partially visible—cleaning apparitions who, as if by miracle, enable the place to maintain its sterling appearance. Meanwhile, at night when lights go on and the place comes alive, a virtual army of mostly white part-time employees greets and caters to fans.

This striking contrast between the visible and the invisible world provides fertile ground for the generation of the kind of urbanesque energy unique to new urban entertainment destinations like Jacobs Field. The nighttime whiteness of the stadium scene and the transition that patrons experience walking from their cars toward the stadium create a tension that has the potential to revive much of the longed-for pleasure of the urban. The partial visibility of the darkness of the area's past offers the space an aura of black magic. This aura, in turn, invests the location with an edge, without which the Gateway might feel just like another suburban shopping mall.

Shrewdly, Indians management and the city manage the tension, employing relatively gentle tactics of containment in place of outright oppression. Management of the plaza next to the Jacobs Field box office constitutes perhaps the prime example of this kind of tactic. In this area, much of which is just outside the

ABOVE: **AS DAY TURNS TO DUSK, STADIUM DAY LABORERS WAIT AT BUS STOPS FOR TRANSPORTATION BACK TO THEIR NEIGHBORHOODS WHILE INDIANS FANS ARRIVE FOR THE GAME.**

RIGHT: **PANHANDLER ON EAST NINTH STREET AFTER A GAME.**

"clear zone" prohibiting ticket brokering within 250 feet of the stadium, patrons can resell their extra tickets at face value under the watchful eye of a few plain-clothed and uniformed police officers. This dramatically limits scalping, or the resale of a ticket for profit, a practice dramatically curtailed by a city ordinance passed in the summer of 2000 subjecting scalpers to prosecution and a fine. The effects of this are several. First, it protects the organization's investment, guaranteeing to the club the ability to regulate prices of tickets bought both at the box office and second hand. Second, it helps homogenize the streets around the park, eliminating a source of revenue for a segment of the urban dispossessed. Typically, as a symbolic gesture to the community, and in an effort to regain the African American market (a group of potential consumers whose interest in baseball has steadily declined during the past half-century) ball clubs will set aside about a thousand free tickets per game for inner-city youth. A common sight in previous decades has thus been groups of African American teenagers and young adults selling complimentary tickets at ball parks constructed in what may have been their neighborhoods. By limiting the profitability of these renegade enterprises, the ball club, in effect short-circuits an important form of urban carnival.

Other cities have gone even further down this path, not just limiting but essentially co-opting scalping activities. In Baltimore, for example, officials created a "scalp-free zone" on Russell Street behind Oriole Park, replacing ad hoc open-air markets with a privatized public space subject to the control and discipline of the corporate and state apparatus. While the basic activities (peddling and negotiating) remain the same, the element of transgression has been severely tempered. Like the myriad fairs and markets brought under bureaucratic bourgeois control in Western public culture during the past two hundred years, the underworld economy of the scalping market around the stadium is contained and repackaged in Baltimore as a tourist attraction.[32] No longer a renegade activity performed by marginal members of the urban economy, scalping now largely serves as an auxiliary form of ticket distribution for the organization. Yet these zones still maintain residual liminality, gesturing back to the thrilling sport of ticket acquisition prior to institution of "scalp-free." In its heyday, scalping was often able to produce an inverted economic order in which the poor and racially marginalized potentially held all the cards, and in which the value of a dollar was a product of a person's skills and savvy, a matter of exchange rather than state-managed fiat. Ball-park scalping reenacted a more fluid, bartering economy, when goods were sold under the table so that the state could not impose taxes. Thus the creation of residual forms of these markets *by* the organization displays how, in the modern American city, the impulse for and the motive force of carnival remain intact even as its realization is appropriated by savvy, legitimized corporate or public entities.

Scalp-free zones have become so popular in fact that they are now a precondition for some ball clubs agreeing to move to downtown arenas. In arguing

IN THE PLAZA NEXT TO JACOBS FIELD, PATRONS CAN RESELL EXTRA TICKETS AT FACE VALUE PROVIDED THEY REMAIN IN THE "CLEAR ZONE," AT LEAST TWO HUNDRED AND FIFTY FEET FROM THE STADIUM.

for the creation of such an area near the new MCI Center in downtown Washington, for example, *Washington Post* family values columnist Bob Levey lamented that he had received dozens of letters from fathers of families who had been "harassed by aggressive scalpers as they walked to the entrances" of other area stadiums. He urged the management of the Washington Capitals and Wizards to "designate an area, hang a sign and watch smiles form—lots of smiles." Levey's concerns are representative of the buzz generated in anticipation of the opening of the sports facility. Like Camden Yards and Jacobs Field, the MCI Center is the centerpiece of redevelopment catering to a largely affluent and white recreational crowd in an area that had been almost exclusively poor and black or Asian. Thus it should come as no surprise that much of the pre–opening night discourse in Washington focused on questions about the safety of the urban location for suburban visitors. Intense surveillance outside the arena, Levey implied, was the only way to negotiate the tension caused by a neighborhood in transition. He insisted that police officers "lurk nearby to be sure no one 'accidentally' forgets the face-value-only rule or fails to mind his manners."

Absent from Levey's analysis, however, is recognition of the social value of carnival for the elite themselves. The underworld economy of scalping is one tangible way that much of the local population would have been allowed to benefit from the construction of this large, crowded arena in their neighborhood. History has shown that tolerance of a degree of underworld activity indeed helps to manage resentment and anger of those on the economic margins of society—a lesson especially important in the areas near the arena that have still not recovered from the race riots of the late 1960s. Nonetheless, Levey's barely submerged fear of the city is extremely representative of the demand on the part of consumers for reassurance that they are being looked after when they enter the liminal world of urban reconstruction. The replacement of young, primarily black scalpers with white suburban families in scalp-free zones is perhaps symbolic of the relatively subtle and unintentional, yet profound, way that stadiums affect a particular downtown evolution.

HOW THE INDIANS PROTECT AND SERVE

Commenting on the process by which the Indians whittle down a pool of ten thousand applicants for two thousand game-night jobs, Dibiasio said, "We really look for those who have good communication skills and appearance (because) you'll go back to where you feel comfortable." His words point out how a careful orchestration of the age, class, and race makeup of the staff is part of the big picture, providing balance to the excitement and attendant fear of the urban. "We look for just the right college kid," who passes a background check and gives off a "courteous, clean-cut appearance." This young, courteous, clean-cut, educated, and predominantly white image of the Gateway at night provides a sharp contrast to the scene of day laborers at the bus stop nearby and to the one at old Cleveland Municipal Stadium, where a notoriously surly lot of moonlighting blue-collar men and career service workers used to serve as ushers and vendors.

Many members of this new generation of employees take stadium jobs as a form of luxury. They choose to work because their small salaries provide them a bit of disposable income to spend at college and, perhaps more important, because the jobs are fun, providing them status and access, a chance to be part of the Indians team. "I don't need the money," confirms Shelly Perkins, the young hotel clerk who in the late 1990s volunteered as a Jacobs Field tour guide. "I just like being a member of the team." Her words describe the extent to which the Indians draw upon successful human resource strategies of the Disney Corporation for creating the desired atmosphere. Like the managers of Orlando's giant amusement park who hire "cast members," not workers, Dibiasio and his colleagues aim for a cheery, elective work force that sees itself as part of the show rather than simply as employees.

Like Disney, the Indians have also learned to use state-of-the-art surveillance methods to ease the mind of potentially anxious visitors.[33] As part of the ball club's agreement with the city, fifty extra police officers patrol the stadium area beginning an hour and a half or so before the gates open. That number of officers in a roughly thirty-acre space ensures that at virtually no time can one be outside the sight of at least one patroller. At the stadium itself, surveillance takes on a futuristic dimension. Instead of tearing tickets, each gate usher passes the entering patron's ticket in front of a scanner that collects data for the organization. This system, which Dibiasio believes was the first of its kind, allows the Indians' marketing team to track zip codes for future sales and promotional use, since most tickets are bought with credit cards. It also allows them to catalogue use patterns of its individual patrons, and it virtually eliminates counterfeiting. But the symbolic content of the scanners is just as important. The technology one encounters when entering the ball park announces plainly that the Indians security detail has its act together. It advertises the fact that the club aims to protect patrons from potential unsavory elements lurking in the surrounding city landscape while also keeping an eye on those whom they protect, in effect discouraging fans from acting on their own transgressive impulses. In other words, the electronic eye both helps patrons ease their ambivalence about feeling exposed when downtown and issues an overt reminder that the ball club is watching them. Like Foucault's "panopticon," the stadium's system of surveillance seems to bring with it the ability to control its patrons efficiently by prompting an internalized belief in the ubiquity of the regulatory apparatus.[34]

Meanwhile, the effects of this symbolic and real crowd control strategy are reinforced by the incorporation of similar technologies helping Jacobs Field workers internalize their own surveillance. Once an employee has been hired, his or her performance is closely monitored and recorded via a comprehensive computer program. Each employee enters in a key card when arriving at work, allowing management to carefully track attendance and arrival habits. Someone who shows up habitually late will find his or her hours cut short, or dropped all together. Compounding the Foucaultian nature of the system is the fact that this discipline is meted out anonymously. The managers do not directly inform people of their work schedules. Instead, they instruct employees to call a voice-mail system in order to find out when they are to report to work. The success of this system is at least partially based on the fact that, if employees find their hours cut short, they seem to have no one to blame but themselves because the computer program acts objectively. Stadium workers (accustomed as such to an atmosphere of efficient surveillance) in turn constitute a virtual army of ocular vigilance maintaining order for the Indians organization. The club employs more than four times the number of part-time employees to work games than it did at Cleveland Stadium. While of course a large part of the reason for this increase is simply that Jacobs Field draws more fans, part of it also has to do with the need to reassure patrons of their safety in this transitional urban space.

AT EVERY STOPPAGE OF PLAY, USHERS, SECURITY GUARDS, AND CLEVELAND POLICE PERFORM A WELL-CHOREOGRAPHED BUNKER MANEUVER.

In fact many of the workers' jobs involve little more than watching fans. Three ushers occupy many of the entrances to the seating sections, and several managers with clipboards and two-way radios shuttle from section to section for quality control. Additionally, thirty-four ushers, a host of security guards, and four Cleveland police officers perform a well-choreographed bunker maneuver at every stoppage of play. Between every half inning, whenever there is a pitching change, or when a manager calls time out to talk with his players, the security force moves with the precision of a team of infielders attempting to cover a double steal attempt. One of the three ushers from the entrance level sprints down to the first row, where he or she assumes a position with his or her back to the field. There, joined by a security guard in every couple of sections, he or she pans the stands looking to head off trouble. On the field, the bullpen doors and the camera well gates swing open and four police and security guards emerge to survey the stands from field level. This level of vigilance, originally employed only at cham-

DURING THE GAME, USHERS AND POLICE TURN THEIR BACKS TO THE FIELD IN ORDER TO KEEP WATCH OVER FANS.

pionship events at the end of games to discourage fans from rushing the field to celebrate with players, has now become so systematic that the average patron simply internalizes it. In order to enjoy a live sporting event, the modern stadium fan must simply accept the fact that he or she is being watched full time.[35]

Nonetheless, as is the case with any large gathering, transgressive behavior does in fact emerge. When this behavior is excessive, however, discipline to the perpetrator is meted out swiftly and efficiently. When there is a disturbance, an usher and a police officer quickly come together to round up the participants and bring them to the concourse or a holding pen in the bowels of the stadium. Jacobs Field (like most new parks built after it) comes equipped with a detention area, meaning that a person can now go straight from a box seat to police custody without ever leaving the stadium. This allows for the concealment of trouble, essential in maintaining the illusion of safety. One of the guiding principles among members of the security force at Jacobs Field is that, if possible, they are not to deal with disturbances in the public eye. "We remove the problem from the general populace," says Dibiasio, acknowledging that security must never be perceived as a problem, given that the club wants to create feelings of safety amid what some perceive to be a dangerous setting. In order to attract the same people whose families fled the city for the suburbs based at least in part on racial panic and fear about the dangers of urban life, the club must carefully preserve the illusion.

Susan Willis details the extent to which safety is largely a fantasy in Disney World, the model for this kind of security/public relations strategy. Despite the presence of an intense surveillance apparatus (i.e., cameras allowing a view from multiple angles at every spot inside the park), crime and violence are actually prevalent inside the "Magic Kingdom." Willis argues that, rather than preventing crime, the cameras primarily benefit Disney by allowing corporate security teams to rush in and remove both the perpetrator and the victim quickly from sight, thereby preserving the crucial illusion of absolute safety in the Mouse's utopia.[36] Indeed, according to Dibiasio, choreographing what the patron sees from the moment he or she enters the Gateway area was among the first priorities for management when they moved to the new park. "We incorporated the city," he said. "We needed the mayor and police chief. Visually, we got bright lights and wider streets." His use of the term "incorporated" is highly suggestive in this context. It implies a dramatically evolving relationship between the government and private business in the post-Fordist city. Within a Fordist regulation model (exemplified by the actions of the Kucinich administration), local governments largely worked as checks on corporate power and abuse. Conversely, within the post-Fordist model (exemplified by Voinovich's, White's, and subsequent administrations), local governments have begun to see themselves partially as service providers for corporations whose products or jobs serve the public. They expand the urban infrastructure and even act as entrepreneurs as they seek to recapitalize downtown.

Publicly funded "bright lights and wider streets" as well as a massive police presence combine with the Indians' cadre of ushers, security guards, and friendly vendors to form a crucial part of the big picture. Together, the city and the ball club have aimed to engineer a transformation of the Gateway from darkness to light, dangerous alleys to well-illuminated thoroughfares, scalping to scalp-free, prostitution to baseball. Through the provision of symbolic images of state power and off-screen-oriented crowd control, Indians management and city officials have sought desperately to reassure visitors that they are safe. Ultimately, their belief is that the truth will follow suit, that life will begin to imitate illusion. Once this illusion of safety is well established, they surmise, more people will indeed come back downtown, which in turn should actually make the place safer.

PRESCRIBING THE EXCESSIVE

When thinking about urban entertainment facilities, it is crucial to keep in mind that safety and regulation can only represent half the story. Management understands that patrons who are increasingly dependent upon informational technology at work come to the park for release. Thus, a large part of the big picture consists of providing an environment highlighting the benevolent and recreational virtues of the very technology that in other contexts, inside and outside the park, represents work or control. In Wahoo World behind right field, for example, a fan can pitch a virtual-reality batting practice session or take swings at a computer-generated Roger Clemons fastball. For twenty dollars, the same fan can sit in an authentic broadcast booth and record a half-inning of play-by-play commentary of an actual ball game. As such, Jacobs Field enables fans to see technology as leisure rather than work, thus producing an atmosphere in which they can master the world of productivity by turning cutting-edge technology into a game.[37]

These benevolent technologies allow visitors to blur the distinction between spectator/participant, player/fan, and broadcaster/viewer, an ability crucial in a culture that finds its professional athletes at a greater physical and psychic remove than in the past. Pro ballplayers increasingly live lives separate from the communities they represent. They are also (as a result of improvements to training habits and the increasing popularity of chemical performance enhancements) much bigger, stronger, and faster than the average fan. Thus, the provision of games that enable spectators to imagine themselves as players helps provide compensatory pleasure.[38] Of course, modern technology aside, the very performance of sports spectatorship has, since the advent of sporting matches as spectacle, naturally bridged the gap between simply watching and performing. Yelling and screaming, rooting at the right time, or waving arms behind the backboard when a visiting basketball player attempts a free throw have long been essential parts of the stadium experience. Fans who attend sporting events in part do so in order to help their teams win games and thus feel themselves as part of the action. One of the most tenuous aspects of the big picture, therefore, is maintaining the balance between the allowance of this kind of performance and the amount of control necessary to make tourists comfortable in an in-process urban space like the Gateway.

In this regard, Dibiasio and his co-workers clearly have their work cut out for them each night. They convene a large gathering of people, then ask them to behave both passionately, when rooting, and calmly, when paying attention to rules of crowd control. When the Indians' scoreboard operator flashes the "Make Some Noise!" sign at key moments in the game, it brings into focus the extent to which the success or failure of Jacobs Field is incumbent upon management's effort to get it right. This scoreboard imploration has been necessitated by the changed demographics of the new stadium. It suggests management's belief that contemporary visitors sometimes need to be reminded and encouraged to cheer. Without cheering, without release, attending a game loses one of its most profound appeals. Yet the flashing message on the scoreboard is not without its pitfalls. By making such appeals, management flirts with alienating patrons who come looking for spontaneous enjoyment. They risk making the audience feel manipulated. In fact, many longtime Indians supporters resent the organization's attempt to overproscribe their experience. "Real baseball fans don't want guys with pretty faces coming up to you saying, 'Hey, are you having a good time,'" said longtime fan John Adams, who along with his wife Kathleen has missed just a handful of games during the past forty years. "And we don't need a scoreboard that says 'I Can't Hear You' to know when to cheer."

The need to satisfactorily script the big picture, to perfectly balance historically central aspects of stadium appeal (release, spontaneity, a looser set of rules and guidelines for behavior) with control and regulation is not unlike the task facing Cleveland officials and speculators as they attempt to revitalize the Gateway. For the Gateway and Jacobs Field to lure people back downtown, Dibiasio and Cleveland officials need to walk an increasingly narrow tightrope. They need to provide a constant supply of substitutions reintroducing the perceived energy of the urban, which an elaborate system of surveillance and discipline, itself necessary for reassurance, threatens to eviscerate.

CHAPTER TWO

BASEBALL'S "BENEFICIENT" REVOLUTION

Jacobs Field is in many ways a historical inevitability. For more than a century, since the inception of city planning as a discursive subject, urban reformers have debated the role of baseball facilities in managing a set of tensions similar to those being worked out in the Gateway. From the time of the first enclosed ball park in mid-nineteenth-century Brooklyn through the present era of the retro stadium, engineers, architects, and baseball management have felt the need to derive strategies for the provision of social insulation. Various pressures—political, social, and economic—have prompted them to shelter wealthier fans while both encouraging and containing oppositional or transgressive forms of behavior among the middle and working classes.

This central paradox between the intensely democratic potential of the ball park and its somewhat less idyllic realization has long troubled baseball fans and social historians and it continues to trouble today. Witness a strikingly ambivalent 1995 article describing the design of Jacobs Field. In "Steeling Home," architecture critic Heidi Landecker initially joins a chorus of voices praising the park. She finds herself pleased with how the new venue, in replacing Municipal Stadium, has brought baseball back to an intimate setting. Seating about forty-three thousand fans instead of eighty-five thousand, putting patrons closer to the action, the new ball park, she writes, is warm and friendly, whereas the old one was cold and alienating. She applauds the park's primary designer, HOK Sport's Joseph Spear, for including a host of witty accents of Cleveland's past: expressed steel beams echoing the many steel bridges still visible from the ball park; the ochre color of its bricks reminiscent of the 1912 West Side Market across the Cuyahoga River; a tall, vertical concourse recalling the Arcade, the nation's first shopping mall, still standing a few blocks away. Though she concurs with Spear's argument articulated in the article that Jacobs Field is not a retro park, not simply a knock off of the same architect's Camden Yards built a few years earlier in Baltimore, Landecker organizes all of her praise around descriptions of the many features of the park recalling old Cleveland.[1]

Yet despite her belief that it endows the new location with authenticity, the old seems to carry some classist baggage for Landecker, ultimately bringing her to qualify her praise. In the final paragraph of her piece, she mentions "the definitive segregation of the Indians' wealthy fans and those in the stands," what she and other critics view as the park's one major flaw:

> A restaurant for club members might have been discreetly tucked out of sight; instead, its glassy, terraced volume hangs ostentatiously over left field. Perhaps such class stratification is also true of Cleveland, long a society of extremely wealthy patrons and blue-collar factory workers. Baseball, after all, is for everyone, and today everyone can enjoy it in the style that he or she can afford. (64)

Landecker's comments seem oddly bifurcated here. On one hand, she laments the symbolism of the overhanging restaurant; the Cleveland wealthy "ostentatiously" advertise their privilege when they sit in the glass Terrace Club looming over the grandstands. On the other hand, she casually dismisses this inequity by suggesting a certain kind of natural justice in the Cleveland caste system. The biggest problem, she asserts, is not the gap between rich and poor, but that, in the stadium, injustice is not "discreetly tucked out of sight." In other words, the club restaurant ruins the illusion—or at least the utopian fantasy—articulated in the passage's final sentence, that contemporary baseball is somehow fulfilling its destiny as the great American democratic game.

The abrupt truncation of her critique is in many ways a product of a thoroughly American form of longing, a desire for democratic public space, combined with the historical power of baseball to generate narratives describing urban ball parks as precisely these kinds of sites. Landecker's quick shift suggests that certain obvious truths about baseball's reality in relation to its mythology are simply too threatening to integrate. In fact, contemporary professional baseball is *not* for everyone. On the field during the past twenty years, the percentage of African Americans playing the game has dropped precipitously, and although major league teams have progressively added more Latino and Japanese players to their rosters, baseball's audience is, more than at almost any time in its history, overwhelmingly white.[2] Furthermore, as Landecker must realize, escalating prices at new ball parks like Jacobs Field have contributed to the virtual exclusion of most of America's working poor.[3]

The particular "style" of baseball that "everyone" can afford has thus become the style of the television consumer. In the early years of the park, when the Indians sold out every game before the season even started, those with

179

THE TERRACE CLUB RESTAURANT OVERHANGS THIRD-BASE-SIDE SEATS AT JACOBS FIELD.

enough disposable income to buy season tickets enjoyed the grace of the new venue. Everyone else watched the games on the tube. The movement of retro authenticity, which, in the 1990s, produced the series of "warm" parks that Landecker praises, has also reconfigured the ball-park experience in order to shift the stadium economic demographic upward, thereby setting up the kinds of troubling juxtaposition she criticizes. Meanwhile, however, the mythology of baseball as the "national pastime," a mythology that informs her optimism as well as her abrupt tonal shift, perseveres.

Landecker's mixed message is emblematic of more than a century of baseball rhetoric attempting to synthesize the game's own ambitions of being the great democratic pastime with some uncomfortable truths about both its own structure and the structure of the larger culture in which it participates. Looking back to the origin of organized professional baseball in the nineteenth century, contemporary critics can see how, from the beginning, its founders set out to establish a dual pattern of physical exclusion and discursive inclusion. Since the mid- to late 1800s, when middle-class business interests began defining the parameters of the sport, baseball has been able to continually generate and propagate a rhetoric of inclusion at every moment it has taken steps to become more exclusive. In short, baseball has been remarkably successful through the years at thinking itself inclusive, whereby thinking has a doubled resonance of "believing" and "making it seem true through the evangelical spread of this belief." As Landecker's sudden shift indicates, the rhetoric of baseball has made its own status as the "great democratic sport" seem axiomatic, so ingrained in the American fan's psyche that it has accumulated the power to overwhelm sensations of dissonance.

MORAL REFORMATION AND THE FIRST BASEBALL STADIUMS

It is clear that baseball, as it became professionalized in the 1870s, helped reinforce middle-class perceptions of a burgeoning revolution of the individual spirit. Once a game played primarily by elite school boys, baseball after 1850 or so began to be enjoyed by working-class and middle-class men as well. Both Union and Confederate soldiers adopted it as their game of choice during the Civil War, investing it with an edge lacking when it was played only by the nation's elite. After the war, widespread reports of violence and betting associated with the sport gave pause to many genteel reformers as they considered whether or not this emergent national pastime was truly a salubrious pursuit for workers who, more than any time in the nation's history, had some leisure time to fill up.

On the professional level, the sport gradually became dominated by a type of ruffian culture, the best players and the best teams known as much for their tactics of intimidation and rough play as for their skill "at the bat."[4] The parks in which they played accommodated cordoned off areas—bettor's pens—where middle-class men were free to shed the decorum of their daily lives and engage in a host of illicit activities such as betting, smoking, cursing, and drinking. Meanwhile, on the amateur level, workers and immigrants ran roughshod over the intentions of the genteel designers of urban parks. In Central Park, for example, dozens of vernacular recreation areas emerged. In these spots, groups of men trampled down their own diamonds and other types of ball fields in order to quench their thirst for "manly" amusements.

Understanding the debates over proper usage of Central Park is key to comprehending the dual promise and threat of baseball in its early years. In the decade prior to the construction of the park, groups such as the New York

Knickerbockers, the largest baseball club in the city at the time, petitioned the Central Park Board to provide space to accommodate ball grounds. These groups, in favor of orienting the park primarily toward such forms of "manly, vigorous" outdoor exercise, had every reason to believe that their requests were to be met. After all, early brochures promoting the proposed park featured drawings of cricket games on their covers, and the winning design entry clearly marked out three separate playgrounds.[5] Furthermore, various parcels of land appropriated by the city for the park were themselves already vernacular recreation areas, for years having been used for baseball and other sporting activities by local residents. Yet the changing demographics of baseball in the 1850s and 1860s convinced the Central Park Board to proceed more cautiously, to redesign the park in order to keep the passionate fans of the game at bay. Advocates of a "quiet, orderly, and decorous park—a park that resisted rather than embraced the variety and spontaneity of the city—generally held the line against such challenges throughout the first decade" (Rosenzweig and Blackmar 247).

In the early 1870s, when pressure continued to build and the demand for active recreational facilities (in particular public diamonds) proved too strong to resist, the park board produced a dubious compromise. It allowed the construction of diamonds but refused calls to let working-class men and youth play. Instead, it gave only well-behaved schoolboys and girls access to the public ball fields.[6] This contradiction shows the extent to which the game seemed a threat to genteel reformers like Frederick Law Olmsted (who designed Central Park) and the aristocratic park board (which controlled it). Although it is unclear whether it was the drinking, the gambling, the cursing, the class makeup, or the pure physicality of the game that threatened Olmsted and the members of the board, one thing is beyond dispute: there was an air of revolution, a revolution in acceptable forms of public behavior, associated with baseball.

At roughly the same time that reformers were attempting to limit access to baseball diamonds, another important social force was added to the mix, intensifying the sense of revolution. Baseball as a professional, for-profit enterprise got its start in these decades, as a slew of entertainment entrepreneurs emerged in order to capitalize on interest in the game. The most important of these men was Brooklyn politician and businessman William H. Cassmeyer, who in 1861 created almost by accident the first enclosed baseball park, Union Grounds. Three years after the opening of Olmsted's Central Park, just across the river yet miles away, Cassmeyer set up his venue as a large ice pond for recreational skating. Then, attempting to augment his profits in the off season, he tried to get the community to use it for summertime boating and horseback riding before a lack of revenue forced him to convert the space to a ball park.

This transformation is important. The kinds of activities that Olmsted had sanctioned in Central Park certainly appealed to Cassmeyer the politician. Ice skating and horseback riding tended to attract a rather decorous crowd and encouraged the participation of women, who were thought to bring out the best behavior in the men who accompanied them. Just as important, these forms of recreation discouraged the participation of the urban working poor, who, for the most part, had neither the means nor the inclination to participate in skating and riding. Yet to Cassmeyer the businessman, the attempt to earn money off the provision of only salutary and gentle recreation proved disastrous. Within a year, severe losses convinced him to have his laborers drain the pond, level the field, and plant sod so that he could provide a recreational space more attuned to the desires of the burgeoning Brooklyn population looking for a more intense experience.

The new baseball park he created out of the quagmire was, from the very beginning, a huge attraction. Local newspapers estimated that eight to ten thousand people attended the park's inaugural match. In turn, this immediate success convinced Cassmeyer to begin charging admission. This was one of the first times in American history that fans had to pay to watch a game, and it served as a watershed moment in the transformation of baseball from an almost exclusively recreational activity to one which is also a spectator sport.[7] The overflow crowd on the first day proved that there was tremendous popular interest in this form of public diversion and that, obviously, there was a great deal of money to be made.

Yet Cassmeyer's dual status as a politician and a businessman complicated matters. On the one hand, as a respected member of New York's emergent mercantile class and as an intimate of Mayor William Marcy "Boss" Tweed, he must have shared a sense of anxiety with Olmsted and other genteel reformers about the dangerous potential of this particular form of public gathering. On the other hand, as heir to a successful leather business and as part of a new breed of aggressive middle-class entrepreneurs, he saw almost limitless potential in his ability to make the ball-park experience appeal to the segment of the population willing to spend money to attend a game. The result of this tension seems to be a compromise between the beliefs about salubrious public amusement voiced by Olmsted and a sense of the need to cater to the desires of a large number of locals increasingly passionate about baseball.

The scene inside Union Grounds was simultaneously controlled and anarchic—a setting allowing the expression of both Victorian respectability and its corresponding underworld. In order to attract ladies to the events and thereby endow the games with decorum, Cassmeyer created two segregated areas. The first was a long wooden shed "capable of accommodating several hundred persons, and benches provided for the fair sex."[8] The other was a "bettor's ring," which confined gamblers and kept them away from more properly behaving patrons. This demarcation is representative of the particular tension shaping baseball in its early years and continuing to inform the makeup of stadiums today. Professional baseball club owners, from the beginning, wanted to distance their product from other forms of popular amusement, but they also needed to market the game to a relatively wide swath of the American urban scene. So they simply segregated their fans.

In writing about the inauguration of the Union Grounds, the *Brooklyn Eagle* went out of its way to praise this "thoughtful" segregation of "ladies" and "bettors":

> The chief object of the Association is to provide a suitable place
> for ball playing, where ladies can witness the game without being
> annoyed by the indecorous behavior of the rowdies who attend some
> of the first-class matches. . . . Wherever their [the ladies'] presence
> enlivens the scene, there gentlemanly conduct will follow. Indecorous
> proceedings will cause the offenders to be instantly expelled from
> the grounds.[9]

The reporter's words are, of course, a bit naïve. The "chief object" of Cassmeyer's association was to make money. Of only ancillary benefit was the provision of a "suitable" ball field amid a general, citywide shortage. What *is* notable is that the *Eagle* seemed to be endorsing a fairly radical compromise that clearly was untenable to the more old-world members of the Central Park Board across the East River.

It is important to understand, though, that the reporter's description of the compromise fails to tell the whole story. Absent in the article's discussion of this "thoughtful" internal segregation is any acknowledgment of the external segregation resulting from the enclosure of the park. Tall fences, admission charges, and inconvenient daytime hours excluded the majority of Brooklyn residents right off the bat. Those really on the margins of society—the working poor, new immigrants, the unemployed, and African Americans—were locked out completely. The "rowdies" inside the park to which the Brooklyn newspaper refers simply could not have been primarily members of Brooklyn's working classes. For one thing, even a ten-cent admission fee would have consumed too much of a laborer's salary.[10] For another, games were usually held on weekday afternoons. Only leisured men and women and white-collar workers with flexible schedules could take time off to attend games. Thus, because this privately owned, quasi-public space was enclosed and regulated, its great experiment in social mixing had to have taken place among a relatively homogenous population.

Nonetheless, this arrangement, though at least as exclusionary as it was revolutionary, provided a venue for a certain outing of an aspect of Victorian middle-class life that theretofore had been hidden in the dark back rooms of male-only saloons and clubs. Men, who most probably lived a respectable public life outside the ball park, stood in an area apart, conducting themselves much more freely than they could in almost any other public space. Smoking, drinking, betting, and cursing openly, they in effect took the behaviors of male-only saloon life into the open air. Baseball parks not only allowed but also invited rough public behavior and large-scale male bonding unavailable else-where even as they excluded the folks labeled "dangerous" for their propensity to enjoy these very behaviors.[11]

RHETORICAL RESPONSES INSTITUTIONALIZED

It is safe to say that the "thoughtful" internal segregation of baseball stadiums only eased the apprehension of genteel reformers temporarily. The pressure to reform the professional version of the game, to eradicate drinking, gambling, and cursing from the ball park, intensified in the late 1860s and early 1870s. Moralists decried the nexus of sport and business, which placed the financial standing and attendant pressure to win at all costs above concerns for the spiritual well-being of baseball participants. By the early 1870s, the National Association of Base Ball Players (NABBP), which had been formed in 1858 to organize the many teams playing the game and to try to keep baseball a recreational amusement exclusive to upper-class gentlemen, had clearly become obsolete. The status a winning ball club afforded a town had long compelled many of the original teams to relax membership standards based on social standing. Teams routinely violated rules about amateurism and began, like Cassmeyer, to charge admission to games in order to pay for the best players. On top of this, the profit motive became irre-sistible. By the late 1860s, it had become apparent that a well-organized club could help an owner make a fortune.

What emerged in the early 1870s from this dual set of pressures—to reform the game and to profit from it—is an aggressive program of consolidation, regu-larization, and propaganda on the part of a small group of owners. Led by Chi-cago coal merchant William Hulbert, this group drafted a constitution and gath-ered support for a new league, the National League of Professional Baseball *Clubs,* to replace what by then had evolved into the National Association of *Pro-fessional* Base Ball *Players* (NAPBBP).[12] The subtle difference in name actually describes a tremendously important distinction between the new league and the one it displaced. The old affiliation had functioned as a loose partnership be-tween management and players. The new association, on the other hand, evolved in part out of an emerging sense in industrializing America that players should not meddle in financial and administrative decisions. In other words, this shift denotes the change from professional baseball as a pursuit that is first and fore-most a sport to one that is a business with a distinct separation of labor and man-agement. Predictably, this shift angered more than a few people. Genteel moral-ists cried foul, denouncing the collusion of profit and sport. Owners of teams that were shut out of the new league also complained, arguing that this association was promoting an unfair monopoly of the game. Finally, many players who previously had shared both profits and decision-making power condemned the new owners for being greedy and selfish robber barons.[13]

To a large degree, the owners' response to these widespread and diverse expressions of discontent was a coordinated package of rhetoric rationalizing the consolidation. To deflect criticism from locked-out owners and angry players, the National League (NL) owners began to promote themselves as symbols of uniquely American ingenuity and prosperity. They publicly hailed themselves as heroic generals, joining other entrepreneurs in leading the culture through an industrial revolution. To allay the fears of genteel moralists frightened by dangerous behavior at baseball parks, they began to construct a mythology of baseball, holding it to be more than just a game. In this way, baseball was promoted as a cure for the physically and spiritually draining experience of living and working in the industrialized city, a way for urban dwellers to connect with the country's rural past, a way to shape and refine the character of the American individual.

This rhetorical movement helped create a special and profound acceptance of sports among the middle classes, one that perseveres to this day. Middle-class prosperity toward the end of the century had prompted a number of observers to speak out against a kind of overcivilization of the American city. More and more, people began to notice a widespread nervous tension and anxiety among the very people who had come to benefit most from progress. Given a name, "neurasthenia," this condition soon came to be thought of as a type of "national disease" among the middle classes. It was said to stifle the individual spirit, creating a "paralysis of the will."[14] A large part of the owners' strategy during this time was thus to sell baseball as a unique tonic for this national disease, a sport that naturally recharged moral fiber and strengthened will.

CONSOLIDATION AND EXCLUSION

Almost by accident, early baseball club owners had struck a chord with important segments of the American public. Forced to negotiate dual pressures for reform and "manly" activity, they generated a rhetoric of simultaneous exclusion and inclusion, which helped them immensely in their pursuit of three main objectives: currying favor among moralists, consolidating power, and regularizing the game. In seeking genteel approval, they attempted to convince a wary public that their reason for forming the new league was primarily to effect a cleansing of the sport and only secondarily to make a profit. To this end, they immediately waged a high-profile campaign against gambling and drinking, claiming that the newly professionalized league would be able to eliminate the sins of the past. This campaign, part of the league's stated goal of making "Base Ball playing respectable and honorable," made it illegal to sell alcohol on club grounds or to bet on games

(Levine, *Spalding* 24). Although it is clear that in reality much of this behavior was tacitly accepted, these high-profile attempts to reinvent the game's image did earn the new league some good favor among local politicians and reformers. In their effort to consolidate power, they went about "reducing the game to a business system such as had never heretofore obtained."[15] The National League raised the annual franchise fee from ten to one hundred dollars in 1875, pricing out collective enterprises and other teams that were not financed by already-wealthy individuals. What had theretofore been a loose affiliation of hundreds of professional teams in the NAPBBP all of a sudden became the National League with but eight teams representing only cities with a population of at least seventy-five thousand. The third objective, of effecting a dramatic regularization of the game, went hand in hand with the first two. After cracking down on gambling and drinking and raising the franchise fee, owners eliminated the so-called lively ball. This measure cut down the length of the game, allowing baseball to increase its appeal to businessmen who had daily appointments to keep while privileging more conservative, defensive play.

The owners' collective efforts initiated a long-term attrition of the game, eventually providing the blueprint for the structure of professional baseball still shaping the sport today. The act of consolidation and regularization by Hulbert and the other owners was the first step in the eventual merger of the two dominant professional leagues. It paved the way for the "New National Agreement" of 1903, after which the baseball public came to consider the American and the National Leagues the two "major leagues."[16] Symbolically, the shift from a wide range of ownership types to a singular one, from the collective and sometimes off-the-wall ownership of the old affiliation to the earnest and disciplinarian middle-class creed of the new National League, is crucial. Emerging out of a perceived crisis period in baseball's history, when rowdy public behavior and the actions of "hot-headed anarchists" (i.e., players who tried to form their own leagues) suggested that the sport truly had far-reaching revolutionary potential, this group of owners immediately set about to promote themselves to an anxious middle class and to genteel reformers as just the ticket to restore order.[17] In other words, in less than fifteen years the primary agents of exclusion from the game had changed dramatically. Whereas the class warriors previously had been elite members of the NABBP, aristocratic and leisured men who wanted to ward off the threat of rowdyism and, perhaps worse, professionalism, they were now middle-class entrepreneurs who saw professionalism itself as the way to preserve the sanctity of the game.

Meanwhile, those on the margins of society, blacks and the working poor (two groups for whom the game had held so much promise), suffered most as a result of this reduction. Coinciding with the owners' perceived need to legitimize and justify their enterprise was the onset of statutory racial segregation. Prior to this period, despite widespread racist sentiment and occasional boycotts by ballplayers and clubs scheduled to play against teams with African American players, many blacks had been able to play the game at the highest levels. African American players such as Bud Fowler, Fleet Walker, George Stovey, and Frank Grant participated for a variety of teams in the professional leagues before consolidation. Although there had been a couple of attempts to establish a statutory color line in baseball—most notably by the aristocratic NABBP, which, in 1867, did in fact bar blacks from participation—most Jim Crow battles were fought individually, team by team, event by event. In reality, since the end of the Civil War, most baseball leagues had almost always chosen to depoliticize themselves, to simply ignore race, easily the most combustible political topic of the day.

In the 1870s and 1880s, however, the climate began to heat up. In 1883, the manager of A. G. Spalding's White Stockings, Cap Anson, perhaps the greatest player to have played the game to that point and a venomous racist, drew attention to the Negro question by threatening a boycott of Chicago's scheduled exhibition with Toledo if Fleet Walker was allowed to play. Though Walker did play, Anson's actions and words brought to the fore rampant antiblack sentiment among a large segment of professional players and owners. In the wake of this ugly incident, as the leagues sought acknowledgment of their reputability, they began to rely on race in the most pernicious of ways. The emergent professionalized ethos of the sport held that the gradual purging of blacks from the highest levels would signal a transformation of the game away from its recent rougher and more anarchic form to one more in line with new American middle-class values of regularity and discipline.

In 1887, one of the top eleven leagues, the International League, made it official: no new contracts would be tendered to any player of color from then on. By that time, as many as twenty-five African Americans were participating in the league. After that fateful moment, however, the color line in the other professional leagues became sharply delineated. It was not until sixty years later, in April 1947, when Jackie Robinson first suited up for the Brooklyn Dodgers, that the line was officially crossed again.[18]

THE FUNDAMENTALS OF RACE

Above and beyond the obvious social injustice that this sixty-year exclusion engendered are questions about how segregation helped construct many of the more odious stereotypes of black athletes still in circulation today. During this crucial era of reorganization and consolidation, the idea of fundamentals began to emerge. Previously, when the professional version of the game was being played by thousands of teams nationwide, rules and strategies were as numerous as the number of games being played. After consolidation, however, the leagues were able to agree on rules and were able to begin to address questions pertaining to the best ways to play the game. Along with this, countless publications such as *Reach's Official Baseball Guide* were founded to both inform a national audience about players and scores from around the various professional circuits and to serve as manuals instructing players on fundamentals.

Proponents of the "organized-play movement" promoted Public School Athletic Leagues (PSALs) as training grounds not just for professional baseball but also for the essential business of the American middle class.[19] PSALs, whose motto was "Duty, Thoroughness, Patriotism, Honor, and Obedience," were established to teach discipline, fundamentals, and, most important, the necessity of "harnessed aggression" to white children. In general, the core belief behind PSALs was that sport would allow for the release of potentially dangerous energy while developing the rigor necessary to compete in the business world.

This belief is central to the place of sports within the developing white middle-class consciousness insofar as it suggests a simultaneous pride in and fear of the spirit of middle-class youth. Anxious middle-class adults felt the need to counter the allure of the modern American city filled with immigrants and other perceived agents of corruption and social unrest by providing simulated access to the more rugged preindustrial world and by constructing commercial pursuits as themselves vigorous and manly.[20] The PSAL curriculum stressed the correlation between success in the world and the mastery of fundamentals. In this way, the youth leagues were a large part of the process by which the white version of the game became increasingly subject to bourgeois discipline and regularization.

Conversely, after 1887, when exclusion of blacks from organized leagues became statutory, African Americans were forced to diversify their act in order to draw an audience and earn a living. Fowler, the first black professional baseball player, who (unlike the sport) really was born in Cooperstown, had made a living playing ball with integrated teams for fifteen years prior to segregation; in fact, he is said to have been one of the best second basemen to play the game in that era. However, after political winds shifted and Jim Crow agreements quickly phased out his access to organized baseball, he had to begin barnstorming. He traveled from town to town, thrilling curious white audiences with exhibitions of his remarkable physical prowess. Instead of just playing ball, however, he now traveled mostly in the Northwest, giving walking exhibitions against skaters and running the mile in under five minutes.[21]

Fowler's traveling curiosity show functioned as a model for black professional baseball players who wanted to play for pay as well. Although exclusively African American teams began playing as early as the beginning of the 1880s, an organized Negro League did not emerge until the 1920s. In the interim, all-black teams traveled the country, often playing three games in three towns in a single day in a perpetual search for competition and a reasonable gate. Along with simply playing a baseball game, like Fowler they were expected to provide alternate forms of entertainment as well. Often, white entrepreneurs would organize a

black troupe that would have to provide a minstrel show, music, and other carnival attractions to go along with their baseball exhibitions. Thus notions of African American showboating, still assailed by many writers and fans today as a
primary cause and indicator of the ruination of the game, are at least in part a
product of sixty years of exclusion forcing blacks to "jump Jim Crow," to earn a
living simultaneously as ballplayers and pickaninnies, while their white counterparts played a version of the sport increasingly defined by regularization and
fundamentalization.

VIRTUE, CLASS, AND THE LANGUAGE OF INCLUSION

Of course, blacks were not the only Americans excluded from many forms of participation in the "national pastime." As part of consolidation, Spalding worked
tirelessly to reduce ball-park access to America's working poor. He convinced
fellow owners to vigorously enforce a fifty-cent admission policy at National
League parks. This sum constituted roughly a third of the average worker's
weekly salary, thereby pricing out most of the people considered by reformers to
be among the "dangerous classes." Adding to the efficacy of this exclusionary
new policy was the fact that the higher price enabled owners to make enough
money six days a week to resist the impulse to open their parks to baseball on
Sunday, the one day workers had time to see a game.[22] Ingeniously, Spalding
spun this move in religious (instead of classist) terms. He claimed that owners
eliminated Sunday baseball out of simple respect for the Sabbath, which in turn
further pleased reformers.

Ironically, at this very moment of widespread and systematic exclusion,
when blacks became statutorily forbidden from playing and members of the
working classes were simply being priced out, owners began to discover the
cultural value in promoting the game as inclusive and democratic. At the end of
chapter 17 in *America's National Game,* Spalding gleefully describes the exclusionary policies of the National League, arguing that by raising ticket prices, the
"patriotic" owners were able to both turn away "the class that is always 'against
the government'" and squeeze out countless teams and cities.[23] Yet despite his
clear expressions of the belief that the league's success was dependent fore-
most upon widespread exclusion, Spalding concludes the chapter by quoting
from former league president A. G. Mills's confident manifesto asserting that
baseball's primary appeal is as an inclusive game "for the people":

> When we behold what a revolution Base Ball has wrought in the
> habits and tastes of the American people we may well denominate its
> advancement a "good work." But a generation ago that large body of
> our people whose lives were not spent in the forest or on the farm
> was marked as a sedentary race, with healthful recreation denied to

all but a favored few. Now, not the least of our claims to distinction among the peoples of the world is our general love of and devotion to healthful outdoor sports and recreations. The deterioration of the race has ended, and the rising generation is better equipped for the duties, the conflicts and the pleasures of life than were their fathers and mothers.[24]

Mills's propensity for essentializing is important to note here. Ignoring obvious distinctions among classes, he conflates the "habits and tastes" (as well as the insecurities) regarding neurasthenia of the American middle class with those of the "American people." He implies that concerns about being sedentary applied to the urban population in general, though, in reality, most steelworkers and other laborers were not worried about their bodies going soft. His use of the word "race" is of course also problematic. Willfully eliding recent historical events—the fact that his league had just excluded an entire race of four million newly free American citizens and that it was finding ways to make itself less and less accessible economically to the millions of immigrants populating urban areas—he chooses to fantasize a mythical, democratic American baseball public. More than anything else, Mills's language underlines the psychological need for the American middle-class man to *think* himself regular, hard working, and disciplined.[25]

Spalding's history and Mills's written beliefs are doctrinal manifestations of the kind of middle-class anxiety fascinating many of their more skeptical contemporaries. Writing his novella *Bartleby* in 1853, Herman Melville anticipates the challenges baseball owners were to face by creating a narrator haunted by this kind of apprehension. The proprietor of a small scriveners firm, Melville's narrator comes face to face with the folly of Mills's brand of ideology through his absolute inability to indoctrinate his new clerk into the ways of bourgeois productivity. Bartleby's preference "not to" (not to work, not to go home, not even to eat) flies in the face of everything that the narrator would have been raised to believe about the ennobling quality of white-collar work.

Nonetheless (Melville's and others' distrust of the ideology notwithstanding), the evangelical belief in the mission of the emergent middle-class entrepreneur gained momentum in the last few decades of the century. Mills makes clear his desire to effect widespread faith in the ability of professional baseball owners to be agents of profound social change, able to lead an extensive, yet not radical, revolution:

And can it be doubted what has been the most potent factor in achieving this *beneficient* [emphasis added] revolution? We have seen Base Ball steadily growing from its notable beginning before the war, accompanying our soldiers in the field, spreading like wildfire throughout the West, until now it is known and loved and practiced in

every city and town within the borders of the United States. Base Ball
is essentially the people's game, in that it is equally accessible to the
sons of the rich and poor, and in point of exhilarating exercise to the
player and healthy enjoyment to the spectator—whether played on the
modern village common or the splendidly appointed grounds of the
modern professional club—it satisfies and typifies the American idea
of a manly, honest, entertaining recreation. (Qtd. in Spalding 248)

The word "essentially" is crucial here. Not quite the "people's game" but rather
essentially so, baseball, with it roots in the martial rigor of the Civil War, had
spread equally to the rich and the poor, according to Mills's formulation. Yet as
Spalding's narrative of the 1870s indicates, the owners' primary charge during
this time was to prevent exactly that, to counteract what was thought to be a
dangerous radicalization of the game. They wished to advance this "beneficient" revolution while short-circuiting impulses toward the more drastic forms
of uprising occurring across the continent of Europe and being discussed do-
mestically by an increasingly organized work force. In this unique period, baseball did seem to be inherently invested with the potential to lead the way toward
some social changes. It certainly enabled a relaxation of some standards of public behavior in the stadium. Plus it helped elevate the status of many men with
working-class roots to that of baseball heroes and it allowed for a certain amount
of class and racial mixing in the stands and on the field when white teams played
exhibitions against barnstorming black teams. Yet, largely as a result of owners'
efforts at containment, the ability of baseball to effect widespread social transformation was limited even as these owners paid lip service to the "beneficient"
revolution.

Of course, in terms of who controls capital, Spalding and Mills never even
bothered to pay lip service. Their words and actions regarding the economics of
professional baseball made it perfectly clear that anything less than a consolidation ending with them in complete command of the business was untenable.
When the National League wrested control from the NAPBBP in the early 1870s,
it prefigured two decades of even more egregious and systematic efforts to
destroy players' attempts at gaining a greater stake in the game's economic
structure. In 1890, for example, Spalding appointed himself head of the National
League "War Committee" to crush a campaign by players to form their own
league. Frustrated by the collusive efforts of owners to fix wages, 80 percent of
the league's players joined together to create the Players League. Favored by the
majority of fans, this league nonetheless lasted only a year, ultimately falling
victim to Spalding's "war effort."

During this pitched war of words, Spalding pulled out the most virulently
anticollectivist rhetoric heating up at that point in American cities as a response to revolutionary rumblings in Europe, threats of labor unrest, and fear
of immigrant activity at home. He called the players "hot-headed anarchists"

bent on a "terrorism" characteristic of "revolutionary movements."[26] Along with these denunciations, he spoke frequently in public about the paternal "vision and daring" of venture capitalists. He argued that only those who were sufficiently capitalized and who had a proclivity for big business could see the big picture, providing for long-term security of players and franchises and ensuring that the game would not become "cheapened" by desperate measures such as Sunday baseball or low admission charges. When the Players League folded the following year, Spalding presented this failure as evidence of his point. He reasoned that only the magnates behind the past decades' economic expansion were capable of successful (as well as moral) organization of capital.[27]

Ultimately, however, it is clear that the failure of the fledgling league had less to do with the inability of the players to organize than it had to do with aggressive, monopolistic actions on the part of the National League owners. By all indications, the players' game was better played and better attended than NL games. Yet the older league survived because its owners had amassed a substantial "war chest" allowing them to ride out the storm.[28] The National League scheduled its games in the same cities at precisely the same times as the Players League, ensuring a split in the fan base and guaranteeing that both leagues would lose money. A model for today's revenue-sharing plans among professional sports franchises, the war chest enabled each and every club to remain solvent, whereas the Players League failed. In the end, the players' uprising proved to be a financial windfall for the National League. When the Players League disbanded in 1891, NL owners absorbed the majority of renegade players back into the league, but at a fraction of their original salaries.

Of course, this narrative of revolt and discipline is not unique to baseball. In a century witnessing an unprecedented reorganization and expansion of capital, the hiring of scabs and collusive attempts to fix wages decimated many attempts on the part of labor to earn a larger share of the revenue. Yet the particular language Spalding and the others used to justify their enterprises cannot be discounted as merely hypocritical. In the wake of violent European revolution, the American opinion-makers truly discovered how to have it both ways. Mills's description of baseball as part of a "beneficient" revolution underlines how the American middle class learned to both manage and contain conflict while appropriating the language of revolt.

BASEBALL AND MIDDLE-CLASS MORAL REGENERATION

Exploring the distinction between the "beneficient" revolution, which Spalding praised, and the economic revolution of the "hot-headed anarchists," which he condemned, helps create an understanding of how the emergent rhetoric of baseball aided the formation of American middle-class ideology and identity.

Throughout the last three decades of the nineteenth century, National League owners sold the game as an endeavor that simultaneously brought about a revolution in the individual spirit and helped to defeat efforts at a more radical revision of the structures of capitalism.[29] The entrepreneurial giants of the NL promoted baseball as "artificial adventure" which would train a whole generation of children to succeed in the great battles now being fought in the boardrooms instead of on the battlefields.[30] At the same time, they suggested that the emergent business structure of ball clubs was an indicator of inherent American organizational and commercial savvy.

Decades later, while reflecting on this crucial period of image transformation, Spalding confidently described baseball's place as not only a shaper of a renewed individual spirit but also a signal of American election. Baseball, he wrote,

> owes its prestige as our National Game to the fact that no other form of sport is the exponent of American Courage, Confidence, Combativeness; American Dash, Discipline, Determination; American Energy, Eagerness, Enthusiasm; American Pluck, Persistency, Performance; American Spirit, Sagacity, Success; American Vim, Vigor, Virility. (4)

His word choice is crucial. As the "exponent" of these uniquely American qualities, baseball does not just prepare the American male for metaphoric battle, it reveals him as the exemplar of natural fitness. Spalding's language fuses a Calvinist discourse of election with the Darwinian logos of survival, two belief systems which emphasize a natural order of things and which were readily adopted by the rhetoric of American neoliberalism. In other words, perhaps less important than any kind of truth about what the game provided for individuals was the fact that it inspired supreme confidence among the consumers and participants of baseball.

Writing retrospectively at the end of the first decade of the twentieth century, Spalding was able to repeat, without reservation or qualification, what had become by then virtual truisms about the value of sport. Baseball, according to his formulation, helped the American (or more precisely, the middle-class American) man restore his preindustrial status as vigorous, adventuresome, and physical. As the frontier closed and memories of the Civil War faded, the cult of the warrior became more internalized. Individuals readied themselves for commercial and sporting skirmishes rather than militaristic battles.[31] All along, this newly elevated form of simulated work justified industrial progress. The origin of the still-common cliché about the unique ability of sport to train men for the business world, this rhetoric melded a critique of modernity with the elevation of virtues of discipline and enterprise. In short, it helped solidify the purpose and place of the rising middle class.

In his book, Spalding makes it clear that promoting this rhetoric went hand in hand with the financial well-being of the league. He describes the owners' efforts at eradicating the "prevailing evils—gambling and pool selling . . . from the grounds and the game" in terms best used to describe the heroism of Union soldiers: "With these and other problems confronting them, the League managers entered upon the discharge of their onerous duties earnestly and vigorously."[32] The expansive quality of this line is highly representative of the rest of his *history* in that it makes clear his purpose of elevating baseball from the status of a mere game to that of a transcendent national institution. His particular choice of metaphors is important. The owners became *generals* "earnestly and vigorously" leading others in symbolic battles. Ballplayers, especially middle-class youth trained in the PSALs, were taught that playing the game involved stakes greater than merely enjoying a satisfying communal activity or blowing off steam. Instead, participation in baseball taught children discipline and patriotism while strengthening their bodies and minds for individual pursuits.

Ironically, the vigorous challenges of the game took place within the context of a sport that was increasingly disciplined and regulated by the same economic forces responsible for structuring the world of industrialized work. Beginning in the 1870s, the structure of organized baseball became more and more controlled by business interests that maintained social hierarchies, enforced racial segregation, and made owners wealthy at the expense of labor. All along, however, the sport's popularity was augmented by a growing belief in the game's "beneficient" democratic, if indeed not revolutionary, qualities.

CHAPTER THREE

EQUALITY VERSUS AUTHENTICITY

Mills's attempt to promote his "beneficient" revolution underlines the extent to which two apparently contradictory impulses—a simultaneous worship and fear of the physicality, individualism, and independence of the American working classes—have been negotiated through the elevation of sporting events to a higher symbolic level. The history of this kind of negotiation clearly informs architecture critic Landecker's bifurcated review of Jacobs Field. It helps explain how her reflexive belief in the power of baseball stadiums to be inclusive can exist alongside her disappointment over the fact that overt markers of class are not more carefully hidden. What she bemoans at Jacobs Field is to a large degree the legacy of tight control of the spatial structure of professional sporting venues. Yet, just as important, what she *senses* must be at least in part a product of an internalized belief system consistent with traditional American sporting rhetoric compelling her to suggest that, despite astonishing evidence to the contrary, in the contemporary stadium, "baseball is for everyone." For more than a century and a half, the stadium has been an important site of experimentation, a virtual battlefield in the dialectic between love for and fear of a crowd. While certain parks truly have accommodated raucous attempts to expand the (demographic and behavioral) limits of acceptable public space, most others have more closely followed the reform model, conducting these experiments in an often repressively tolerant way.

REPRESSIVE TOLERANCE

From the beginning, large crowds at baseball games forced owners to find creative ways to manage them. Lithographs and eyewitness accounts depicting the scene at urban ball parks arising prior to the era of Spalding and the National League suggest the continual presence of a kind of ruffian culture just beyond the outfield. A drawing published in *Harper's Weekly* illustrating a 1865 game between the Brooklyn-based Atlantics and the Philadelphia Athletics at Athletics Park at Jefferson Street in Philadelphia shows how much of the event's action took place behind the roped-off line of spectators forming the boundary of center field.[1] As top-hatted men (with a few women here and there) watch the game, a dozen or so others exchange blows, play leap frog, or make wagers in the grassy area behind the playing field. In the earliest incarnations of baseball parks, the outfield appears to have been a relatively anarchic space, bringing people together and allowing them the opportunity to perform behaviors unacceptable in most other public locations.

However, borrowing from existing models of crowd control, the owners of the Athletics moved quickly with measures to keep the barbarians at the gate. Another drawing depicting a game between the same teams at the same park just a year later shows a significantly changed atmosphere. By this time, the outfield had been enclosed by a wall limiting by several thousand the number of spectators.[2] Along with this, team management had elevated ticket prices to an almost unthinkable one dollar, thereby excluding the majority of Philadelphia's population. What is portrayed in the second drawing is thus more like the controlled anarchy characteristic of other enclosed ball parks at the time (e.g., Cassmeyer's Union Grounds). The 1866 lithograph shows a small grandstand on the third-base side where the ladies sit fronted and flanked by what appears to be well-behaving men enjoying an afternoon of fresh air and harmless leisure. These men stand, sit in chairs, or even recline in their carriages parked inside the grounds in foul territory down the third-base line. Conversely, on the first-base side, men from the Victorian middle-class sporting community jostle, toss objects toward the field, and make bets. In the foreground of this particular lithograph, one group of men, faces beaming in amusement, passively watches an angry patron grab another by the throat. As in other parks, the violent behavior of this particular sector of middle-class Philadelphia society seemed to be not only tolerated but in fact sanctioned through the creation of a separate space inside the park to accommodate it. Kept at bay from the ladies and their more respectably acting suitors, these men were free to blow off a bit of steam.

Nonetheless, according to newspaper accounts of the scene, Magee's drawing fails to tell the whole story. Absent from the lithograph is the apparent mob scene forming that day around the newly enclosed ball park. One writer estimates that during the game "there were over 20,000 people in the area in trees, on roof tops, on trucks, and in second floor windows."[3] A more rigidly enacted exclusion seems to have produced an effect diametrically opposed to the intentions of the ball-park owners. It created a violent outsiders' culture in numbers even greater than in previous years.

THREE ROWS OF LUXURY BOXES BEHIND HOME PLATE AND ALONG THE THIRD-BASE LINE SEPARATE THE LOWER BOXES FROM THE UPPER CONCOURSE AT JACOBS FIELD. THIS KIND OF SPECIAL ACCOMMODATION FOR WEALTHIER FANS FIRST EMERGED IN 1883 IN CHICAGO'S SECOND LAKE FRONT PARK.

A decade later, Spalding brilliantly figured out a way to resolve this problem. He constructed a park that simultaneously was able to promote and contain these threatening forms of public interaction. His Lake Front Park, built first in 1878 then dramatically refurbished in 1883, featured two enormous stand-alone boxes in the outfield, the largest bleacher sections in baseball at the time. These bleachers served as extremely creative forms of genial containment. They provided a way to incorporate and even profit from a potentially dangerous section of the population given to congregating just outside the walls of enclosed parks. In Spalding's park, the subversive activity beyond the wall at Athletics Park was brought, literally and figuratively, within the confines of the stadium. His bleachers, which in the second version of the park accommodated six thousand spectators, allowed for an unprecedented number of people to see a game, all the while sheltering the more elite Chicago fans. Accommodating thousands of members of Chicago's increasingly large immigrant population instead of leaving them to congregate outside the park, Spalding was able to make enough money to provide for a comfortable segregation.

When he renovated the park in 1883, Spalding went even further, perhaps creating the template for the modern baseball stadium that Landecker finds problematic. A precursor to Jacobs Field and other modern arenas, the second version of Lake Front Park was the first venue to incorporate primitive forms of luxury skyboxes. Spalding provided eighteen plush saloons above the third base grandstands where wealthier patrons sat in comfortable armchairs and were waited on by White Stockings' staff members. To ensure the safety of these upscale fans, the owner hired an unprecedented forty-one-guard security team to keep watch over the bleachers and the standing-room-only sections. In short, rather than simply repressing or excluding the more dangerous factions of Chicago's baseball faithful, Spalding chose gentler, more profitable forms of crowd maintenance.

The structure of his ball park serves as a physical manifestation of what Spalding (like Cassmeyer before him) perceived to be one of his central missions—a negotiation of the disparate pressures faced by middle-class baseball owners. As a businessman, he looked to cash in on the widespread popularity of the sport. As a social climber, he had to manage the stadium environment in such a way to avoid the displeasure of genteel reformers. Finally, as a member of an anxious middle class, he had to allow for enough raw energy within the stadium to satisfy the longings for raucous experience among his peers.

"DER POSS PRESIDENT" AND EMERGENT CARNIVAL

By creating separate sections accommodating the "dangerous classes," Spalding walked a fine line that the reduced National League had itself established. Clearly, however, when rival owners or leagues crossed that line, when they took measures to accommodate too many working-class fans or when they allowed for too much expression of sentiment undermining emergent bourgeois values of order and discipline, Spalding and his fellow owners took strong measures to destroy them. Chris Von der Ahe, the renegade, populist owner of the American Association St. Louis Browns, was in this sense the antithesis of the NL breed. His Sportsman's Park, dubbed the "Coney Island of the West" and replete with roller coasters and a Wild West Show, represented a spectacular attempt to promote, celebrate and, in essence, *feature* activities typically found on the wrong side of the razor wire.

While Spalding was successfully experimenting with crowd control, bleacher segregation, and posh amenities in an effort to attract and insulate Chicago's wealthier baseball fans, Von der Ahe was focusing on the masses. Whereas Spalding imagined the public space of a baseball stadium as one which reinforced social order while allowing for a modicum of release and primitivism among members of the middle classes and a few thousand bleacher fans, Von der Ahe looked to provide a place that allowed for a wide range of pleasures available to as diverse a fan base as possible. To appeal to the "millions" in the 1890s, he installed rides, built a racetrack, constructed a honky-tonk, hired a "glamour girl" coronet band, and arranged for prize fights at the park.[4]

In contrast to the National League, which was founded in part as a way to extirpate excessive drinking from baseball stadiums, Von der Ahe openly promoted public drunkenness. He created a beer garden in the outfield, then refused to cover it with a roof because, in the sun, thirsty patrons would drink more. Remarkably, in the earliest incarnation of his Sportsman's Park, originally constructed in 1881, this beer garden in right field was in play.[5] During games, opposing outfielders would have to chase fair balls into an area where men and women sat at picnic tables eating and drinking. Von der Ahe's refusal to enforce a firm separation between player and spectator, which was becoming more and more rigid in a burgeoning epoch of professionalization, was a central part of the experience at his park. In the early years of the age of mechanical reproduction, when fewer and fewer people consumed what they produced, this refusal to rigidly separate consumer and producer—spectator and ballplayer—must have provided at least a degree of psychic compensation.

Von der Ahe's primary strategy, it seemed, was to embellish the stadium experience—indeed, the experience of rooting for the Browns—with the topsy-turvy world of carnival. On the way to games, he paraded his players in front of the fans in open barouches adorned with St. Louis Browns blankets. He hired as his player-manager the legendary Charles Comiskey, who in turn recruited the wildest bunch of characters in baseball, known for their tactics of intimidation on the field and for their hell-raising behavior off it. Visiting teams were forced to suffer torrents of abuse from both the aggressive home team and the passionate, crass, and drunken fans. In so many ways, the baseball season in St. Louis gave a large segment of the population a chance to turn the social order on its head. It allowed for the elevation of formerly blue-collar and marginal baseball players to the status of heroes. It accommodated and sanctioned public displays of hostility and resentment toward authority figures (e.g., umpires and opponents' managers), and it helped blur the distinction between producing and consuming, perhaps the most important new line being drawn by emergent industrial capitalism.

On top of all this, in the lampoonable figure of Von der Ahe himself, St. Louis fans were given a king figure to simultaneously revere and mock in a country allegedly without royalty. "Der Poss President," as he was known because of his thick German accent and over-the-top sense of his own grandiosity, adorned himself just like a carnival monarch. He wore a stovepipe hat, gaudy waistcoats, and a slew of diamonds. At once an embodiment of the town's wealth and a symbol of the decadence caused by this wealth, he was given to storied largess as well as excessive frugality. More often drunk than not, he threw lavish public parties one day, selling off his most expensive ballplayers the next. He was both of the people, an inspiration to the largely immigrant and poor St. Louis populace, and a grotesque stand-in for the monarchy the people left behind when they emigrated from Europe. He even carried physically the grotesquery of carnival. His large nose and thick accent, for example, made him the frequent subject of cartoon caricature in local newspapers.[6] This image of a decadent, drunken king (which seemed to intensify as Von der Ahe grew more and more enchanted with his own power) became progressively more insufferable to Spalding as the National League ramped up its program of image reconstruction. Eventually, the NL owners would have to find a way to shut him down entirely.

THE ESTABLISHMENT

Even before the Browns were reluctantly allowed into the league as part of the 1891 merger between the American Association and the NL, the public rivalry between Von der Ahe and Spalding had approached its boiling point. Although for years the St. Louis owner had been making public sport out of Spalding and his cultivated professional image, his pique perhaps reached its zenith in 1885. In what should have been the deciding game of that year's controversial World Series between the Browns and the White Stockings, Von der Ahe allowed Comiskey to protest an umpire's decision by having his team walk off the field, leaving the competition deadlocked. Spalding, who immediately pledged to have nothing more to do with Von der Ahe, finally agreed to have his club play the Browns the next year, provided the St. Louis team consent to a provision stipulating that the winner would take all the gate. Von der Ahe not only accepted but also offered to bet an extra ten thousand dollars of his own money.[7] When the Browns did indeed pull the upset, Von der Ahe flaunted his success not just by buying champagne for his team but also by giving money to a few Chicago players who had lost their shirts betting on themselves. This gesture of largess helped solidify his image as a populist owner who seemed genuinely interested in the players and fans; it also threatened to make a mockery of the National League propaganda campaign claiming that gambling and drinking had been eliminated from the sport. The forces already weary of Von der Ahe's antics were thus motivated to mobilize more actively against him.

As the propagandistic and consolidating strategies of the National League owners began to affect the general climate around baseball, something like an establishment (comprising so-called legitimate owners, stable conservative baseball publications, and public figures such as Theodore Roosevelt and Mark Twain) began to emerge.[8] Von der Ahe's adversarial relationship with this establishment, despite his widespread public approbation, doomed him when his business (and personal life) later began to unravel. Alfred Spink, Von der Ahe's close friend who had originally convinced him to invest in a ball club and park, famously turned against him after he created the "Coney Island of the West." As editor of the *Sporting News* (widely accepted as the top sports journal of its day), Spink ordered an article titled "The Prostitution of a Ballpark." In this and other columns, Spink's newspaper relentlessly went after Von der Ahe, claiming that he had turned his park into the "resort of disreputable men and women" and suggesting the establishment conduct "warfare on him" with "but one result": a hostile takeover of the franchise.[9]

This clarion call from the increasingly important opinion maker proved to be the beginning of the end for Von der Ahe. In 1898, when a fire broke out in Sportsman's Park with close to four thousand spectators in the stands, Von der Ahe's kingdom began to crumble. Spectators were trampled and burned as they rushed to exit the park, and Von der Ahe's saloon and ticket office were completely destroyed. In the fire's aftermath, Der Poss President was faced with a stream of lawsuits and a barrage of creditors looking to recoup money they had invested in the park. By this time, the owner was also buried in a financial crisis involving his Depression-ravaged real estate investments and embroiled in personal scandals related to adultery and divorce proceedings.[10] Yet without a push from the baseball establishment, it seems entirely possible that he could have weathered the storm. Trying to court investors for the club, he was outraged when the Browns instead passed into court-ordered receivership. He claimed conspiracy. The deal, he maintained, was brokered by the National League, which was trying to ruin him. The other owners were envious of his success, he reasoned, and would stop at nothing to force him out.

In fact, history suggests that his claims have plenty of merit. Just as Spink had proposed, the league quietly arranged a transaction involving a third party and traction magnate, Frank Robison, the owner of the Cleveland Spiders. The arrangement allowed Robison to take control of both franchises. Seeing the potential of the passionate fan base in St. Louis that Von der Ahe had cultivated, Robison then raided the Cleveland franchise, sending the best players west and filling up the Spiders primarily with the has-beens Von der Ahe had accumulated during his last couple of years. On paper, the National League expelled the old Browns franchise and replaced it with an expansion one awarded to Robison. Although Von der Ahe did not give up without a fight, bringing an unsuccessful suit against Robison and trying to collect twenty-five thousand dollars from every visiting team that played the Browns that year, he had clearly been checkmated by the league. Humiliated and broke at the turn of the century, Von der Ahe symbolized the extent to which the "beneficient" revolution had begun to shape the stadium landscape.

CONEY ISLAND OR CENTRAL PARK

The battle between Spalding and Von der Ahe for the right to define the parameters of a healthy public sports facility mirrored larger fights about public space occurring around the nation. John Kasson, in *Amusing the Million,* argues that the success of Coney Island (the model for Sportsman's Park) constitutes at least in part a popular, grass-roots reaction to excessively genteel forms of public space designed for the masses. Places like Central Park were originally built to be "rural retreat[s] in the midst of the city . . . easily accessible refuge[s] from urban pressures and conditions" (Williams, *Country and the City* 12). They were to provide suitable public space remedying the effect of city life on the individual. Consequently, they were to be filters, controlling threats to public order from the dangerous classes.

Coney Island (and by extension, the "Coney Island of the West") provided more dynamic alternatives. During this era of popular amusement, when the shortened work week and a transition from an agricultural to a manufacturing based economy began to forge a clear distinction between work and leisure time, amusement entrepreneurs such as Von der Ahe and Frederick Thompson (the manager of Coney's Luna Park) attempted to provide recreational spaces virtually free from the discipline of everyday life and normative demands. They created venues mocking the world of productivity insofar as their attractions were almost all deliberately unproductive or a-functional. According to Kasson's argument, their roller coasters and shoot-the-chutes turned the relationship of worker to technology on its head. Slaves to the machine by day, workers spent evenings and Sundays riding big contraptions that did not produce anything tangible or consumable and that existed solely for their frivolous enjoyment. Yet despite its widespread appeal, Sportsman's Park was a bad fit for baseball at the time. As the *Sporting News* had made clear, the Browns' home of the 1890s had become too hospitable to "disreputable men and women," too much like Coney Island and not enough like Central Park. Von der Ahe's public spectacle of excess simply had to be closed down as part of baseball's transformation.[11]

The nature of the stadium event, metaphorical war or a primitive release, privileged the corporeal or the authentic. Coinciding with acceptance of baseball as the "national pastime" was the formation in consciousness of an American middle class, a class heavily invested in becoming arbiters of this authenticity. Widespread perceptions of a softening of manners throughout the latter half of the nineteenth century had created the environment from which sports emerged as a restorative, a cure for the pervasive panic caused by a shift in emphasis in the life of the middle-class man from production to consumption, from creation to negotiation and salesmanship. The worship of force in controlled form appeared to help many middle-class sports fans deal with what seemed to be a repressed envy of the working classes.[12] Reputable baseball stadiums allowed middle-class owners to think themselves part of what felt like an ongoing revolution. Not real battles, but simulated ones, baseball games helped inform sensations of commonality—revolution as symbol divorced from material conditions. At the same time, unlike Sportsman's Park, the stadiums hosting these metaphorical wars allowed owners multiple ways to contain unrest. Bleachers, high ticket prices, daytime baseball, security forces, and the elimination of renegade ownership helped keep poorer members of society either outside the gates entirely or tucked safely in segregated areas.

The degree to which middle-class moralists and even genteel reformers seemed to be willing to overlook the supposed sins of the game suggests how important these physical manifestations of the "beneficient" revolution were perceived to be. In *Popular Amusements,* a moralizing monograph treating the problems of popular diversions, Richard Henry Edwards provides a revealing taxonomy, cataloguing and discussing, type by type, all major forms of American popular amusement and ranking them in terms of their "goodness." He declares some amusements (such as "men only" shows) worthy of intense scorn, sites of absolute debauchery, intemperance, immoral sexuality, crime, and late-night hours. He calls others (e.g., bowling) good, wholesome amusement. When he gets to baseball, however, he becomes oddly ambivalent. After cataloguing the various sins and abuses transpiring nightly at ball parks, and after expressing extreme wariness about a sport that had become distressingly professionalized, he ultimately finds it necessary to give the sport an uneasy nod in the affirmative. Though he has seen enough rowdy behavior and gambling at games to provoke condemnation, he ultimately concludes that "rowdyism . . . is usually the rowdyism of a small section of the crowd rather than of the players. . . . The morality of American professional baseball, especially in the major leagues, is on the whole nothing less than a national achievement and expression of America's love of clean sport in honest, hard-fought contests" (15).

The dissonance between the evidence he presents and the conclusions he draws is not unlike that found almost a century later in Landecker's treatment of Jacobs Field. Consuming and propagating Spalding's fiction—that baseball is the "national game," a uniquely American sport reflecting a singular set of values and skills—Edwards, like Landecker, shows himself willing to overlook both baseball's underworld and its exclusionary practices most likely because the stadium environment was so successful at reassuring middle-class Americans that national democracy was alive and well. Wary of the social forces splitting the country along class, ethnic, racial, and regional lines, he seems to find great assurance in the series of compromises at baseball stadiums like Lake Front Park that at once maintained certain crucial segregations and gave off the scent of classlessness. In short, he comes to see most baseball parks, as Spalding did, as necessary components of urbanization, as clever syntheses of the impulses behind both Coney Island and Central Park.

OVERLY DEMOCRATIC MULTIPURPOSE STADIUMS

A century after Edwards wrote his monograph, retro baseball parks, modeled after many of the originals created during the "beneficient" revolution, have emerged at least partly in response to similar stimuli. The boom in downtown ball-park construction has occurred in the wake of an unprecedented widening of the gap between rich and poor in America, a gap in large measure the logical conclusion of an economic crisis in the mid-1960s and the oil shortages of the early 1970s, which forced American businesses to reinvent themselves. In the wake of this period of economic uncertainty, capital was forced to become increasingly disorganized, flexible, and global in scope. As a result, the American manufacturing base, long the engine driving the economy and providing steady if unspectacular jobs to the masses, moved across the borders. In its place, a service-oriented economy of lawyers, financiers, technocrats, and global entertainment entities emerged, producing unprecedented prosperity for many during the 1990s along with widespread despair for those left behind.

New old baseball stadiums, virtual signposts for the decade, have become the centerpieces of efforts to renew the American city previously torn apart by racial riots, suburban flight and the exodus of capital. They are dramatic symbols, manifestations in brick and steel, of the need to cleverly choreograph an experience attracting and satisfying a still-expanding suburban population, prosperous and comfortable but perhaps uneasy about both economic inequity and its own contribution to the surrounding physical world.[13] New stadiums in part relieve these anxieties by serving as physical markers of the antimodern, holding working-class-inflected notions of authenticity to be a source of salvation. They thus ease patrons' adjustments to a culture defined increasingly by consumption and service and allow them psychic connection with members of economic classes excluded by the new world order but often imagined as more free or independent. The most important contemporary representations of baseball's mythical resiliency and creativity, new urban parks serve as dramatic texts articulating American utopian longings invested in the national pastime.

Ironically, however, the very stadiums that have been replaced—the massive, sterile, multipurpose venues like Milwaukee's County Stadium or Baltimore's Memorial Stadium—at one point in their short history offered many of the positive qualities that Landecker reflexively equates with baseball. As they began to decline in popularity throughout the 1960s, 1970s, and 1980s, these enormous venues presented a wide range of vernacular and spontaneous forms of pleasure on the model of Sportsman's Park and Coney Island. After their heyday, but prior to their demolition, these parks provided die-hard fans the freedom of exile and the ability to invent their own ways to enjoy the game. For years, virtually alone in these cavernous buildings, groups of fans famously bet on games, banged on drums, danced, heckled, and partied in spaces they had come to see as uniquely their own. During this brief time, these parks also accommodated large degrees of social mixing merely gestured toward by historical baseball rhetoric. Cheap tickets, wide public concourses, and a lack of segregated seating enabled an unprecedented degree of fan diversity and mixing.

Of course, the creation of this kind of free-for-all was not the original intention of multipurpose stadium designers. Aesthetically, these parks were meant to reject historicist belief in the timeless quality of the sport and instead embrace a kind of postwar, up-to-the-moment, modern life ethos.[14] Economically and socially, they were built to provide controlled accessibility. Feeling pressure to accommodate huge live audiences before the reality of the 1950s decline in baseball attendance had sunk in, their architects *supersized* them, in part because revenue from ticket sales was still substantially greater than money from television contracts.[15] All the while, the need to increase the number of spectators was balanced by a kind of troubling selectivity. Promising the ability to attract crowds of seventy to eighty thousand, many of these concrete leviathans were designed to lure long embedded teams from urban locations to suburban and exurban sites near other cities. When the Braves moved from Boston to Milwaukee, the Dodgers from Brooklyn to Los Angeles, the Athletics from Philadelphia to Kansas City, the Giants from New York to San Francisco, and the Browns from St. Louis to Baltimore, they all did so largely as a way to escape city neighborhoods.[16] Racial panic had led some owners to believe that declining attendance was largely a result of the fact that white audiences were becoming progressively less comfortable with visiting black city neighborhoods. When most games were moved to night, this sense of panic intensified. Owners such as the Dodgers' Walter O'Malley failed to see any future for a game asking white audiences to come to black sections of town after nightfall.

Along with the perception of the need to provide for this kind of economic and spatial segregation, baseball owners were prompted by the dawn of automobile culture to close the book on the Polo Grounds, Ebbets Field, and several other parks of their generation. The Federal-Aid Highway Act of 1956 completely remade the American landscape, providing an unprecedented subsidy to suburban development and making the construction of these distant stadiums all but inevitable. Surrounded (as most of them were) by huge parking lots and attached to the emergent federal highway system, they were easily accessible to O'Malley's desired demographic. They attracted the burgeoning postwar, suburban white audiences of the 1950s in record numbers while at the same time leaving behind much of the urban population reliant on public transportation.

Indeed, in the early years, enormous crowds filled venues such as County Stadium in Milwaukee and Candlestick Park in San Francisco, making owners who had moved their teams seem like visionaries. Jilted fans in Boston and New York had to acknowledge that, at the very least, their beloved clubs had achieved a level of prosperity impossible at their old parks. However, as these new suburban locations began to age, the novelty gradually wore off. Mirroring greater societal and economic trends of the 1960s, 1970s, and 1980s, the infrastructure around them started to decay and erstwhile urban problems began to sprawl out toward them. Predictably, attendance dipped along with this decay.

As this happened, the enormity of the multipurpose parks became a liability for owners and a bonus for many fans. Because games rarely sold out, tickets were cheap and ready available, meaning that, for perhaps the only time in baseball's history, live professional games did in fact seem to be "for everyone." With so much space to fill up, these stadiums usually provided enormous bleacher sections where tickets almost always could be purchased on game nights for less than ten dollars. In some cases, the deal was even better than that. "They let us in for free," says longtime Indian bleacher fan Craig Mahovlic, "so long as we would drink a lot of beer."

Adding to this sense of inadvertent classlessness was the fact that, because they were built primarily to attract mass audiences, multipurpose stadiums lacked specialized revenue-producing mechanisms characterizing arenas constructed for post-Fordist audiences. Unlike Spalding's Lake Front Park and unlike new parks, these stadiums tended (and still in some cases still tend) to flatten out consuming alternatives within the park. Even though some of these older parks were eventually retrofitted with a few revenue-producing luxury suites, the focus was on a kind of lowest common denominator of seating options. Though box seat tickets still cost more than bleachers, the majority of the seats were relatively evenly priced.

Similarly, the concession alternatives, the standard baseball fare of hot dogs and domestic beer, suggested a kind of egalitarianism of consumables. Rich and poor alike ate Ball Park Franks and drank Budweiser. In Memorial Stadium, residents of posh suburban Bel Air waited in the same lines as folks from working-class South Baltimore to buy mass-manufactured felt pennants and Orioles replica hats. In short, although they are now categorically dismissed as cold eyesores (and indeed, could be ugly and uncomfortable), these relics of an age of American mass production did not generally set up the kind of symbolic hierarchies that trouble Landecker at Jacobs Field.

THE DESIRABLE UNDESIRABLE IN CLEVELAND

Hidden but still present in Landecker's qualified praise of the new park is recognition of the loss felt by some when the Indians moved. "I liked the old park," says Darin Good from his seat in the Jacobs Field bleachers. "It had a lot of history. Plus, it's like when they [the Indians] weren't that good, you know it was the real fans who would still come out to support the team." During the last twenty years of Cleveland Stadium, Good and his father would come to about five or ten games per year to sit with the other "real" fans braving the sometimes obscenely uncomfortable conditions created by a freezing wind whipping in off Lake Erie. Good still comes faithfully to support the Indians in the new park, but he is quick to point out how a changed demographic took him and his father by surprise during the early years of Jacobs Field. "There were a lot of people who came here just because it was the thing to do." In this regard, Good is not alone in his thoughts. Most longtime fans discussing the switch to the new park repeat this sentiment. "When it was the thing to do in '95 to about 2000, people jumped on the bandwagon," says Mahovlic. "For all but the real baseball fans, what was going on was just a social event."

Although most longtime Cleveland fans like Good and Mahovlic are grateful for Jacobs Field, embracing the newcomers, enjoying the comfort and beauty of the new park, and taking pleasure in their team's recent successes on the field, they make a distinction between "real" baseball fans and those attracted to games at the new park because they are trendy activities. Mahovlic's describes a "real" fan as one who "comes down regardless of how the team is doing . . . who comes down to watch baseball in its purest form and doesn't care about mascots and music." John Adams, who according to Mahovlic's definition is perhaps the most "real" fan of them all, agrees wholeheartedly. Adams, who has banged his bass drum from the bleachers in support of the Indians for four decades while missing only a handful of games, likes the fact that the new park has attracted an expanded fan base for his beloved team. But he gets impatient with new-comers who do not eventually come to take an interest in the game itself. "Look around," he says. "You still get people who just come to chat. It's like, why take up a seat?"

Carting his drum to the top row of the bleacher sections nightly in support of the Tribe, Adams has long been a treasured, albeit unofficial, member of the Indians team. He has been featured numerous times in the team's game day pro-gram and nightly receives visitors who come to pay their respects. "I came all the way from Madison to see the Indians and to meet you," Bill Chmelka told Adams upon approaching him in between innings at a June 2003 game. "I've been an Indians die hard all my life, and I've always wanted to tell you how much I appre-ciate you being out here night after night." Adams loves the team and is gener-ally supportive of its management, yet he feels that the move to the new stadium invariably created a degree of tension between club officials and "real" fans. "The truth is, the guys running the show don't really know about Cleveland baseball," he says. "Cleveland is a family town, a big city with small-town values. We're not yuppyville, but they don't understand that." Adams enjoys the new park tremen-dously and does not express much outright nostalgia for Cleveland Stadium, yet his words underscore a certain amount of adjustment necessary when new meets old. He resents the extent to which Jacobs Field management feels the need to recreate and package for new patrons the kind of energy that he believes

LONG-TIME INDIANS FAN AND BLEACHER DRUMMER JOHN ADAMS.

"real" fans provide naturally. "You can't have controlled spontaneity and authenticity," he says. "The cleverest stuff happens directly from the fans." Like Mahovlic, Adams dismisses the sensory blitz of dancing mascots, rap music and electronic clapping as needless distractions, diminishing the potential for fans to create their own responses to the game. The move to Jacobs Field, while viewed on balance as positive, has regularized and mechanized the kind of pleasure he and his friends had already been enjoying.

Underscoring this tension is the fact that, as Indians tickets became hot commodities and Jacobs Field sold out nightly, management made Adams purchase a season ticket for his bass drum. "I'd bet that it's the only season ticket anywhere for an inanimate object," he laughs. Having to restrict himself and his drum to two assigned seats suggests the extent to which the environment changed for the "real" fans when the Indians moved to the Gateway. For years in old Cleveland Stadium, Adams, Mahovlic, and a handful of other faithful fans would, night after night, assemble in the huge, and mostly empty, center-field bleacher section, a section so distant from the action that in the history of the park, no player ever hit a home run there. Dwarfed by the enormity of this outpost (which was built to accommodate almost eleven thousand fans), this small group of creative loyalists cheered wildly for their beloved yet woebegone franchise. For their efforts, they were commemorated in *Major League,* a widely dismissed 1989 feature film. This movie, largely derivative of the more critically acclaimed 1988 hit *Bull Durham,* nonetheless manages to articulate something essential about the experience of longtime baseball fans in the changing world of modern sports.

In a stirring opening credit sequence, the film deftly uses images of baseball to explore some of the ironies and tensions involved in downtown Cleveland's process of gentrification, its own "beneficient" revolution. The director juxtaposes shots of the rising new glass, stone, and steel downtown of renaissance Cleveland with images of working people playing ball on a small patch of dirt outside their soon-to-be-closed refinery. Meanwhile, a group of bleacher crazies is shown readying headdresses, baseball mitts, and megaphones—accouterments of vernacular forms of stadium pleasure—for yet another season of exile in Cleveland Stadium.

The credit sequence makes it perfectly clear that this is a time of profound transition. While workmen lay the final bricks of a new corporate office tower (which in real life will come to form part of the backdrop to Jacobs Field), a few local factory workers who share a passion for the Tribe engage in their annual spring rite, speaking hopefully about the upcoming Indians season over coffee and pie in a diner. Meanwhile, the movie offers up Rachel Phelps, the new owner of the Indians and the locus of greed and class privilege against whom the fans will be pitted. In the film's first few moments, it is revealed that Phelps has entered into a secret arrangement with the city of Miami to move the Indians south if she is able to escape her lease with Cleveland. It paints her as the very personification of years of greed and mismanagement, annually conspiring to dash the springtime hopes of the dwindling Indians faithful.

A former showgirl who inherited the team when her husband died during the off season, Phelps announces her diabolical plan in her posh Cleveland Stadium office filled with effete signifiers of privilege: servants, expensive tea settings, and fancy furniture.[17] Having sold off all of her good ballplayers, she orders her general manager to assemble the biggest bunch of losers he can in order to make the team so bad that attendance drops below eight hundred thousand for the year, thus allowing her to act on a fine-print clause in her contract and leave Cleveland in favor of the sweetheart deal in Florida. The comfort Phelps enjoys in her office of course stands in sharp contradistinction to the modest environs of the working people seen during the film's opening; it also contrasts strikingly with the plain, neglected old stadium just outside her window.[18]

In 1989, this character seemed more than just a bit preposterous, a cardboard cutout of greed and nouveau riche whimsy. Yet it is fair to say that in the 1990s, life imitated art. Art Modell packed up and took Cleveland's beloved (NFL) Browns to Baltimore because the state of Maryland gave him a sweetheart deal on a new stadium, and Jeffrey Loria, owner of baseball's Montreal Expos, conducted annual fire sales of players in an effort to leverage the city into paying for a new stadium and/or to lower revenue sufficiently to make a case for being able to relocate.[19] Miami not only got an expansion team but also was able to buy enough talent in its fifth year of existence (Moises Alou from Montreal and Bobby Bonilla, originally from Pittsburgh, were the cornerstones of the new team) that it won the World Series title in 1997. Shockingly, right after this victory, Wayne Huizenga, the Florida Marlins' owner, proved to be a real-life Rachel Phelps. He immediately dismantled the team, selling off all but one starter in order to lower the club's payroll so that he would profit more when he sold the team afterward.

Of course, the fact that real-life owners would eventually stoop to Phelps's level does not excuse the fact that her portrayal remains problematic in several ways. For one thing, she is at best two-dimensional. All the things that make working-class Clevelanders suffer—economic decline, an uncertain future, a bad ball club, and greed among the powers that be—are invested disingenuously in a single individual. As Hollywood films are prone to do, this one suggests that getting rid of/reforming a single greedy person can somehow take the place of more laborious economic reform and development. On top of this, as a woman who craves power in the male-dominated world of professional sports, Phelps is too easy of a target for a just barely submerged misogyny. Blaming a striving woman for the bleak prospects of the working classes in post-Fordist Cleveland constitutes an almost inexcusable cheap shot.

Nonetheless, the fact that her character is so easily recognizable by a popular film audience as the consolidation of forces conspiring against poor people in general and long-suffering baseball fans in particular is important. It suggests widespread mourning over the passing of cultures as downtown Cleveland revitalizes and the Tribe goes upscale. Throughout the movie, the evil owner is forced to confront Jake Taylor, a washed-up, working man's catcher holding on tenuously to one more year in the big leagues. Jake of course is the dramatic embodiment of the kind of constructed authenticity emergent in over a century's worth of baseball rhetoric. In one highly representative scene, Jake tails his former girlfriend, the erstwhile working-class Lynn Wells, who has left her old life behind and now directs a special collections room in the Cleveland library; she drives a Volvo while he still lumbers around in his beat-up Buick. He follows her to what he believes is her apartment in a revitalized downtown neighborhood and ends up at a snooty dinner party in the newly restored luxury condominium of her new fiancé, a rich, young attorney. Jake, in his jeans, t-shirt, and disheveled sports coat, is forced to engage in pleasant conversation with what the movie suggests are representatives of the empty suits and cocktail dresses of new downtown Cleveland. While *Eine Kleine Nachtmusik* plays in the background, Jake is confronted with not-so-subtly demeaning questions about his financial plans after baseball. The movie portrays him as the regular old guy, juxtaposed with an undesirable, uptight respectability.

Of course, by the end of the film, Jake wins back Lynn's affection, mirroring the resurgence of the outcast Indians. Typical of underdog sport films, this movie shows fans gradually warming up to Phelps's ragtag collection of players who defy the odds and force a playoff game with the Yankees for the American League East championship. A full house packs cavernous Cleveland Stadium, banding together with the team against the evil owner who is, by now, furious that her plans have been foiled. Panning around the crowd, showing the movie audience what Phelps sees, the camera captures visions of retreating working-class Cleveland. It reveals a sea of bad haircuts and fake leather jackets, a mixed bag of bleacher faithful in Native American head dress, bikers, sheet-metal mechanics, and secretaries, all of whom identify with the underdog outcasts on the field. In the end, the overachieving Indians miraculously (but predictably) win the pennant through hustle and guile, drawing big crowds and invalidating Phelps's contract with Miami. Goodness—the goodness of working-class, baseball-crazy, old Cleveland—triumphs over evil. In the movies, of course, average Joe machismo routs yuppie pretension most every time.

In real life, however, it was only after taxpayers paid to replace Cleveland Stadium with Jacobs Field that the Indians stopped threatening to move. Once the Indians cut their deal with the city and moved into the new park, they began to attract a bigger, more affluent crowd. In the process, they generated sufficient revenue to buy themselves a contender, breaking their four-decade-long slump and finally winning a pennant. Yet despite the inevitability of such trends, despite the fact that the decade following the movie's release saw a relatively straightforward correlation between increased capital and on-field success, the movie clings desperately to the type of fantasy contained within the century-old baseball rhetoric.[20] It holds on to the belief that "pluck, verve and vigor" will help ordinary Americans win despite odds decidedly stacked against them. This seems to be the main point of the film, the essence of its mythology. Cleveland and baseball itself, both traditionally unaffected, are threatened by emergent downtown culture represented by Lynne's fiancé and friends and by greedy owners like Rachel Phelps.

The movie is, obviously, an exaggeration. Adams and Mahovlic have never been as down and out as their fictional counterparts. The former is a longtime systems analyst with the phone company, and the latter has held a steady job with the postal service throughout his time rooting for the Indians. Additionally, neither of them seems to feel overwhelming class animus. In fact, they both appreciate the fact that the Cleveland bleachers have always been very welcoming to all stadium visitors, be they fans of opposing teams or yuppie newcomers. "We're a family town," says Adams. "People from Chicago would come and say 'hey, what is this?' In other places, the bleachers are like a halfway house. But here, even back in the old stadium, it was always a nice place for the family." Nonetheless, the film does point out the extent to which Cleveland's old stadium, and indeed the many multipurpose stadiums being replaced around the league, represent (or represented) something like a sanctuary for a particular kind of pre-post-Fordist solidarity, a place existing in a time before a bass drum needed its own season ticket for entry.[21]

Intentionally or not, the movie chronicles the passing of an age in which *unappealing* urban and suburban public spaces like multipurpose stadiums expanded behavioral freedom for a generation of fans. The cavernous quality of these parks provided the possibility of vernacular forms of pleasure to countless spectators enjoying their status as exiles or castaways. It thus helps to offer insight into Landecker's qualification of her praise for Jacobs Field. Even though she is a deep admirer of the energy and beauty of the Jake, she cannot help but be a little nostalgic for the outsider eroticism of Cleveland Stadium and its crew of lovable outcasts left alone in the outfield bleachers.

Massive multipurpose venues like Cleveland Stadium, dismissed by Landecker and other critics as little more than black marks on the history of stadium architecture, in fact serve as good symbols of consumption patterns in an era of relative economic parity. By allowing for the inclusion of more fans and by flattening out the range of consumer choices available, older venues like the now-demolished one in Cleveland did in fact accommodate a greater degree of ball-park democracy than almost anything before them. Leaving fans alone in virtual exile, they invited the behavior that became the model for what Adams considers to be pernicious attempts to engineer "controlled spontaneity" in contemporary stadiums. These new parks, constructed as part of baseball's retro movement, on the other hand, renounce the immediate past in order to pay homage to stadium architecture from a previous era. They refer back to a time of smaller, more intimate venues built when higher ticket prices relative to average salaries, daytime-only games, and in some cases, statutory segregation, made them accessible primarily to those in the middle classes and above.[22] They thus shift the main characteristic of ball-park appeal from equality to authenticity. Whereas the multipurpose stadiums constructed in the middle portion of the twentieth century were large enough to accommodate huge crowds, but in a somewhat bland and uncomfortable setting, the new parks promise the "warm" architecture of the distant past to an often more exclusive audience.

Yet as the inconsistency in Landecker's remarks suggests, this shift unsettles contemporary fans on an instinctual level. After all, some modern notions of authenticity are themselves infused with romanticized ideas about the virtues of working-class life and "real" baseball fans, if not with a thoroughly utopian desire for equality. America itself was born as an experiment in classlessness, its institutions and politicians producing a rhetoric praising equality over privilege even if they sometimes have failed to achieve their lofty ambitions. Landecker's dissatisfaction with the overt and visible segregation at Jacobs Field demonstrates how baseball stadiums have become charged particles in the psyche of the American baseball fan, powerful reminders of America's democratic, yet perhaps not fully realized, potential.

CHAPTER FOUR

BLEACHERS:
WHERE THE OUTSIDE IS IN

Let me first call your attention to the bleachers. This is the place to be, the place where the *real* fans sit.

—Jacobs Field tour guide

By beginning the tour of the Cleveland ball park this way, the young tour guide encapsulates much of the fantasy behind retro ball parks. Uttering this line on the first stop of the excursion, the state-of-the-art pressroom on the mezzanine level of the stadium, he asks tourists to consider the weighty juxtaposition he has set up. Surrounded by cameras, video-replay monitors, headsets, microphones, and so on—the technology mediating the experience for television viewers—the tourist looks out onto the no-frills bleacher section and is asked to consider it a final refuge of authenticity. Where the "real fans sit" is fundamentally different from the couches of television viewers, or the lounges of the luxury suites flanking the press box, or the fancy dining-room tables of the Terrace Club Restaurant overhanging the concourse on the third-base side. It is encoded as both a site of unmediated experience and a place where real fans can reject an overabundance of comfort in skyboxes and living rooms in favor of some previous order of things.[1]

A huge, stand-alone box, perched entirely in open air underneath the Jumbo-Tron video screen (part of what was built to be the world's largest freestanding scoreboard), the bleachers form the only section segregated from the rest of the park, the only outdoor seating area requiring a specific ticket for entrance, and the only one with its own concession stands, restrooms, and other amenities.[2] Passage into this exclusive zone therefore marks bleacher inhabitants as special within the inverted psychic economy of the ball park. The corporate and upper middle classes have their luxury skyboxes, true, but the real baseball fans have their bleachers.

Of course, the tour guide's notion of realness is a product of a projection—and a deeply contestable one at that. It is clear that nobody attending a game in

THE BLEACHERS UNDER THE JUMBOTRON AT JACOBS FIELD.

other sections of the park would consider him or herself "unreal." Plus, as longtime Cleveland bleacher dwellers John Adams and Craig Mahovlic point out, even in the bleachers there are many Indians supporters who draw their own distinction between "real" fans who have more than just a passing interest in the game and unattentive newcomers who show up at to the park simply because it is the "place to be." Nonetheless, the tour guide's words imply the ball club's desire to offer certain patrons the opportunity to engage in a fascinating form of nostalgic practice. Exposed to the elements, segregated from the rest of the stadium, Cleveland bleacher patrons can purchase a taste of the working class (or at least anti-elitist) experience in its most attractive form—in a scenario in which marginalized culture holds an exotic appeal. The tour guide feels that, to a large degree, fans choose this section—always the first to sell out during the Indians' championship seasons and more than twice as expensive as the cheapest seats at Jacobs Field—in order to tap into the outsider eroticism of ball parks past.[3] He suggests that memories, stories, and legends of unscripted and often delightfully eccentric behavior in the cheap seats of earlier decades overlay modern patrons' experience, promising them psychical fellowship with traditional bleacher inhabitants. In this way, purchasing a ticket to this section enables participation in a simulated culture of the castoff, one that gets its cachet from ghosts of the past—laborers, African Americans, die-hards, and immigrants who historically occupied the section out of statutory or economic necessity but then found the space able to accommodate a wide range of behaviors unacceptable in more reputable social venues.

In short, the tour guide's script reveals the extent to which retro stadium managers and architects have felt the need to package vestiges of the historically *unappealing* in modern, appealing forms. Franchises with new parks now routinely spend a great deal of time and creative energy imagining ways to replicate vernacular forms of pleasure available in older ball parks. They thus attempt to offer for ready consumption much of what Adams and Mahovlic experienced for years in the nether regions of old Municipal Stadium. Contrary to Heidi Landecker's claim that the symbolic juxtaposition of bleachers with the gaudy club restaurant diminishes the pleasure of the new park, this contrast seems to enhance the stadium experience for many fans.[4]

BLEACHERS PAST AND PRESENT

To understand the promise of contemporary bleacher sections, it is first necessary to comprehend the history of bleachers, learning how they gradually became invested with what the tour guide describes as the authenticity of the urban outcast. The term "bleacher" first emerged in the middle of the nineteenth century, probably as a double entendre. Its most obvious meaning derives from the fact that these sections were uncovered. Thus, a lack of protection from the sun and rain guaranteed that a patron in this part of the park would be "bleached."[5] However, a less- known trope of the word refers directly to the people populating the sections. In the late nineteenth century, the term "bleacher" also would have signified "slacker" or "bum," after the colloquial meaning of the verb "to bleach," which meant to skip or to cut. So, for example, Harvard students whom "attended morning prayers more in 'spirit' than in body" were called "bleachers."[6] This double meaning is crucial. The sections were not simply devoid of amenities such as a roof and concessions, but they were also coded as safe havens for transgressors. Thus part of their appeal from the very beginning was that they were a place to dress down, the place to be after checking one's sense of decorum at the gate.

An extension of the "bettor's ring," or the pens constructed in earlier enclosed ball parks to both accommodate and contain unruly behavior, these sections allowed for and even promoted illicit activity. Baseball owners made sure beer flowed freely for the sun-parched fans in the bleachers, many of whom were already "bleaching" from work. The bleachers as an innovation thus further institutionalized a large part of the appeal of baseball as a spectator sport for many Victorian men. The sections afforded them a public space free from the prohibitions characteristic of many of their lives outside the stadium. They gave men a refuge, a place to drink, curse, spit, gamble, and even loudly voice discontent with authority in the form of umpires and management. In short, bleachers allowed "saloon behavior" in an open space with a slightly better reputation than clubs and brothels.

When immigrants began to take an interest in the sport, and as a few African Americans were able to afford tickets to ball games, bleachers gradually also became a site of a modicum of social mixing impossible in many other public venues. Though hardly a radical space (after all, they were constructed to insulate wealthier and more decorous fans while profiting from the desire of poorer citizens and members of the Victorian male sporting community to see games), they facilitated a certain brotherhood. They allowed men from various neighborhoods, occupations, ethnicities, and sometimes even races and classes to temporarily join together, rooting for the same team or jeering the same umpire. In a nutshell, they enabled a degree of solidarity among the economically exiled, as well as among those middle-class men who chose to exile themselves.[7]

This dynamic of simultaneous exile and energy (as well as cheaper entrance fees) made bleachers most popular in towns with large ethnic, particularly German and Irish, populations. The two Lake Front Parks in Chicago, built in 1878 and 1883 respectively, housed the largest bleacher sections in the major leagues in order to accommodate masses of fans from the South Side and Bridgeport. The five incarnations of the Polo Grounds in New York also had large, mostly German and Irish, bleacher sections.[8] But perhaps the wildest bleacher section of the late nineteenth century could be found in Chris Von der Ahe's original Sportsman's Park. Selling a "scuttle of suds" for a nickel and a baseball ticket for two bits, the former tavern owner built his St. Louis Browns around "a keg of beer and a barrel of pretzels" (Lieb 6). His bleacher section gave fans a space where they could act out in resistance to the newly professionalized ethos of both baseball and the middle classes that came to dominate it. This spot hosted the inversion of social status by orchestrating a type of *anti-privilege,* whereby the worst seats in the house became the best, the most marginal patrons the most storied. Reaching its heyday in the late 1890s, when Von der Ahe turned the whole park into his "Coney Island of the West," the St. Louis bleacher section helped establish this area in the ball park as a world apart, an island for workers, immigrants, African Americans, and self-isolating middle-class white men. Compensating spectators who sat there with freedom from larger societal restrictions, this section was such a tremendous draw that toned-down versions of it appeared in most of the concrete and steel parks built during the first couple of decades of the twentieth century.[9]

In these now-revered venues (such as Brooklyn's Ebbets Field and Boston's Fenway Park, two of the direct models for contemporary retro parks), the characters and rituals found in the bleachers became a central part of the experience of attending a game. For example, some Dodger fans, such as Eddie Battan (who constantly tooted a tin whistle) or Jack Pierce (who would loudly scream "Coooookie" in honor of his favorite player, Cookie Lavagetto), became as famous as the ballplayers themselves. Because their team was so bad year after year, because they felt that, after the 1925 death of founder Charles Ebbets,

Dodger management cared more about the bottom line than about the ball club or the comfort and enjoyment of the ball park's patrons, Brooklyn bleacher bums took it upon themselves to invent their own forms of pleasure. The unauthorized Dodger "symphony" brought in kazoos, pots, pans, or whatever else they could find in order to form their unique version of a baseball marching band. They paraded around playing parodic music, mocking players, insulting management, and heckling umpires.[10] In a time before the public relations arm of baseball teams hired men in chicken suits to stir up stadium energy, fans themselves, particularly those in bleacher sections, were largely responsible for creating atmosphere.[11]

The Jacobs Field tour guide's suggestion that the bleachers are the last refuge of the "real" fan is clearly invested with nostalgic notions of "Dem Bums" in Brooklyn and other storied bleacher faithful. It elevates to mythical status more than a century's worth of patrons in St. Louis, Brooklyn, Chicago, and elsewhere whose exiled status inspired and invited picaresque and creative activities while allowing freedom to protest the status quo. His words imagine a desire among Jacobs Field visitors to experience the fantasy of being on the outside looking in, of being people who, with nothing to lose, are able to express themselves freely. They gesture toward what some feel is the central irony of attending a game at a retro park. The bleachers at old Ebbets Field truly were a refuge for people who were economically or statutorily denied entrance to other parts of the park. Blacks-only sections in the bleachers and dramatically stratified admission charges elsewhere in the stadium enforced segregation. In contemporary parks, on the other hand, segregation is often more of an elective. Like middle-class men in the Victorian sporting community, many modern bleacher dwellers choose their own exile; they choose to place themselves spatially in a location just opposite the markers of the elite—luxury sky boxes and elite dining clubs. In fact, they often pay extra for the privilege.

FROM SUBURBIA TO THE BLEACHERS

Many of the oppressive forces creating the need for the outcast culture of the bleachers in the early part of the century appear to have been replaced by more subtle stimuli today. In testimonials describing why they choose the bleachers, many fans stress their desire to perform acts that are sometimes unavailable in their day-to-day lives. Some says they were drawn by the ability to take part in a large group effort. "We get to influence the game," says seventeen-year-old John Popovich from suburban Parma. "The other day my buddies and me went down to the railing and yelled at [Royals center fielder Michael] Tucker to try and distract him." Others seem to appreciate the feeling of community offered by the bleachers. "This section is friendly," says Darin Good from outside of

Canton. "There is a lot of high-fiving with your neighbors when something good happens."

In Lonnie Wheeler's 1988 testimonial, *Bleachers: A Summer in Wrigley Field*, the writer describes his summer-long quest to find, in the storied Wrigley outfield, a "real place . . . one that feels different from other places" (1). He looks to the bleachers to provide him temporary access to an antithesis of the world he was forced to grow up in, a "cookie-cutter suburban universe" where every shopping mall was like another, "with five shoe stores, a chocolate-chip cookie shop, and patient husbands sitting around the fountain" (12). As such, he provides clues to the psychic lift suggested by Popovich and Good and promoted by the Jacobs tour guide at the new park's bleachers, a section the guide said was "directly modeled after Wrigley."[12]

Wheeler begins his description of his pilgrimage with words reminiscent of the expansive tour guide's commentary:

> The bleachers seemed . . . like baseball's stomping ground—companionable, passionate, fundamental, unaffected, and gloriously human.
> I imagined them as the place where the game met the people; as the place where a ballgame felt like a ballgame, and a season felt like
> a season. (2)

Wheeler's words bespeak a desire for elusive forms of human connection, which he expresses to the reader through the most insider of rhetorical devices, the tautology. Anyone in the know instinctively understands the feeling of a "ballgame" or a "season." Excessive language or description thus becomes unnecessary, decadent, an antithesis to the "fundamental."

His confidence about the signifying potential of this tautology mirrors one of baseball's (and other sports') primary appeals: the fantasy of pure signification or an immediately understandable world. When a center fielder leaps at the wall and fails to come down with the ball, everyone in the stands perfectly and instantly understands the feelings of impotence and disappointment signified by the expected drop of the player's head; likewise, when a first baseman digs out a low throw and raises his glove delightedly, every spectator, in unison, fully comprehends the meaning of his triumphant pantomime—be it in Cleveland, San Diego, Duluth, or the Bronx. Cultural difference and semiotic ambiguity vanish in "baseball's stomping ground," providing spectators a respite from the more complex system of signification they are faced with in the outside world.

But the purpose here is not simply to recast poststructuralist arguments into the stream of baseball discourse.[13] Instead, describing some of the linguistic assumptions central to Wheeler's fantasy enables an examination of widespread cultural constructions of the bleachers as a utopian place of the "people," where entrance, like the understanding of a tautology, codes one instantly as an insider. Wheeler's longing for a place where "a ballgame felt like a ballgame" signals his desire to experience the sensation of community associated with signifying certitude among those in the know. According to his formulation, semiotic homogeneity makes a suburban mall too inclusive, the meanings it generates available to anyone regardless of the intensity of their investment or attention. A "real place" like the Wrigley bleacher section, on the other hand, rewards invested members of the clan with hyper-understanding, or a common, unique system of signification. Wheeler writes that, growing up in suburbia, he had always felt cheated out of participation in a community of people with a unique cultural tradition and language—a set of communal assumptions endowing them with instant and profound understanding of their world and of each other. So he came to Wrigley to experience the sensation of being a cultural and linguistic insider, one of the mythical "people" that the game comes to meet in the bleachers.[14]

Shortly after arriving at the ball park at the beginning of his quest, Wheeler befriends one of these insiders, Mike Murphy, a sales representative and self-described "bleacher historian" who gives him a firsthand account of the beginning of "Bleacher Bum" renown. According to Murphy, the Chicago bleachers had always been an interesting place, but their spot in baseball folklore was not established until the mid- to late 1960s, when fifteen to twenty loyal and lonely Cubs fans came to recognize in each other a shared tragi-comic sensibility. "We were a raucous group . . . a little friendship among people . . . with nothing to do but talk to each other," he tells Wheeler, describing how, by that point, he could often count on two hands the number of people attending games in the right-field bleachers. He then describes to the writer just how an accidental group of outcasts emerged from this isolation, learning not only to accept but also to enjoy their marginal status. Sitting together, they made an art form of taunting opponents' outfielders and conducting dollar wagers among themselves. The outcome of the game mattered much less to them than the camaraderie they enjoyed (13–14). Producing their own meanings from the stimuli offered by the game, instead of simply succumbing to the dominant semiotic world of wins and losses, the bleacher bums derived pleasure from their exile. They created their own subculture.

However, after a year or so of this, the fun was diminished when a strange and unexpected thing happened—the Cubs started winning and the outside became *in*. The team "became a hot story in '69, [and] all of a sudden everyone wanted to join the bandwagon":

> There were four newspapers in town then, and they were all trying
> to get an angle on the Cubs. One time a reporter came out and
> asked, "Who are you guys?" We said, "Ah, take a hike. We're just a
> bunch of bums out here." The next day the headline said something
> about "bleacher bums" this or that, and all of a sudden all these TV
> crews are out there looking for the Bleacher Bums. Before we knew
> it, NBC was out there, the Wall Street Journal. We started wearing

yellow helmets because when we went to St. Louis the Cardinal fans threw things at us; pretty soon, they're selling yellow helmets on the street corner. The Bleacher Bums became synonymous with Cub fans in general. We didn't set out to make ourselves a group. The press made us a group. The press created us. (Wheeler 13–14)

Here Murphy demonstrates many of the qualities implied by Wheeler when he imagined the bleachers as "passionate, fundamental, unaffected, and gloriously human." The colorful bleacher historian carries a healthy suspicion of power; he is independent, defiant, and, above all, nonchalant. Being a true bleacher bum requires one to think him or herself but an accidental member of a group of outsiders. Membership cannot be bought on a local street corner, and it cannot be self-conscious. Thus the concept of Bleacher Bums itself becomes a theoretical impossibility at the very moment that the Bums become recognizable as an entity. Self-consciously marginal behavior differs enormously from instinctive behavior. It forces one into a quid pro quo economy. Motivations become tainted; actions become more tied to performance than simply being.[15] The simplicity, the "unaffected" quality fantasized by Wheeler, is subsumed by the logic of exchange. Therefore his attempt to enter and understand this community is, by nature, problematic. He will, regardless of his earnestness, always be on the outside looking in at his beloved outsiders.

It is easy to see the extent to which the pilgrim's quest (just like the nightly quests promised to the Cleveland bleacher contingent by the tour guide) is a naïve one. Whereas Wheeler rhapsodizes about old ball parks providing him an escape from his "cookie-cutter suburban universe," Murphy remains sanguine (4). The bleacher historian senses that the energy of an authentic place is, by nature, ephemeral and accidental. To him, the demise of the real Bleacher Bums began to occur shortly after they were formed and was only hastened when the press commodified them with a name. By simply coming into consciousness of themselves as a group, the Bums were faced with the end of the delightful sense of independence and anonymity giving this loose collection of working-class and white-collar romantics its gusto.

When the Cubs' on-field success began to attract a wealthier clientele, their enjoyment waned further. New patrons to the park, like Wheeler himself, could perhaps mimic the ways of the Bleacher Bums, shouting down opponents' outfielders and making dollar wagers during the game, but they would never share the original Bums capacity for irony; they would never be able to tap into the extreme sense of marginalization and spontaneity that created the initial group solidarity in the first place. Murphy's words clearly demonstrate that he recognizes the significance of the campy yellow helmets sold on street corners. Like other commodified tokens (such as pottery or other sacred remnants of vanquished Native American culture purchased at gift shops on land once actually inhabited by natives), the helmets, to the original bleacher bums, represent imminent replacement—of themselves by consumers, of their ephemeral experience with an object that concretizes as it commemorates.

It was fun while it lasted. During the first year or so, Murphy and his friends had managed to produce oppositional meanings of self-empowerment.[16] Creative manifestations of pleasure had provided the Bleacher Bums a way to counter psychically the effects of the hierarchy mapped by the social and economic segregation of Wrigley Field as well as the inevitable heartbreak of yet another losing season. Virtually ignored by stadium management just like their progenitors in Brooklyn, the Bleacher Bums in Chicago found themselves relatively free to engage in unauthorized yet charismatic behavior such as heckling, betting, and shouting down figures of authority. In exile, they were able to safely vocalize their discontent and imagine nothing short of a new order for themselves. It is this kind of energy—the creative energy of the exiled—that Wheeler seems to long for when he exits suburbia. Unfortunately for the pilgrim, however, the very fact that he is predisposed to see the Wrigley bleachers as an authentic place seems to undermine this section's ability to produce a rarefied experience for him. The "fundamental" form of energy and community accessible previously by Murphy and the gang can come to Wheeler only in commodified form, as part of baseball folklore. Wheeler's pilgrimage and the book he wrote after it, as well as the Jacobs Field tour guide's linguistic shorthand for describing the bleachers as a site of unmediated and unselfconscious communal experience, all result from and perpetuate that folklore.

It is important to understand that, although the Cleveland bleachers were modeled after the ones in Chicago, there are many crucial distinctions between the two—distinctions that Adams thinks the tour guide fails to grasp. "He was just making assumptions about the place," says the bleacher drummer, lamenting the fact that many people on the outside bring with them similar generic expectations. "We don't have idiots here like in Chicago. We've always been about the family. We don't throw things or cuss at opposing fans." Bill Chmelka, a longtime Indians fan but also a frequent visitor to the Wrigley bleachers, agrees. Although on balance he feels that "no bleachers top Wrigley's," that "cold beers and acres of bikinis in the sun make them the best," he is impressed by the family-values-style passion at Indians games. "This is pretty good, as much energy as Wrigley, but different," he says in reference to the atmosphere in the Cleveland bleachers. "People at Cubs games mainly want to make sure they get the beer down while it is still cold. The people here just want to see the Tribe win." In other words, in Cleveland, the tour guide seems to have mistaken the Jacobs Field bleacher contingent for the Wrigley "Bums." Like Wheeler, he is guilty of a degree of middle-class presumption, basing his projection of the bleachers on overly broad ideas generated by twentieth-century bleacher folklore.

Of course, individual motivations for choosing the bleachers are almost as numerous as the people making this choice. Some sit in the Jacobs Field bleachers because they like the elevated vantage point above the "little green monster," the left-field wall; some simply like the extra amenities found in the bleacher concourse. Nonetheless, multiple conversations with bleacher patrons suggest that for many people a primary motivation for their seating choice does in fact have to do with the reworked psychic economy of the modern stadium. Many patrons who choose the bleachers do so in order to connect with the Murphys of the past, to sample a taste of what baseball mythology has constructed as "the bleacher experience." Young John Popovich and his friends from Parma come to the bleachers to try to relive some of Murphy's rowdy behavior. Similarly, Good and his family come so that they can "high-five" with neighbors, connecting in an almost tribal way with members of their community. The tour guide thus seems to have gotten it at least partially right. Inside a themed urban space with an appeal directly linked to virtual reality—experiencing baseball, the transcendent game, once again played on an idyllic urban pastoral landscape accented with simulated forms of the turmoil and energy of the retreating twentieth-century city—many patrons flock to the bleachers because they promise to be the epicenter for the reconstitution of the real.

TO BE REAL

In contemporary America, being "real" brings with it enormous cultural cachet. Hip-hop culture idolizes figures such as NBA player Allen Iverson, who refuses to disassociate from childhood friends, instead preferring to "keep it real" by hanging out with his "homies." Similarly, gay and transvestite culture has made camp superstars out of gender benders such as the late Divine, who are able to exquisitely and ironically pass as "real" members of the opposite sex, in the process making a mockery of standard notions of masculinity and femininity. But perhaps nowhere is the desire to be real more powerful than in mainstream culture. Shows like *Survivor* and its many clones on network television suggest the extent to which American mass audiences hunger to consume something like unmediated reality. Trends such as "restoration hardware" (selling products by spinning yarns about the history of an old oil lamp or cherry wood dresser) and the cult of Martha Stewart (harking back to the Arts and Crafts movement of the late nineteenth century) equate being real with being in touch with the act of fabrication. In a world in which identity is increasingly defined by consumer choices, many forms of popular entertainment are, to a degree, tied to providing ways to counter psychically this crisis of unproductiveness.

In this sense, one of the most attractive benefits of sitting where the "real fans sit" has to be in part nourishing the fantasy of having influence, of being a producer or player.[17] When a sports owner or coach proclaims "our fans are the best in the league," he or she implies that the stadium environment—with its boister-

FLOODLIGHT POLES, STEEL TRUSSES, AND EXPOSED BEAMS REMIND JACOBS FIELD PATRONS OF THE NOW-CLOSED MILLS ACROSS THE CUYAHOGA. ONE OF THESE DORMANT MILLS IS SEEN HERE FROM THE STADIUM CONCOURSE.

ous partisans acting as a sixth, tenth, or twelfth man, depending on the sport—goes a long way toward affecting the outcome of the game. Sports fans do not just spectate, they participate. Of course, this fantasy has obvious heightened psychological value in Cleveland. A city whose workers throughout much of the twentieth century crafted the raw material to build a nation has undergone a rebirth that, to a large degree, renounces large-scale feats of production. Instead, in its new incarnation as a haven for tourists, sports fans, service providers, and conventioneers, Cleveland has become a site primarily of large-scale consumption. Whereas one's civic duty in earlier eras was to produce, one's most important function now is to consume. So sitting underneath floodlight poles, exposed steel beams, and mammoth trusses meant to remind visitors of the now-closed mills just across the Cuyahoga from the stadium, some bleacher patrons look to gain a kind of ancestral connection with a more muscular past. In turn, this form of participation, saturated with meanings from a previous epoch, satisfies many other needs missing from the fabric of a consumer-based existence—from catharsis to cathexis to nationalistic tribalism. Bleacher fans are not only invited but expected to scream out daily frustrations in a place that, for the most part, welcomes such behavior. In doing so, and in bonding with their neighbors, they are able to feel part of a movement that is larger than themselves.

It is precisely this kind of tribal fantasy that is captured in *Bleacher Bums,* a play written by Joe Mantegna in 1977 to celebrate the exploits of the Wrigley fans. Though set in Chicago, this play captures much of the essence of the mythology that seems to prompt both the Jacobs Field tour guide to speak so appreciatively of the new bleachers and the boys from suburban Parma to visit them. To begin with, Mantegna's play deifies working-class baseball fans, suggesting a serious-ness to their endeavors transcendent of mere fandom. Unlike Wheeler's account, which was primarily laudatory of the psychical benefits of bleacher life for the bleacher dwellers themselves, Mantegna's version implies that "the bums," like workmen, actually perform the heavy lifting, helping the ball club win games and making the ball-park experience more pleasurable for the other fans.

In this sense, the most important stretch of the play comes when a charac-ter identified as "Cheerleader" returns to the bleachers and begins to lead the regulars in homophobic, personal attacks on the opponents' right fielder as well as deleterious schemes to affect the outcome of the game. Previously, Cheer-leader had been ostracized and exiled from the section when he had attempted to lead the bleacher bums in a series of positive cheers. "We don't do no singing here. Go back to left field," he was told by Zig, one of the regulars in the bleach-ers. This rebuff underlines how an outsider to the world of the Chicago bleach-ers would fail to understand the tragi-comic ethos of the section. History has told the bums that their team will, somehow, find a way to lose, so the regulars focus not on standard results but on their own ends. They make bets with each other on the outcomes of each plate appearance; they occupy themselves with smaller acquisitions, getting their friends to buy them hot dogs and chocolate malts; and they make unwanted advances toward the occasional woman who lands in the right-field stands. Many even bet against the Cubs as a way to off-set the inevitable disappointment of losing.

The Cheerleader's attempt at being a team player, allied in spirit with the Cubs' organization and mainstream audience, shows him to be ignorant of the dynamics of pleasure in this male-dominated, antiestablishmentarian under-world. His behavior augurs the imposition of the ways of the legitimate world just off stage and, by extension, the unwelcome colonization of the bleachers by a less-marginal crowd so thoroughly bemoaned by real-life bleacher bum Murphy. Yet when the Cheerleader returns in the later innings, he brings with him a more edgy attitude and thus comes not only to be accepted by the bleacher bums, but lionized. This time, rather than imploring the outfield cynics to cheer for the Cubs, he bets them that his verbal abuse will get the opponents' outfielder to "climb the vines," or get so mad that he turns his back on the game and tries to enter the bleachers (44).

Pulling out a book of facts he has compiled on all major league players, the Cheerleader climbs down toward the Cardinal center fielder Anderson and begins to hurl a stream of homophobic insults:

> Hey you look pretty good in your uniform now, you know that? You should keep those dancing lessons up. I bet you look good in tights and a tu-tu. Too bad you can't play baseball. Hey, isn't your mother ashamed of you? She thought you were a regular guy and now she hears you're going out with Lou Brock. You fruitball turkey! You're stuffed, Anderson, you're stuffed like my dummy here! (45)

By calling into question Anderson's sexual orientation, the Cheerleader not only angers the outfielder but also publicly reinforces his own hetero-masculinity. Throughout the play, Mantegna has made clear the gendered component of the enjoyment of bleacher exile. All of his main characters, but especially Zig—based on real-life Murphy—react strongly against threats to hetero-masculine privilege in the bleacher underworld. They harass the few single women who dare to enter this boy's club, and they close ranks swiftly when the wife of any of the bums enters unexpectedly. Throughout most of the play, the one thing that seems to produce constant solidarity amid the steady bickering, betting, and bad-mouthing is a shared sense of gender identity leading to a circling of the wagons around masculine primacy.[18] Thus the Cheerleader's public display of homophobia allows him instant insider status. He really does belong in the bleachers now that he too has testified to the sanctity of bleacher hetero-normativity, now that he has renounced gender bending and embraced a paranoia that helps keep this space exclusive of women and gays.

Yet despite Mantegna's tendency to view the Wrigley bleachers as primarily a sanctuary for masculine fellowship, eventually in the play class solidarity comes to subsume other politics of identity. Toward the end, the playwright uses the reaction of his bums to another of the Cheerleader's exploits as a litmus test helping to gauge their class affinities. This time the Cheerleader engages in an activity aimed at helping the main characters, a collection of unemployed, formerly blue-collar workers, actually influence the outcome of the game. He gives high-pitched whistles (perhaps Mantegna's homage to Dodger fan Eddie Battan) to every one in the section and has them blow simultaneously when each Cub batter swings. This temporarily deafens the St. Louis outfielder, blocking his ability to hear the crack of the bat, which subsequently throws off his timing. He misplays a fly ball so badly that it becomes a rare inside-the-park home run for the home team:

Cheerleader: An inside the park homerun. We did it! (Everyone goes nuts.)

Richie: That wasn't fair.

Cheerleader: All's fair in love and baseball!

Zig: We did that! Marvin, you owe me! (36)

Two crucial ideas are at play in this passage. The first, the notion that "we did that," points to the transcendent and rare thrill of having influence. The enervating feeling of being merely a consumer was temporarily replaced by the sensation of producing. No longer invisible, unproductive, irrelevant outcasts, the bleacher bums for this one fleeting moment make an impact on the visible, inside world. It is a joyous moment in which the dichotomies of oppressor/oppressed, athlete/spectator, powerful/powerless, bum/citizen, and corporation/consumer are turned topsy-turvy. In fact, Cleveland bleacher fan Adams, although denouncing the particular "profane" style of the Chicago bleacher bums, suggests that this kind of behavior is universal in bleacher sections. "A lot of the yuppies in the early years of Jacobs Field wouldn't ride the outfielders," he says. "But eventually the real fans came out. You find out something about the outfielders and you needle them. Real baseball fans know how to get into a guy's head." To Adams, the pleasure of heckling is clearly enhanced by sensations of class solidarity that transcend love of a particular team. "At the end of the day, they [the players who are heckled] are all still millionaires and we have to go to work in the morning."

The second idea at play in the passage, the one articulated by Richie's words, is perhaps just as important. It serves to register a reminder that the economy of the bleachers, an underworld economy among a tight-knit clan, stands in direct conflict with the fair play ethic/passive spectator mode prevalent in other parts of the park and the rule of law represented by the ball club's administration.

To emphasize this, the playwright brings on stage a security guard shortly after this incident:

Guard: Yeah, I'm looking for whoever was heckling that outfielder down there. We got a complaint from the St. Louis bench. (Cheerleader moves away from him.)

Decker: (Pointing to the other bleachers.) Uh, I think it must've been somebody over there—

Guard: If I don't find out who it was, I'm gonna have to clear out this whole section.

Richie: It was him. (Points at Cheerleader.)

Guard: Alright, come on. Let's go.

Cheerleader: I didn't do nothin.

Decker: Hey, hey, wait a minute, officer, it was me. I did it.

Guard: Okay, you're coming too.

Zig: No, wait, officer, it was me.

Rose: No, no, it was me.

Melody: No, it was me. . . . (Security guard leaves in disgust during this melee.) (49)

This exchange points to several important aspects of the bleacher underground. As in mafia culture, the ethos of *omertá* prevails. Literally translated "honor," the Italian term more abundantly signifies "loyalty to one's clan above all else." The security guard, like Carabinieri and government officials dispatched historically from Rome to bring Sicilian culture into the fold, represents the unwelcome imposition of legitimate authority onto a closed, fully functional, yet renegade system. His very presence ensures solidarity amid endemic internal turmoil. The Cheerleader as well as the two women present, Rose and Melody, had previously been ostracized because they represented elements of the antimasculine. But now they are embraced by the community. In Mantegna's fantasy of the bleachers, identity tied up with class and community—a community comprising a collection of working-class underdogs and outsiders—supersedes troubling differences based on gender and sexual orientation.

In Cleveland, although the bleachers have traditionally been much more welcoming to outsiders—women, children, "yuppies," and even the occasional fan rooting for the opposing team—this sense of commonality also unites bleachers patrons. Recounting a dark moment in Cleveland bleacher history, Adams describes his anger when the Indians organization tried to turn the screws on him and his friends in the mid-1980s. "I duked it out in the press with [former team president Peter] Bavasi," he recalls. "He closed the bleachers and said it was full of nothing but drunks and pot heads. But he didn't know anything. He never lived in Cleveland." According to Adams, Bavasi, like the tour guide, was making an assumption about the Cleveland bleachers based on the behavior of patrons at Wrigley Field. Yet despite getting the details wrong, Bavasi's criticism identifies something unmistakable about the bleachers. In Cleveland, Chicago, Baltimore, and elsewhere, there is a sensation of implied solidarity and identity among bleacher patrons. There is a belief that their "stomping grounds" are fundamentally different from the other sections of the park, that they exist at a greater remove from official authority. This belief, perhaps as much as anything else, promotes feelings of realness in the bleachers.

THEMED CLASS CONSCIOUSNESS

If, then, the appeal of bleacher exile is informed by something akin to class identification and a shared outsider status, the Jacobs Field *imagineers,* trying to offer the experience to an increasingly mainstream audience, would seem to need a substitute.[19] In this sense, they do not disappoint. Consciously or not, the designers of the ball park and Indians management have managed to offer up just such a series of replacements. The ocular arrangement of the bleachers vis-à-vis the rest of the park encodes sensations of class otherness—ironically, the very setup that disturbs Landecker. In this island of liminal identity, the orientation of the bleacher benches turns patrons' heads slightly to the right, coaxing them to look up from their hot dogs and sodas in order to witness spectators dining on double-cut lamb chops and fine wines in the glassed-in four star restaurant overhanging the left-field concourse. Additionally, when looking toward home plate, bleacher patrons see other fans ordering champagne from the waiters catering to them in the rows of luxury boxes ringing the mezzanine.[20] Although this juxtaposition is mostly an illusion (in reality, many bleacher patrons are just as well off as fans in the boxes and the restaurant), this strategic ocular arrangement invites Cleveland's bleacher contingent to distinguish the details of their environs from symbolic markers of wealth and privilege found elsewhere in the park.

Yet as important as what bleacher patrons see is what they do not see. The arrangement of the bleachers ensures that its spectators are the only ones turning their backs on the mother of all televisions, the 150-foot JumboTron perched behind them. This symbolic refusal to watch the game as television affords bleacher patrons a fair amount of psychic lift. Not bombarded with advertisements, sheltered from the constant repackaging of the event via instant replay, reverse angles, slow motion, and so on, they are freer to imagine a more one-to-one relationship with the game. Facing away from the JumboTron, unable to see the superimposed images on the left-field wall below them, bleacher patrons are the only spectators who have a view of the game more or less unmediated by television technology. In the rest of the park, on the other hand, televisions are everywhere. In luxury boxes, club restaurants, and even above urinals—660 televisions broadcast the game to its live spectators. This is significant. Televised versions of sporting events have changed how fans process games. Tele-screens in indoor stadiums, packages of replays throughout televised events, all-night *SportsCenter* highlight reels, and even instant replay used to reverse calls in NBA and NFL games mean that less of a premium is placed on the live occurrence of any particular play. Instead, modern spectators rely on mediating technology to complete the action. The presence of so many televisions in Jacobs Field is recognition that most fans expect their stadium experience to come replete with the hyperrealistic omniscience of the television viewer. Bleacher fans, on the other hand, reject this perspective in favor of a less mediated vantage point.[21]

ON MOST NIGHTS, A SMALL GROUP OF BLEACHER FANS WILL INSPIRE THEIR SECTION MATES TO START A "WAVE" CASCADING AROUND JACOBS FIELD.

Unquestionably, this lack of mediation inspires a fair amount of energy among Cleveland's bleacher patrons. Although ushers and security guards, as well as a history of fan intolerance of bad language in the Cleveland bleachers, are quick to curb too much cursing, fans, like the boys from Parma, do sometimes yell relatively tame insults at opposing outfielders. Similarly, bleacher spectators often organize themselves in impromptu yet coordinated cheers for their team. On most nights, a small group of bleacher fans will work up a sweat getting their fellow section mates to start a "wave" cascading around the ball park.

Perhaps, though, it is Adams, banging his bass drum in simulated Indian war chants at appropriate moments of the game, who best symbolizes the determination of bleacher fans to create a boisterous yet organic home-field advantage for their beloved Tribe. In contrast to the rest of the park, where on average nights cheering tends to happen primarily as a response to goading by the scoreboard operators ("I can't hear you!" and "Let's hear you roar!" are two frequent implorations), the Cleveland bleacher section, rhythmically following Adams's lead, remains more connected to the game.[22] During late-inning pitching changes, when Indians management blasts "Wooly Bully," the 1965 hit by Sam the Sham and the Pharoahs, over the park's loudspeakers, Adams even plays over top of the piped in music. It is an act that is steeped in meaning. His performance means that fans sitting nearby are able to hear a live rendition of the pulsating beat produced by one of their own, largely drowning out the official version. Adams's drumming generates kinetic energy in the section, inspiring widespread dancing in much the same way that live music at clubs, often more than recorded music, inspires movement. When describing his motivation for producing this kind of vernacular pleasure, Adams barely can contain a bit of antiestablishmentarian sentiment: "You gotta leave the real fan alone to do his thing. . . . Get that 'I can't hear you' stuff out of here." He has come to the bleachers in part to escape the overscripted quality of the rest of the park. Yet as the tour guide suggests, Adams himself has been scripted into the experience. He is a "real" fan whose independent actions provide an unofficial but crucial form of pleasure for other patrons.

BLEACHERS FAMILY STYLE

Like Adams, most Cleveland bleacher patrons are proud of the fact that, in contrast to Chicago, nearly all of the rowdiness of the Cleveland bleachers comes across as relatively tame fun for the whole family. Gesturing back to the Wrigley Field original, the Jacobs Field outfield section retains vestigial traces of outsider eroticism, but it largely substitutes child's energy for adult animus, middle-class commemoration for working-class esprit de corps, and a degree of pleasant consumption and respectful replication for picaresque original production. In short, it offers for family enjoyment the liminal experience of blissful exile, enjoyed by Murphy and Adams and fantasized about by Wheeler, Mantegna, and the tour guide.

Of course, as Murphy's eulogy for the bleacher bums and Adams's impatience with management's efforts to overscript behavior suggests, the pleasure dynamic of any attempt to recreate original experience is rife with a central irony: the very idea of the bleachers is most powerful as long as it remains just an idea. Actually attempting to reconstruct the bleacher experience in effect blurs and distorts the past by tying memory up with the present. The danger of constructing such a good simulacrum is that both the original and the copy run the risk of being rendered artificial. The past comes across as too shabby or "other," and the present comes across as too tidy. However, leaving these sections as memory, purely products of the symbolic order, would have required a renunciation of a bedrock consumerist belief in the power of acquisition and simulation. Reconstructing the bleachers of past eras, contemporary architects and stadium managers attempt to restore a visible order and, by doing so, assure consumers that the tendency to accumulate has meaning.[23]

This paradox stands at the center of any discussion of pleasure at retro ball parks. Designed above all to be family-friendly, the Jacobs Field bleachers share some traits in common with Disney World. Whereas Disney was designed as a replication of New Orleans—keeping the parades, the architecture, and the theme of celebration while renouncing the bawdy, the rude, and the gluttonous—Jacobs Field was constructed with places like Wrigley in mind. Both Disney World and Jacobs Field are utopian in vision, each attempting to permanently reproduce the communal and celebratory energy of the city in a space that is clearly not supposed to be suburban but does not quite seem to be completely urban either. Each represents an attempt in part to package the experience of marginalization and community to folks such as Wheeler, who feel their middle-class suburban upbringing denied them the opportunity to be of the "people." The Jacobs Field bleacher section promises patrons the ability to experience the fantasy of being real baseball fans of the past, the people who knew instinctively when a "ballgame felt like a ballgame, and a season felt like a season."

CHAPTER FIVE

CONSUMING BLACKNESS

In 1990, when Rickey Henderson was on the doorstep of breaking the major league record for stolen bases in a career, the speedy African American outfielder began to appear in an interesting television commercial.[1] In this advertisement for an antacid, a white catcher sits virtually alone in a dark room watching a loop of eight-millimeter film showing Henderson stealing base after base off him. Like Marlow floating down the river toward the heart of darkness, the catcher finds himself in preternatural fear of the other.[2] He trembles, he slumps low in his chair, he pops antacid after antacid. The other players and even most of the coaches have deserted him as he attempts to use an outdated technology to find some weakness in Henderson for the next day's game, some way to stop the assault, or, short of that, some way to soothe his panic attacks (through pharmaceuticals). He represents the last line of defense against a virtual epidemic of theft, yet the advertisement implies that his quest is quixotic. The gates are open; the fortress is indefensible. He will never be Henderson's equal. Better to just scarf down heartburn medicine and accept it.

The catcher's dilemma links two standard white dystopic narratives: white men cannot compete physically with black men and whites must work harder to earn what they have. The first notion of course has its roots in the history of slavery in America. For two hundred years, the muscles of black men and women were a primary means of wealth creation in colonial America and in the slave states and territories after the Revolutionary War. Then, for a century after Emancipation, once African American bodies were no longer subject to statutory control, racists used lynching as a way to retain a degree of mastery. The black male body, hanging lifeless from a tree, reassured murderers and spectators alike that black physicality could still be rendered powerless. The second narrative, suggested by the fact that the catcher sits alone at night, still dressed in his dirty uniform long after just about everyone else has gone home, points to a nonlethal remedy for this quandary. The endangered white athlete, unable to match the physical prowess of his black opponent, must find other means in order to keep up. The catcher employs technology (still disproportionately in the hand of whites in an age of continued economic disparity) and good, old-fashioned hard work (again, traditionally associated with the white athlete) to reclaim his advantage.

The commercial, intended to sell its product by portraying the catcher as a kind of work-a-day everyman, overstressed by pressures at work and threatened daily by the dangerous world outside, invites the viewer to identify with the dyspeptic protagonist. Its director positions the camera immediately behind the catcher, allowing the viewer to see the Henderson threat through the white player's eyes and thus take on the racial dilemma as his own. In this way, the advertisement constructs the gaze as white and suggests race as a central factor underlying the anxiety of the contemporary American white man, left chewing or guzzling antacid behind desks, on couches, in dugouts, and in board rooms.

Yet in the catcher's face, the viewer sees something significantly more complex than simple fear and loathing. He or she also sees a profound reverence for Henderson's godlike athleticism. The catcher's clenched jaw drops and he manages a brief, uneasy smile at the sight of the beautiful base-stealing predator. He, and by extension the viewer, watches in awe as Henderson, muscles rippling through his tight uniform, explodes out of his crouch toward second base, where, with characteristically reckless abandon, he slides head first underneath the throw. In many ways, this tableau enacts a standard psycho-visual relationship between the white spectator and the black athlete. The catcher feels the threat of African American physicality so acutely that he literally becomes ill. Yet because Henderson's movements are so graceful, a Platonic ideal of the athlete, the beleaguered warrior cannot take his eyes off of him.

By juxtaposing the two figures in this darkened room, the commercial generates a series of racially coded dyads underscoring the essentialism of American sports discourse. Its central set of antitheses, the catcher and the base-stealing outfielder, organizes a barely submerged belief system regarding the respective qualities of the races. The white catcher is cerebral, defensive, disciplined, protecting, fundamentally sound, and perhaps not very athletic by nature. Conversely, the black outfielder is physical, offensive, reckless, stealing, flashy, and graced with an innate natural athleticism. These dyads help give shape to a peculiar love-hate relationship between the white spectator and black athlete. In large measure a historical byproduct of institutionalized segregation, these pairs of traits help some spectators distinguish themselves from, and in some contexts identify with, black male athletes.

This dance of admiration and hatred, censure and identification, is exceptionally important at new urban stadiums. A central component of pleasure for many members of the audience seems to be the ability of the stadium and the area around it to reproduce vicissitudes of fear, admiration, and mastery of "blackness." During the past decade, in the face of overwhelming evidence that the stadium scene is becoming more and more white, baseball management, local merchants, and city officials have, perhaps unintentionally, introduced blackness as a replacement for black people. From hip-hop music piped in between batters to high-topped, shade-wearing, and pelvic-thrusting mascots, the contemporary stadium environment is replete with images and sounds suggestive of standard white projections of African American hipness. The choreographers of this liminal urban space replicate, and make genial, multiple forms of black oppositional culture in order to manufacture sensations of edginess; in so doing, it seems, they hope to simultaneously titillate and reassure their audience.

Stadiums such as Jacobs Field, constructed literally on top of razed areas of legitimate and illegitimate black-owned businesses—check-cashing shops and open-air drug markets alike—invite audiences to "black up," to inherit what is imagined as the cool abandon, the vitality and esprit de corps of the erstwhile dark city, or at least to come into contact with it. In other words, even as large-scale urban projects such as Jacobs Field work to recolonize the city according to the desires and tastes of young, upwardly mobile, and primarily white consumers, there remains an inevitable white/black dialectic—much like the one enacted in the Henderson commercial. Unpacking this dialectic helps provide an understanding of the cultural cachet of black simulacra at retro ball parks and shows how urban renewal centered on sports facilities is invariably tied up with complex, often contradictory, and deeply ingrained American beliefs about race.

INSTITUTIONAL SEGREGATION

Amazingly, during the 1997 season, a year Major League Baseball dedicated to the late Jackie Robinson, who had heroically crossed the color line fifty years earlier, not a single starting catcher was African American. Considered the quarterback of baseball, the catcher calls pitches, makes positioning adjustments, and serves as a counselor/tutor to the pitcher. Often less impressive athletically, the catcher is supposed to be the brains and the heart of the team. He must not only organize his side, but also do the gritty, dirty work of blocking the plate when an opponent barrels into him. Despite the existence of some brilliant African American catchers since integration (Roy "Campy" Campanella of the Brooklyn Dodgers comes immediately to mind), this position, like the quarterback in professional football, has remained largely white. Conversely, in the outfield, where Henderson plays, a position demanding pure speed and/or power with an emphasis on good offensive skills, two-thirds of the league's starters are African American. Cause and effect is of course complicated. Something less than overt racism is the primary factor contributing to this positional segregation within the game. Yet residual attitudes and lingering beliefs about African American athletic and intellectual capabilities versus those of whites on the part of management and scouting staffs surely contribute to this racial dynamic.

Understanding this complicated dynamic, grasping the racial coding abundant in the Henderson commercial, begins with a description of the history of baseball's institutional segregation. Baseball had been blossoming as America's most popular recreational pursuit for close to forty years before the exclusion of blacks became statutory. However, in the 1870s and 1880s, when a group of owners consolidated themselves into a singular entity, the National League, the race question began to take center stage. Facing pressure from genteel reformers to clean up their act, to make the experience of watching and playing baseball a more salutary endeavor, this new breed of middle-class entrepreneur engaged in a simultaneous housecleaning and propaganda campaign designed to make baseball resonate as a pursuit that transcended mere sport.[3] The 1887 agreement among International League owners to "approve no more contracts with colored men," which set the stage for the quick displacement of the twenty-five or so black professional ballplayers at the time, coincided with a widespread effort to package baseball as a signifier of American election (Peterson 28). No longer just a game, the sport was promoted as the "national pastime," both a source and a reflection of the cherished qualities inherent in the white American male.

Clearly, it was at this point that the black game and the white game began to diverge. Locked out of the organized leagues, still without a league of their own, most African Americans who wanted to continue to play for pay took to the barnstorming circuit. Jack Marshall, who played for, among other teams, the Cincinnati Clowns, describes his experience as a player/entertainer in an itinerant baseball troupe during these tumultuous times:

> A white Canadian named Rod Whitman . . . wanted two Negro
> ballclubs, he wanted a minstrel show, and he wanted a band. . . .
> So I organized this group for him, and I got a five-piece band and six
> other people as the minstrel show. . . . At six o'clock the Texas Giants
> and the New York All-Stars would play a game. . . . Now, when this
> ballgame was over, then the midway would open up again. While the
> midway was open, he would put this colored minstrel show on. With
> the midway and the minstrel show going on at one time, this man is
> coining the money! Now, when the midway closes, then the band
> would play for the dance. That's another admission, and the dance
> would go till one o'clock. Damndest operation you ever saw!
> (Peterson 8–9)

Marshall's description of his experience makes it clear that African Americans had to be versatile entertainers to play the game professionally. They did not have the luxury of devoting themselves entirely to perfecting the craft of ball playing. In an era when organized white baseball was literally recreating its own image—undertaking comprehensive rhetorical campaigns equating baseball playing with such earnest pursuits as soldier and leader training—itinerant black operations had to play to the tastes and desires of provincial audiences, rabidly enthusiastic about minstrel shows and clown demonstrations. These spectacles helped soothe white anxieties about blackness by infantilizing African American performers and confirmed emergent notions of racial difference. In other words, African American ballplayers were forced to participate in the naturalization of racist beliefs about black style over substance in order to "coin" money for whites.[4]

Blacks such as Marshall were paid to shuck and jive at the very moment that the white professional game was becoming increasingly regularized and disciplined. What had been a loose affiliation of hundreds of leagues became, by the beginning of the twentieth century, a monolith with agreed-on rules and codes of conduct. As such, this erstwhile fluid game with numerous techniques and strategies became highly rationalized and predictable. During this time, the very notion of fundamentals, or the application of *proper* technical and tactical approaches for dealing with the game's many challenges, was able to emerge because the white version of the sport was creating the institutions—youth training leagues, instructional magazines, spring training programs—that defined these fundamentals and set their limits.[5] This institutionalized separation of baseball training methods was one of the first seeds sown in the cultivation of the racial dyads giving meaning to the Henderson commercial. Without this separate and unequal history, it seems doubtful that today, the catcher position, for which fundamentals are considered paramount, would still be an almost exclusively white domain.

COONSBURY RULES

Of course, these particular constructions of racial traits did not arise, and still do not occur, in a vacuum. Baseball is part of a larger culture that has often ensured that a poor black man's "only capital is his body."[6] Historically denied access to power and wealth, their bodies the vehicles with which slave owners accumulated vast fortunes, African Americans have long responded to oppression in part by creating rich cultural forms emphasizing action, dynamism, and kinetics. From the second-lining rhythms of the bayou, to the brilliant paintings and dance emerging out of the Harlem Renaissance, to bebop, hip-hop, boogie woogie, and break dancing, black American dynamic or kinetic expression has been in the vanguard of American culture for more than a century.

Many of these twentieth-century cultural movements rely on the employment of forms of riffing—or the reconstitution of and slight variation on well-known melodic themes in jazz music. Poet and cultural icon Amiri Baraka argues that this gift of riffing is precisely what constitutes the genius of black American expression. Improvisation, necessitated by exile, has been brought to bear on static, largely white, cultural forms and has thus revolutionized them:

> Instead of the simplistic though touching note-for-note replay of the ballad's line, on [sax legend John] Coltrane's performance each note is tested, given a slight tremolo or emotional vibrato (note to chord to scale reference) which makes it seem as if each one of the notes is given the possibility of "infinite" qualification . . . proving that the ballad as it was written was only the beginning of the story.[7]

In this passage, Baraka emphasizes Coltrane's adeptness at "versioning" or going beyond the mere replication of a tune. Released from the shackles of music "as it was written," able to make scribed ballads merely "the beginning of the story," Coltrane fashions a satisfying response to a long legacy of brutal repression and segregation. Often without access to classical musical training or education, many African American jazz musicians came to rely on other, more personal and less rigid, forms of inspiration. Translating music that had been heard but not read, Coltrane, and other jazz greats before him, such as Charlie Parker, were freer to stretch the limits of their genre.[8]

This kind of freedom correlates to the so-called Coonsbury Rules popularized by Negro League and black barnstorming baseball players in the early 1900s. A term mocking the regimented Queensbury Rules (named for the famously uptight Marquis of Queensbury and describing proper boxing fundamentals and conduct), Coonsbury Rules referred to baseball play based on instinct, cunning, improvisation, and pure physical ability. Abruptly cut off from the very institutions (PSALs, textbooks, and leagues) that created and enforced fundamental play, black professional baseball players came to rely on riskier, cagier, more physical methods. Speed, aggressive base running, and "tricky ball," or "any way you think you can win, any kind of play you think you can get by with," became characteristic of the less organized, largely barnstorming black version of the game.[9] For close to sixty years, black ballplayers were statutorily denied access to the fundamental, rational, and regularized version of the game. However, from this position of exile, they (like Coltrane and Parker) were able to push the limits of their craft, expanding their repertoires by providing for the "possibility of 'infinite' qualification" to accepted methods. Yet despite the attendance of huge mixed crowds at barnstorming events and Negro League games—underlining the extent to which the white public was fascinated with Coonsbury Rules—few elements of "tricky ball" found their way into Major League Baseball until after integration.

RELUCTANTLY ASSIMILATING TRICKY BALL

When Satchel Paige arrived in the major leagues two years after Robinson crossed the color line, he brought with him the excitement and unorthodoxy of Coonsbury Rules. Arguably the greatest pitcher ever, Satchel Paige was also perhaps its greatest showman. As a rookie for the Cleveland Indians at the incredible age of forty-eight, he came on the scene with a well-earned reputation for flamboyance and innovation. After all, for thirty years, during an era when most black barnstormers were fortunate to make $150 per month, Paige had combined his "Stepin Fetchit" coon act with exceptional success on the mound, drawing record crowds and pulling in about forty thousand dollars per year.[10] His act included naming his pitches; the "bee ball," which he said buzzed when he threw it, and the "trouble ball" were among his favorites. It also included pulling stunts like calling in his outfielders to taunt opposing batters and speaking to the press using minstrel show one-liners. Above all, however, his routine called for him to dominate opponents. In 1934 and 1935, he toured opposite Dizzy Dean, thought to be the best white pitcher of the decade, and beat Dean's team, composed of the finest white hitters in the game, four out of six times. A full decade later, he did the same and out-dueled Cleveland Indian great Bob Feller.

Yet Paige's treatment by the baseball establishment once he finally got a chance to play in the majors makes it clear that tricky ball was accepted only reluctantly. Time and again, Paige had to endure charges among the baseball establishment that his unorthodoxy was making a mockery of the game. The *Sporting News,* the quintessential sporting magazine of the baseball establishment and the country's most popular source of information and opinions about baseball for more than half a century, opined that Paige's appearance demeaned the "standards of baseball in the big circuits."[11] Because the magazine had previously come out in favor of integration, it was unable to use race as the ostensible reason for condemning Paige. Instead, its writers criticized his actions based on more nebulous yet racially inflected arguments about propriety. They suggested that Paige's advanced age and his unconventionality made him simply a kind of carnival attraction, a publicity stunt. They even insisted that, had the pitcher been white, Cleveland owner Bill Veeck would have simply overlooked him.

The magazine's stance was of dubious merit, however. A handful of white stars such as Ty Cobb and Cy Young had signed large contracts in their mid-forties without having had to endure similar criticism. Plus, Veeck's Indians had already been drawing large crowds and thus did not desperately need an attendance boost, even if Paige's arrival was sure to improve the bottom line by a certain percentage. Instead, the "standards of baseball" that Paige was supposedly demeaning were surely ones of technical orthodoxy. Ignoring or having not been privy to technical "advances" of the past few decades, Paige still wound up his arm as if he were cranking an old automobile. Sometimes this cranking would last six revolutions, sometimes two. Sometimes, instead of pitching overhand, he threw sidearm or even underhand. Often, he would hesitate during his pitching motion or wiggle his fingers on the ball in order to throw off the timing of opposing hitters. This employment of Coonsbury Rules incensed many opponents and members of the white baseball establishment whom Paige kept off balance all summer during one of the most captivating pennant races of all time. Never-before-seen crowds, sometimes in excess of eighty thousand and by some estimates up to 40 percent African American, came to see this almost half-century-old rookie pitch, swagger, and joke as he helped the Indians move to the top of the American League. Yet after a few rough outings in September, he was abruptly dropped from the Indians' rotation. Unable to reproduce the fabulous results of the summer months, Paige all of a sudden found his off-the-field behavior a subject of severe public scrutiny. He was criticized by members of both the black and the white press for refusing to give up his playboy life-style and for arriving habitually late to team functions.

Common sentiment among these critics was that his actions stood to jeopardize the still tenuous position of other black baseball players looking for acceptance in the league. After all, in 1946, Brooklyn Dodger general manager Branch Rickey had chosen Jackie Robinson to step across the color line over a plethora of similarly and more accomplished African American ballplayers largely because he felt the young second baseman was possessed of an almost superhuman amount of poise. He knew that, if his "noble experiment" were to work, his martyr would need to be someone capable of maintaining a low profile and turning the other cheek to the torrents of abuse and indignities he was destined to suffer.[12] Sure enough, during the first few years, when Robinson carried with him the hopes and dreams for the advancement of millions, when he was cleated regularly at second base, beaned by opposing pitchers, and forced to stay in separate hotels and eat in separate restaurants, the second baseman did more than just live up to expectations. A former collegiate football and track star with but one season of experience in professional baseball with the Negro League's Kansas City Monarchs, the young player set the league ablaze. He provided the game with a theretofore unseen combination of power, speed, and daring base running; and, perhaps more important to Rickey and the other white liberals who initiated and closely monitored the experiment, he comported himself quietly and stoically off the field, helping to contradict prevailing racist attitudes about the black athlete. In fact, almost all the young black players who succeeded in the first few years of integration—Robinson, Roy Campanella, Larry Doby—walked a middle ground on the field, displaying a hyper-keen awareness of fundamentals while only selectively infusing the sport with some of the daring and innovative play of Negro League tricky ball. Outside the stadium, to a man, they all also behaved extremely cautiously, aware of their roles as racial ambassadors. Paige, on the other hand, accustomed to the freedom of his barnstorming days, refused (or was unable) to walk the line. Although this intransigence probably cost him the right to pitch in the big leagues into his fifties, it did open up a wider space for athletes who followed him. Paige, during his brief stint with the Indians, more brazenly and unapologetically than his younger contemporaries—Robinson, Campanella, and Doby—helped introduce the legacy of Negro League and barnstorming crafty play into the mainstream American sports scene.

THE POLITICS OF SHOWBOATING

Paige cracked open a door that, a decade and a half later, boxer Muhammed Ali (born Cassius Clay) barreled through, injecting a strong political component into Coonsbury Rules. Going well beyond the behavior sanctioned by Rickey and the other baseball owners who spearheaded the "noble experiment," Ali refused to capitulate to the desires of liberal reformers. A converted Muslim, Ali shocked the establishment, lost years off his career, and even risked jail time for refusing induction into the military. He spoke openly against oppression and racism, attaching the rhetoric of sports braggadocio onto a burgeoning discourse of black power.

Nonetheless, in his showboating he found perhaps his most unique and efficacious language. Not content to suppress his personality to placate the largely conservative sports community, he danced and taunted, insulted and baited as he found a way to set down one opponent after another. Arguably the most crafty and intelligent heavyweight of all time, Ali brought the legacy of tricky ball into the modern era of televised, excessively hyped sports. His showboating was both political expression and part of a brilliant system of smoke-and-mirror tactics enabling him to beat bigger, stronger, and faster opponents. He refused to box according to the standard idioms of the establishment. His "rope-a-dope" (playing-possum) trick, like Paige's bee ball, advertised in front of a national television audience that African American culture could draw from a rich history of strategies and ideas at least equal to those of white culture. In other words, Ali strongly suggested to the world that the white way (seen as fundamental) was not necessarily the right way to play the game.

Of course, Ali's ascendance into the sporting pantheon has been extremely gradual. Subject to scorn, racial hatred, sanctions, and frequent death threats during his boxing career, Ali has only recently come to be widely seen as one of the greatest living American sports figures.[13] In large measure a product of evolving white attitudes toward African Americans and in part because, afflicted with Parkinson's disease, he is nearly speechless and thus less of a threat than he was when he was young and vocal during the heyday of black power, Ali only now seems to be understood and embraced as having been an agent of positive social change. Yet the intensely uneven response to the flashy, and sometimes unorthodox, behavior of black athletes following Ali suggests how the sports world's longstanding ambivalence toward the legacy of Coonsbury Rules lives on.

Cocky and brash, young Rickey Henderson arrived on the professional baseball scene in the late 1970s, prior to widespread mainstream assimilation of urban culture. Early in his career, he cultivated an image that drove white audiences and some teammates to distraction, in turn infuriating, befuddling, and amusing them. When a pop fly came to him in the outfield, for example, he brashly employed his signature "snatch catch." A boldly antifundamental gesture, the snatch catch entailed using only his glove hand to grab a pop fly before sharply snatching it down as if to add insult to the batter's injury.[14] Similarly, as a base stealer, he danced, he feinted, and he taunted opposing catchers and pitchers, throwing off their rhythm and destroying their concentration. Off the field, he revisited the role of the barnstormer, becoming one of the first players to take full advantage of newly liberalized rules about free agency. He jumped from team to team, selling his services to the highest bidder, arriving just in time to help solidify an organization's pennant hopes. In the process, he often pretended not to know names of teammates and coaches, and he continually mocked the obsessive physical regimen of less-gifted players, on one occasion even listing "eat plenty of ice cream" as one of his four rules for a long career.

Throughout his years as a professional ballplayer, he employed many linguistic tropes characteristic of minstrelsy when speaking with teammates, fans, and the media. He almost always referred to himself in the third person, frequently masking extremes of cunning and guile behind studiously ungrammatical or syllogistic speech. For example, when electing to sit in the back of the team bus after arriving in San Diego, he was told it was his right to remain up front. As he walked past Tony Gwynn, his fellow veteran said, "Rickey, you sit up here. You've got tenure," to which Henderson replied, with all the subversive wit of Stepin Fetchit, "Ten? Rickey got 20 years in the big leagues."[15]

All of these words and behaviors shared one thing in common. They all were suggestive of a studied and ironic self-deprecation that made one thing perfectly clear: Henderson could succeed luminously without exerting maximal effort, without needing to employ many of the tools held onto tightly by his adversary, the catcher, in the antacid commercial. Producing brilliant epigrams in the vernacular, he mocked the world of standard language. Turning unorthodox technique into unstoppable offense, he called into question the benefits of fundamental play. Professing disloyalty to all the clubs for which he played, he scoffed at reverence for (historically white) baseball institutions. Telling people he had remained the most physically dominating player in the game for two decades simply by eating sweets, he ridiculed the increasingly technological world of performance enhancement.

In a way, then, the totality of his act allowed him to effect a kind of reverse mastery of the masters. He outplayed and outwitted opponents, fans, and owners but did so in a way that amplified to absurdity many of the otherwise oppressive beliefs about black athletes. Just as Paige had done previously, he was able to avoid being pigeonholed into one of the several problematic roles, such as "coon," "uncle Tom," or "the angry black man," that had been abundantly available to black performers.[16] Not subservient but not obviously revolutionary, not ignorant but not easily recognizable as brilliant, not obsessed with his own physicality but still one of the best athletes on the planet, Henderson defied stereotypes just as he seemed to reinforce them and thus frustrated attempts to keep him in his place.

Yet as he approached retirement age in the late 1990s, the base-stealing king dramatically toned down his act.[17] In 1998, at the Athletics' spring training compound in suburban Phoenix, Henderson comported himself as a model citizen. Day in and day out he extended his hours on the field in order to chat with children in the stands, sign autographs, and pose for photos. Nonetheless, at every step he was taken to task by mostly white male fans suspicious of his transformation. Throughout the seven innings he played in one particular game against the team he had left the year before, the San Diego Padres, Henderson was heckled mercilessly by a group of spectators for, ironically, hustling and not showboating. "You're not fooling anyone, Rickey," one of the fans yelled after thirty-nine-year-old Henderson sprinted down the first-base line to beat out an infield hit. "We know you're just sucking up to get into the Hall [of Fame]." Rejecting a conversion narrative—a bit surprising given the plethora of similar narratives in sports—these fans held fast to their anger toward Henderson of past years. They could only see his transformation as just another form of tricky ball.

This fascination with Henderson's motivation of course points out just how clever he had been throughout his career insofar as now, toning down his act, he found himself suddenly subject to the double bind he had previously avoided. Leaving behind his showboating and residual minstrel ways, he came to be accused of cynically trying to curry white favor. Perhaps letting go of their animus toward Henderson would have, for these white fans, psychically diminished the importance of baseball's hard-working journeymen (like the catcher) with bodies like their own, who have overachieved and held fast against the intrusion of the uncontainable athleticism and subversive wit displayed by the outfielder in his younger days. Perhaps, too, their refusal to accept his transformation was simply just an essential part of sport, a spectacle that produces satisfying binaries offering the ability to clearly see, and distinguish between, good and evil.

Yet clearly something else was at play as well. The fans' ruthlessness toward the base-stealing champion seemed to display a kind of profound admiration, an intense identification with, and longing for, his brand of devil-may-care independence. In multiple conversations with members of the group who mocked Henderson in Phoenix, each admitted privately that the speedy base stealer had always been one of his favorite players to watch. And why not? After all, images of the young outfielder—strutting casually after launching a ball over the fence, darting swiftly from base to base, yanking fly balls down with his snatch catch— above and beyond their simple grace, serve as powerful reminders of the extent to which Henderson was able to defy the limitations of behavior, self-expression, and cultural inheritance imposed upon Robinson and the first generation of African American ballplayers in the modern major leagues. His aggressive style and unique personality are part of a heritage of language and gesticulation underlining the ability, and in many cases the necessity, of talented African Americans to re-create and redescribe the world into which they were born. They thus are inspirational of at least submerged appreciation from American white men raised in a national culture that has long elevated the rebel to mythical levels.[18]

THE WHITE NEGRO

Norman Mailer, by attempting to connect the coolness of 1950s hipsters to something essential about the African American experience in his controversial 1957 essay "The White Negro," provides insight into this kind of white longing for identification with the black male body and spirit:

> It is no accident that the source of Hip is the Negro for he has been living on the margin between totalitarianism and democracy for two centuries. . . . And in this wedding of the white and the black it was the Negro who brought the cultural dowry. . . . Any Negro who wishes to live must live with danger from his first day, and no experience can ever be casual to him, no Negro can saunter down a street with any real certainty that violence will not visit him on his walk. . . . Knowing in the cells of his existence that life was war, nothing but war, the Negro (all exceptions admitted) could rarely afford the sophisticated inhibitions of civilization, and so he kept for his survival the art of the primitive, he lived in the enormous present, he subsisted for his Saturday night kicks, relinquishing the pleasures of the mind for the more obligatory pleasures of the body, and in his music he gave the infinite variations of joy, lust, languor, growl, cramp, pinch, scream and despair of his orgasm. . . . So there was a new breed of adventurers, urban adventurers who drifted out at night looking for action with a black man's code to fit their facts. The hipster had absorbed the existentialist synapses of the Negro, and for practical purposes could be considered a white Negro. (340–41)

Mailer's comments attempt to explain the dynamics underlying white consumption of black oppositional cultural when it hits the mainstream. His notion that

1950s hipsters sought a "black man's code to fit their facts" describes at least part of the appeal of contemporary forms of black cultural products consumed largely by young white audiences. "Gangsta rap" as well as attitude on the playing field appeals especially to white youth, in large measure, because they relate to it as a better signifier of oppositional attitudes and sensibilities than anything else to which they have access. Many whites look to black culture, whose forms have emerged from centuries of hardship and opposition, because it provides a more realistic and resonant description of their experience vis-à-vis traditional bour-geois cultural forms.[19]

Mailer's ideas of blackness are, of course, invariably tied up with troubling notions of sexual and racial essentialism. His belief that "Negro consciousness" could become a revolutionary force in this country is a product of the kind of envy/fetishization of the black man critiqued by Eric Lott in *Love and Theft*. Lott argues that the writing and performance of a large number of twentieth-century white icons such as Mailer, Mick Jagger, and Elvis Presley would be impossible if it were not for a legacy of black-faced minstrelsy. Minstrelsy, like Mailer's notion of the "white Negro," was a product of white worship of a projected image of black masculinity. This image, of black men as more sexually potent and free, is tied up with longings for a return to a mythical, preindustrial past, when white masculinity was defined in more physical terms. The postindustrial emer-gence of bourgeois culture, while providing for greater luxury and ease, stripped middle-class men of their ability to influence their world through physicality and made them subject to oppressive forms of rational control. White male love of minstrelsy therefore was to a large degree a form of simultaneous oppression and idolization. It reinforced ugly stereotypes of black men as uncontrollably sexual and often dim-witted, all the while revealing a widespread envy of African American freedom to stay in sync with physical urges.

In the mid-1990s, two generations after the publication of "The White Negro," Major League Baseball got in on Mailer's act, inaugurating a promotional cam-paign intended to bill the sport as an endeavor for the interracially cool. Faced with a crisis related to declining interest in the game and trying to combat a sense that, in comparison with other sports, baseball was unhip, the major leagues took a page out of the provocative writer's book. As baseball began to see the need to cultivate a younger demographic—not just teenagers with money of their own to spend but also twenty-somethings longing for the lost erotic charge of the adolescent outsider—its advertisements began to feature black stars known at least partially for their swagger. It set one of its promotional spots to a rap beat and aggressively marketed bad boy baseball stars such as Albert Belle (with his icy glare) and Barry Bonds (with his slow, cool home run strut).

In the mostly white modern baseball environment (suddenly billed as a hip amusement space for families), black forms, so often subject to censure in other contexts, reemerged as sources of meaning and pleasure, albeit in bowdlerized and/or sublimated iterations. The promotional campaign, which, like Mailer's piece, elevated projections of the "primitive" to an art form, perhaps reveals a great deal about middle-class white anxiety during periods of relative peace and prosperity. The co-optation of black subjectivity, the absorption of "the existential synapses of the Negro," by the "hipster" and, by extension, the white baseball fan, shows how much white America relies on a commodified versions of the black experience as sources for its own pleasure.

But, of course, this particular commodity is difficult to package without revealing some jagged edges. In the historically regularized world of professional baseball, exaggerated examples of brashness or swagger on the part of black players still occasionally run headlong into an intense desire to preserve something akin to the tradition or integrity of the sport. In May 1990, during a game between the Chicago White Sox and the New York Yankees, baseball rehearsed a real-life morality play between a white catcher and a black outfielder. Carlton Fisk, the former Red Sox legend at the end of his career, considered a throwback player for his hustle, hard work, no-nonsense attitude, and willingness to play with pain, engaged in a fascinating verbal scuffle with young "Neon" Deion Sanders.[20] Sanders, perhaps the flashiest player in the major leagues at the time, after hitting a towering fly ball, began walking perfunctorily down the first-base line. This enraged Fisk who got out of his crouch, ran behind Sanders and started screaming at him to "run it out." Although Sanders was too stunned by Fisk's actions to yell back, the catcher's words almost incited a brawl between Fisk and Sanders's Yankee teammates in the dugout.

The next day, after almost uniform expressions of public outrage, Sanders called a press conference to apologize. Yet the outfielder's renunciation of his act (or more appropriately, his nonact) fails to dull the double-edged nature of Fisk's criticism. On one hand, Sanders's action (or inaction) defied the ethos of fundamental play. Baseball orthodoxy maintains that a player should run out every play under the assumption that the opponents, in theory, could drop the ball or commit a throwing error. Additionally, players are expected to run it out because the very act of hustling, especially in a lost cause, is seen as fundamentally ennobling. On the other hand, Fisk's condemnation of Sanders is complicated insofar as it is an instance of a white man criticizing a black man for failing to perform publicly, for failing to move quickly and gracefully. The catcher's criticism both falls short of accounting for the political component of Sander's calculated conservation of energy and refuses to acknowledge the extent to which baseball management had been reliant on promoting itself as accommodating of this kind of cool reserve. Clearly, Sander's slow saunter, like Bonds's easygoing home-run strut in the ubiquitous advertisements, was, at least in part, a form of meaningful and stylized casualness.

While, of course, few would argue that Sander's nonact was something to categorically applaud, the sports pundits who were intensely critical of the young ballplayer ultimately failed to recognize that it meant more than simple laziness or disrespect. By not running (like Henderson not covering his glove with his opposite hand and Ali keeping his arms at his side instead of using them to cover his face), Sanders on some level, attempted to deliver his metaphorical coup de grace, letting his opponents know he can beat them without having to give everything he's got. In this sense, Sanders's inaction is akin to "playing the dozens," a rich African American tradition of engaging in verbal battles where the goal is to beat down an opponent without resorting to violence or losing ones' cool. Across the country, on playgrounds, in schoolyards, and in comedy clubs, men (primarily) cap, crack, bag, diss, hike, jones, rank, rib, serve, signify, slip, sound, and snap in battles for respect. Successfully playing the dozens requires delivering a knockout blow so suggestive of one's verbal agility or wit so as to discourage future challengers.

In this sense, baseball seems to have reaped what it has sown. Using images of race to signify its own hipness, attempting to appeal to a wider segment of the population (blacks and nonblacks who appreciate the energy of oppositional culture), it created the conditions under which its more "old school" practitioners were bound to lose their cool. Fisk saw Sanders's nonaction as taunting, as a sign of disrespect, as a prelude to violence. Conversely, members of the audience (black, white, and brown) more acculturated to hip-hop culture and "the dozens" were perhaps prone to see just the opposite.

BLACKING UP

The intensity of the tension palpable when Fisk took on Sanders or when, as often happens in professional sports, a black athlete is perceived to have crossed the line of appropriate decorum, suggests something like a national obsession with racial difference. The amount of attention these acts receive underlines the extent to which the American sports world is struggling to reconcile subconscious beliefs about fundamental and respectful play with the intensely charismatic and creative performances of many contemporary African American athletes. In 1999, ESPN, the nation's first all-sports channel, while celebrating its twentieth anniversary, initiated a dialogue examining the complicated nature of highlight-reel-inspired showboating behavior. A common supposition among sportswriters interviewed for the show was that players now pre-plan their acts in order to become looped into *SportsCenter*'s repeat footage.[21] Almost to a person, *SportsCenter* anchors past and present lamented this dynamic, renouncing antimartial self-aggrandizement. Yet they also acknowledged that these acts play well. They all agreed that the ability to see film loops of creative showboating behavior keeps audiences tuned in to their show, often for multiple nightly viewings. In other words, their ideas suggest that, not unlike Jack Marshall of the

Cincinnati Clowns, today's athletes continue to "coin" money for owners (and now cable networks), promoting their acts to an audience that cannot take its eyes off them. Of course, what has changed since the time of Marshall's minstrel shows is that, by any standards, today's athletes coin money for themselves as well. The fact that ballplayers now earn up to $25 million a year by playing ball and taunting opponents ups the ante for viewers. Large salaries, while made possible to a large degree by the appealing flamboyance of particular stars, also give certain members of the audience, perhaps nostalgic for the unassuming quality of Fisk, another rationale for demanding what they construct as higher (often conflated with whiter) standards or behavior.

Two of the most popular sports movies of the 1990s, *White Men Can't Jump* and *Jerry Maguire,* attempt to defuse this tension. Both look to the contemporary American sports scene for clues to relieving the hostility between black and white, pizzazz and fundamentals, money and honor. The fact that both movies are only able to do so semicoherently is perhaps less a statement about the relative skills of their filmmakers as it a reflection of the fundamental insolubility of these dichotomies.[22] In *White Men Can't Jump,* the defining moment arrives when a white ballplayer somehow elevates enough to dunk a basketball during a heated contest. Previously, his inability to jump high combined with his African American partner's lack of shooting and passing consistency had created a seemingly insuperable chasm separating the two. Dunking the ball, rather than simply laying it in, though counting for the same two points, affords Billy Hoyle respect in the black-dominated playground basketball scene. It also serves as the catalyst for his getting his life together. The dunk lets him win a competition, pay off debts, and, perhaps most important, lose his insecurity about a perceived lack of physical acumen. These gains allow him to provide stability for himself and his live-in girlfriend Gloria and, crucially, regain his sexual potency with the biracial Rosie Perez character.

Similarly, *Jerry Maguire* dances desperately between white condemnation and worship of black athleticism and style. Ostensibly a heterosexual love story between two white protagonists, the movie gets its primary energy through attempts by its titular character, a white sports agent, to come to grips with the flashy behavior of one of his black male clients. Having marginalized himself by writing a treatise on the need to restore integrity and simplicity to the world of sports management, the erstwhile agent to the stars finds himself confronted with his own Neon Deion–type character.[23] Desperate for a client, Jerry Maguire meets up with Rod Tidwell, a talented wide receiver from the Arizona Cardinals who, because of his reputation as a player unwilling to give maximal effort during practices or games, risks exile from the NFL. Prior to getting to know the receiver, Maguire had been engaging in a largely bathetic quest to reconnect with the ideals of simplicity and fair play, loyalty and honesty. However, this earnest pursuit of a return to the values of yesteryear is short-circuited by the football player's irrepressible charisma. The agent's (and the theretofore unsuspecting audience's) world is truly turned topsy-turvy by Tidwell's famous "show me the money" dance. Speaking on his cordless phone, dancing gracefully around his kitchen with the pulsating beat of his boom box in the background, the football player raps his truth for the agent.[24] In his song, he reminds Maguire that his window of opportunity for earning a living at his craft is slim and that extremes of charisma and style have set him apart from the thousands of other young would be professional receivers aiming to take his job. Through his rap, the football player forces the agent, and by extension the viewer, to consider a more complex perspective about sports and character.

Sure enough, listening to the wide receiver's words, Maguire is transformed, coming to recognize what Fisk did not. Throwback behavior and showboating are but two different paths to the same result: the use of one's particular physical capital to achieve financial security from a professional sports career. Although Tidwell also capitulates somewhat to Maguire's perspective later in the movie, playing hurt to help his team win, his "show me the money" dance endures as the most electric and revelatory moment of the film.

Jerry Maguire is certainly not a great movie, but it is a great movie for the age. Setting out on a project to extol the virtues of an idealized American sports value system, the film becomes as confused about race as America currently is. Ultimately, Tidwell's magnetic personality subsumes Maguire's fundamental values. The teacher becomes the pupil as Maguire learns to be cool, to adopt some of his client's shade-wearing, jive-talking swagger. Showboating, the movie seems to suggest, is simply part of being a man in America. Once Jerry Maguire stops trying to reform his client and instead adopts some of his attention grabbing behavior (coded as black), he is able to differentiate himself from the institutions that oppress him, inherit his birth right as an American individual, and thus reclaim the fortitude necessary to do right by his wife. In short, both main white characters in *White Man Can't Jump* and *Jerry Maguire* regain their potency in the professional and, most important, the domestic spheres by incorporating aspects of Mailer's "white Negro."

Perhaps both movies, as well as other contemporary cultural products, similar in nature to the Henderson antacid commercial, suggest widespread white masculine insecurity. All three of the white characters—the catcher, the sports agent, and the basketball hustler—struggle to overcome extreme sensations of emasculation. In the beginning of the respective narratives, both Maguire and Hoyle strain to satisfy their partners sexually and emotionally while the catcher contemplates losing his job and thus being rendered unable to provide for his family. Unlike the catcher, however, the two white movie characters come to discover that the only way out of their dilemma, the only way to regain their potency, is to black up. Perhaps if the antacid commercial were to be made into a feature film, the catcher would eventually come to learn this lesson as well.

WHITE (BASEBALL) FLIGHT
AND THE RETURN DOWNTOWN

Recognizing the propensity of white male American sports aficionados to symbolically put on black face as Jerry Maguire and Billy Hoyle did is key to understanding much of the appeal of new urban baseball stadiums for many visitors.
City spaces surrounding new ball parks, as well as the ball parks themselves,
place (primarily) suburban visitors in the same subject position of the catcher and
the two movie protagonists. Just like Henderson's dyspeptic rival, many baseball
fans return to the city extremely wary of theft and ambivalent about changes to
dominant culture brought about by the gradual merging of Coonsbury Rules into
the mainstream. "Most people from Akron are afraid to come to Cleveland," ad-
mits Jacobs bleacher fan Dave Barta. Yet Barta, himself from Akron, and millions
of other fans from outside the city, do return downtown, anxious to "absorb" the
perceived edge and passion of the city as did the protagonists in *Jerry Maguire* and
White Men Can't Jump. New urban spaces allow outsiders the critical capacity of
Fisk, judging African American panhandlers and petty vendors critically for unruly
behavior. At the same time, these residual traces of the city underworld invest
new urban spaces with life, providing an alternative to the often dull, parking-lot
environment of suburban stadiums.

On the surface, from the perspective of anyone interested in improved American race relations, baseball coming back downtown would seem to be an unequivocally positive development. Bringing a hub of social activity and an economic anchor back to majority-black locations reverses a long trend of white
flight. After all, between 1950 and 1970, the critical indicator of whether a baseball team moved was not stadium age, team record, or even attendance, but the
racial composition of the neighborhood. Teams that left went from areas with an
average black population of 49 percent to ones that were just 16 percent black.
Those that stayed put were in neighborhoods that had, on average, a 24 percent
black population.[25]

Since the beginning of the 1990s, however, the trend has reversed. Widespread dissatisfaction with suburban locations has brought teams back to the
streets of Mailer's city in search of an integrated experience in which patrons can
once again combine dining, shopping, and walking with an evening at the ball
park, where they can soak up a dose of city energy as part of their experience.
Yet the city spaces to which baseball has returned are often articulated as *urbanesque* rather than urban. That is to say, they are carefully controlled, relatively
homogenous environments, sometimes barely resembling the areas around the
ball parks after which they are modeled and lacking much in common with the
landscapes they replaced.[26]

For about twenty years prior to the construction of Jacobs Field and the adjacent Gund Arena in Cleveland's old east-side market area, the activity in that sec-

POSTER OF AN AFRICAN AMERICAN BOY ON THE CLEVELAND URBAN DESIGN COLLABORATIVE BUILDING.

tion of downtown had taken place among a predominantly African American crowd. Many of the vendors in the rundown market were black, as were a large percentage of the patrons, most of whom preferred it to the more modern west-side market because it offered slightly better prices. Additionally, the area was full of discount retailers providing merchandise targeting local black customers. Afro-wig stores, cut-rate shoe suppliers, and beauty supply shops selling hair care products for African Americans dominated the area around East Ninth Street. More marginally, black prostitutes and drug dealers took advantage of the forgotten and neglected quality of the district in order to market their particular wares.

Today, of course, all evidence of the market has been buried underneath the footers of the new ball park, leaving the distant, more upscale west-side version as locals' only option. The prostitutes and drug dealers are almost all gone as well, having been pushed to more depressed areas of the city. Homeless panhandlers working the streets in the evening as visitors arrive for games serve as residual traces of the area's former underworld, begging for money in the shadows of the new sports facilities. Similarly, many of the old stores hang on tenuously, continuing to sell their products by perpetually advertising "inventory reduction sales." Of course, many have simply gone out of business, leaving behind faded remnants of their old signs still partially visible underneath new ones advertising condominium units available in their old buildings. Perhaps more eerily, throughout

POSTER OF A SAXOPHONE PLAYER IN A EUCLID AVENUE BUILDING WINDOW.

the area, photographic commemorative photos of African Americans who used to walk the streets there hang in empty storefront windows of boarded-up buildings soon to be converted to new commercial uses for a changed demographic.

Meanwhile, in the resurgent Gateway of the new millennium, next to the two sports arenas, dozens of new restaurants have opened for business. Rows of sports bars, Irish pubs, and themed diners are packed with patrons on game nights. A few new daytime businesses have relocated to the area as well. The Caxton Building on Huron Road is 90 percent filled to capacity with the offices of such enterprises as SABR, the Society for American Baseball Research. On practically every street, old buildings are being converted to condominiums in an ambitious attempt to make the Gateway more than just a commercial space. Though most remain only partially full (it is still a tough sell, given that there is not a single grocery store in the vicinity), those who do buy apartments in these buildings are almost exclusively white.

During this crucial period of transition for the Gateway, a dramatically in-creased security presence has emerged in order provide reassurance for people like Barta and his neighbors from Akron. As Indians vice president Bob Dibiasio aptly put it, ramping up security in the Gateway was an essential element in the success of Jacobs Field from day one because "people return to where they are comfortable." Making visitors to the city feel "comfortable" has required the presence of more police officers and restrictive policies against ticket scalpers, panhandlers, and other residual inhabitants of the area's recent past looking to get in on the action. Combined with the replacement of black business and patrons with (primarily) white residents and visitors, increased security has worked to, literally, change the face of downtown.

As they evolve, however, spaces like the Gateway run the risk of too closely resembling suburban shopping malls, a central paradox of gentrification. When people arrive there, they find many of the fundamental facts of city life swept under the carpet, sent into exile, or bricked over and covered up by fancy yet faux historic materials like aluminum wrought-iron sheathing. Architects, politicians, urban planners, and business owners looking to attract people back to downtown areas clearly find themselves in the position of maintaining a delicate balance between the provision of comfort for visitors and the tolerance or celebration of those elements of city life distinguishing it from the suburbs. Questions of race naturally make this balance an exceedingly difficult one to maintain. As the cultural pendulum swings, as urban spaces become once again de rigueur, and as forms of African American culture continue to occupy significant bandwidth in the mainstream, African Americans in these new urban spaces are largely disappearing from view.

WHITENING CITY, WHITENING GAME

The dramatic whitening of the physical space around new urban stadiums mirrors significant trends within the game itself. With great fanfare, Major League Baseball celebrated the fiftieth anniversary of the integration of the league in 1997. At ball parks around the country, banners bearing the face of Jackie Robinson were hung next to gift shops selling official Negro League team jackets for $240. President Clinton and Robinson's widow Rachel took the field at New York's Shea Stadium to throw out the first pitch at the official game commemorating the former Brooklyn Dodger's first appearance. Players and umpires attached patches bearing the words "Breaking Barriers" to their uniforms. The league organized parties, sponsored lectures, produced television specials, and enforced a league-wide retirement of Robinson's jersey number. Yet the official dedication of the 1997 season to Robinson was largely the culmination of a decade-long effort on the part of the major leagues to window dress a racial house of cards.

Ten years earlier, Dodger vice president Al Campanis had touched off a firestorm of protest by telling Ted Koppel on *Nightline* that blacks lacked the "necessities" to manage major league clubs. This forced a reluctant league to examine its record on racial hiring. What it found was not at all promising. In the aftermath of the Campanis debacle, it was revealed that, forty years after Robinson had crossed the color line, African Americans were still virtually shut out of high-level decision-making and managerial jobs.[27] Yet the dearth of high-level positions filled by black men and women was only the tip of the iceberg. Even more troubling were trends suggesting a possible disappearance of African Americans from even the most visible sectors of the American baseball scene. Even as affirmative action programs had opened up a few spots here and there for minorities in baseball administration, the percentage of African American players populating big-league rosters was steadily decreasing. For every highly visible and marketable African American star like Ken Griffey Jr., countless young black children were tuning out, playing other sports, and ignoring baseball. The numbers of African Americans in the major leagues dropped from 19 percent to 17 percent in the season preceding the year of Robinson. On top of this, two years before a beaming President Clinton threw out that first pitch in front of a national television audience, two teams, the Philadelphia Phillies and the Minnesota Twins, went through the majority of their seasons without even one African American on the active roster.

This downward trend seems likely to continue. More than 90 percent of Little League baseball teams come from mostly white suburban and rural areas. Urban ball fields, which only three decades ago were producing a generation of stars such as Eric Davis, Darryl Strawberry, Ozzie Smith, and Eddie Murray (all from South Central Los Angeles), now lay largely fallow and neglected. If followed to their logical conclusion, these trends suggest that the major leagues could once more be absent of African American players by the seventy-fifth anniversary of integration. In the stands, despite the promotional use of icons such as Belle and Bonds, black spectatorship is way down as well. In the early 1990s, statistics clearly showed African American fans staying away from the parks in record numbers. By 1987, only 6.8 percent of baseball game attendees were black. In majority black cities such as Atlanta and St. Louis, executives discovered that only 4 percent and 3 percent of their respective team's patrons were African American. "It's pretty much a white crowd out here, and ballplayers notice that," said former Braves third baseman Terry Pendleton (Smith).[28]

Explaining the virtual disappearance of African American fans and players from the game today requires one to take into consideration a complex matrix of factors. Clearly, young African Americans are more frequently choosing basketball, football, and even soccer—sports without quite so protracted a history of exclusion—over baseball. In this sense, comments like those by Campanis simply help fuel the belief that baseball is a white man's sport. Of course, the game's infrastructure also works against large-scale African American participation. Says Reggie Brown, a teenager who recently moved to Flushing, "Around here you have to take a couple of buses just to get to a field" (Smith). Additionally, inner-city blacks who do play the sport are largely overlooked by the old-boy network of scouts working for major league teams. Joe Morgan, one of the best second basemen ever to play the game and currently one of the most well-respected baseball color commentators, sees this as a thinly veiled backlash against hip-hop black teenage identity. "A black player's attitude is always the first thing judged by white scouts and it's something they don't understand" (Smith). Finally, simple economics must be understood as a large part of the etiology. Admission costs at major league ball parks have risen dramatically in the past few years, excluding lower-income fans who are disproportionately African American.

INTEGRATION OR APPROPRIATION?

Perhaps the most complicated, yet least talked about, development associated with baseball's renewed interest in downtown is the increasingly common appropriation of African American culture by agents of gentrification. In the new urban playgrounds around stadiums, the cultural cachet of blackness, much more than the actual presence of African Americans, helps remind its visitors that they are, indeed, in the city. Blackness, to a large degree, has become a commodity investing new old baseball venues and their surroundings with the electricity of the urban. Faced with overwhelming evidence that the game is becoming more white, baseball and stadium executives have begun offering up abundant forms of African American culture, in often sanitized form, in order to endow the stadium scene with elements of hipness. Fans dancing to hip-hop music piped in between batters or genially playing the dozens with a "G"-rated team mascot are heirs to Mailer's white Negro. Yet unlike Mailer, who saw white love of blackness as a potentially galvanizing force, many of today's fans who consume and mimic elements of African American culture generally seem to do so without reflecting on the political nature of their actions. Mailer's beliefs about the revolutionary potential of blackness are, to a large degree, a product of his historical moment. Writing after a decade of baseball integration produced hope that sport might lead the way toward a truly integrated culture, during a time when the grass roots of the civil rights movement were taking hold, Mailer could afford to see white admiration of African American masculinity as a potentially revolutionary form of energy. Today, however, even though there is no longer statutorily imposed segregation, the logic of simulacra has allowed for the commodification of this love, in turn both easing the pain of segregation now based largely on economic disparity and providing often troubling forms of compensation.

In Cleveland, in a gentrifying space that has become as homogenously white as it has been at any time since Robinson first crossed back over the color line, Indians management nightly substitutes for the lost thrill of urban racial integration by creating multiple simulacra of blackness.[29] To re-create the energy of the city for its mostly white audience, management injects a large percentage of the stadium's package of extracurricular images and sounds with borrowed elements of chic hip-hop culture. For example, the music excerpted and piped in as each Indian hitter approaches home plate is often rap that has been selected by the players and censored by management to be non-offensive to its audience while still containing the perceptible energy of the genre. Increased security, a more affluent demographic base, and the general friendliness of Clevelanders have eliminated most of the subversive heckling and cat-calling so much a part of the stadium experience at earlier incarnations of urban ball parks. Thus the rhythms and sounds of the city are replicated by music coding similar sentiments of aggressive confrontation, yet in a form now controlled and authorized by the establishment.

This use of rap by corporate America underscores the awesome power and adaptability of capitalism, which shows time and time again an ability to co-opt most forms of avant-garde or oppositional culture. It appropriates the single most recognizable form of contemporary popular art being produced primarily by African Americans, then uses it to squelch the potential for angry speech by drowning out any attempts at heckling. In short, the between-batter music at Jacobs Field both reconstitutes and represses ball-park anarchy in a manner acceptable to management. It safely articulates, and then brings within organizational control, a type of energy that has been meticulously orchestrated out of this new urban space. In the most ironic of shifts, it then also plays a tangible role in crowd control by silencing traditional verbal gestures of discontent.[30]

This replacement is also manifested materially. The Indians' mascot Slider is all "attitude," a vaguely hip-hop character giving form to the vanquished African American presence and helping the audience master it at the same time. Conceived in the offices of a public relations firm employed by management as a gesture toward outraged Native American groups agitating for an end to the infamous Chief Wahoo mascot, Slider is part human, part beast, yet also none of the above.[31] Vaguely aardvark-like, fuchsia with fuzzy yellow whiskers doubling as a mouth, and with a rotund midsection bulging out of his too-tight Indians shirt, Slider struts around the park in enormous, untied high-top tennis shoes. He displays an "urban" attitude by wearing his baseball cap sideways and, occasionally, donning dark sunglasses. He is a grotesque amalgam, a middle-aged "wigger" (the name popularized in the early 1990s by teenagers to describe adolescent white male wannabees) with a gigantic body proportionately similar to that of an out-of-shape forty-year-old former jock who wears the clothing of his rap-obsessed teenage son.

Slider's act at times calls for him to pose as a predatory and polymorphous sensualist, acting out taboo sexual fantasies to the delight of his audience. Dancing to disco, he will often cruise the ball park, groping teenage girls and retirees, young ushers and balding thirty-something men alike. Sometimes he dances the "Freak"—a pelvic thrusting 1970s predecessor of the lambada—his ambiguous genitalia sandwiched in between those of his two escorts, the Slider Girls, dressed provocatively in short wrap skirts or spandex. At other times he sneaks up behind unsuspecting patrons or ushers and consumes them under a "golden shower" of whiskers.[32] His appetite for flesh is insatiable; his actions fly in the face of restraint.

Slider's otherness is largely related to his sprite-like acting out against normative standards of gender and beauty. Part of his shtick requires him to appear completely, decadently comfortable in his grotesque body. When he poses for a picture, for example, he stretches out in mock languor, one arm akimbo, the other brushing his hair out of his eyes, as if posing for a bathing suit pinup. Often, when police and stadium workers are surveying the crowd between innings, he will assume a position behind a male usher or policeman on top of the dugout. He will then rub the man's head or seductively hug him from behind, caressing his chest with his fuzzy arm wrapped around him. With this gesture, of course, he takes the edge off the feelings spectators might have of being overly policed and brings into the level of discourse the obvious existence of ball-park homoeroticism. Balding men, police, and other figures of authority are brought low through campy gestures of the homoerotic. Consistent with this motif, the mascot dances to the most swish music of the 1970s—K.C. and the Sunshine Band, Queen, and Donna Summer. He is at once Tony Manero, Barney, Lady Chablis, and Biggie Smalls.[33] Officially considered an attraction for children, Slider more accurately twists and contorts, gyrates and thrusts in order to express the submerged potential, the repressed erotic energy of the bourgeois spectator class.[34] In an atmosphere of willed family values, he is an open signifier of all the demons of a hyper-normative and racially insular, if not repressed, life-style. His costume and act at once allow him to engender elements of the hip-hop, queer, adulterous, and free-spirited.

As such, he is a creature straight out of the collective unconscious of his audience. As a nonrepresentational, nonhuman character, he is free to transgress most boundaries of decorum and taste. Sure, he might shake his grotesquely large midsection in the direction of a teenage boy or girl, but he *is* only a fuzzy mascot, after all. In fact, the better part of Slider's act revolves around this kind of humor generated by the juxtaposition of children's character and runaway sexuality. His fuzzy costume simultaneously allows for the prurient sexualization of such standard icons of American innocence as the teenage girl and the elderly woman and provides cover as he gives form to elements of the barely submerged homoerotic impulse omnipresent at sporting events among men. In short, he is what cultural critics from Bahktin to Stallybrass and White would consider the rearticulation of suppressed longings of the bourgeoisie through reemergent carnival.[35]

Clearly, it is Slider's hip-hop clothing that instantly alerts a spectator to his liminal status. He is both innocence and experience, presexual and libidinous, cuddly and dangerous, a harmless stuffed animal and a potentially dangerous teenage boy (the second of each pair of dyads coded by his "gangsta" garb).

Slider's presence, in a transitional space increasingly bereft of African American culture actually generated by African Americans, reinforces stereotypes of the young black male as dangerous, overtly sexual, and not to be trusted—in other words, the opposite of innocence. Conversely, the presence of otherwise threatening African American music, dance, clothing, and swagger mediated by a harmless children's character, helps members of the audience contain their fear about the space they have entered when coming downtown for a ball game. In short, at Jacobs Field, hip-hop attitude is assimilable within a type of carnivalesque minstrel show, consumable fun produced for the pleasure of the whole family. Polymorphous and powerful sexuality, once again tied up with images of African American masculinity, both titillates and dissipates within the same act.

THE LIMITS OF COMMEMORATION AND REPLACEMENT

There is a fair degree of dysfunction in a culture that replaces hope for and belief in true integration with simulated forms of racial mixing and with opportunities to culturally cross-dress in order to compensate for anxieties about both race and masculinity. For two decades, baseball has become whiter on every level, yet one of its primary responses has been to generate cultural substitutions. Although the major leagues have taken some real steps toward recultivating an interest among black youth players and fans and worked to reform its hiring practices in the 1990s, its greatest efforts on race have gone into the production of a culture of commemoration and replacement.

In many ways, the Indians' mascot is a less-offensive reenactment of a century-old baseball sideshow with extremely disturbing racial overtones. Slider's historical antecedents, the first mascots in baseball, were African American men paid to make fools of themselves in front of white audiences during late-nineteenth-century games. Some blacks who were hired originally to clean locker rooms and perform menial tasks for the organization, were eventually "adopted" as team "mascots . . . crowd pleasers and good-luck charms" (Levine, *Spalding* 101). They were expected to act as idiot children for the amusement of fans, performing such stock vaudevillian roles as "pickaninnies," "coons," and "nigs."

Perhaps the most famous of Slider's predecessors is Clarence Duval, the mascot of the Cincinnati Reds, who amused the home crowd for more than a decade:

> Because his grin is broad, his legs limbre [sic], and his face as black
> as the ace of spades. . . . Whenever anything goes wrong, it is only
> necessary to rub Clarence's wooly head to save the situation, and call
> on one of his celebrated "double shuffles" to dispel all traces of care,
> even on the gloomiest occasion. (Levine, *Spalding* 101)

In thus praising Duval, the *Cincinnati Enquirer* writer underscores the types of pleasure enjoyed by white audiences in this specific type of minstrel situation. Because he performed *for* them, because "his grin is broad," Duval embodied fantasies of genial blackness, African American masculinity diffused of its most dangerous potential. Like Slider's, his body appeared grotesque to the white audience as he contorted and shook his "limbre" legs. Yet this grotesqueness, a visible manifestation of racist fear of otherness, was thoroughly contained because he performed not only for the audience's amusement but also in their interest. Rubbing his "wooly" head, the patron crossed a taboo threshold by initiating physical contact with a black man and was able to turn Duval's frightening otherness into a talisman that *served* the expansive white fan.

Duval and other African American mascots allowed baseball players and fans to reenact fantasies about a return to the country's pre-Emancipation past, a notion made clear through an examination of his racist treatment during A.G. Spalding's groundbreaking international baseball tour of 1888–89. As part of its act, members of Spalding's American all-star team claimed they had "captured" Duval in Omaha, "recovering" him to "serve" them during the trip. Overseas, these same ballplayers forced the African American man to wear a catcher's mask and gloves while parading him about the Cairo railway station, tethered by a rope, "as if he were some strange animal let loose from a menagerie" (Levine, *Spalding* 101). Though it is unclear what Duval was doing in Omaha when he was "recovered," the players' language almost requires no glossing. Their description of how he joined the traveling group, as well as how they treated him on the trip, references the tragic plight of many escaped slaves and freed blacks prior to Emancipation.

Duval's experience exemplifies how the power dynamic between baseball audiences and their mascots have historically involved some kind of mastery. Smiling and thus appearing to condone his bondage, Duval allowed the white players and fans to revisit slave-based patterns of race relations by that time statutorily forbidden throughout the United States. Today, Slider—a carnival character whose identity is dependent to a large measure on the iconography of young black masculinity—allows for similar fantasies of mastery, albeit in a form much more diffuse and carried out subconsciously.

CLEVELAND'S NEW WELFARE KINGS AND QUEENS

Perhaps this fantasy of mastery resonates in direct proportion to sensations of being overly regulated or controlled on the part of contemporary audiences. Of course, gentrification requires intense crowd control and surveillance in order to allow the new and the old to coexist peacefully. From the elimination of scalpers and panhandlers on the streets, to electronic monitoring devices mounted throughout the stadium, to higher ticket prices ensuring a wealthier audience, the Indians and the city intentionally and unintentionally suppress many of the more edgy elements of the culture being replaced. In doing so, however, management potentially endangers one of the baseball stadium's central appeals: access to forms of antiestablishmentarian pleasure or the rehearsal of behavior outside the normative. It is clear that many of the older fans, those who spent years and even decades in Cleveland Municipal Stadium, bristle at the suppression of this kind of pleasure and its replacement with mascots and music. "Owners are all control freaks," says bleacher drummer John Adams, describing the often overscripted nature of the stadium event. More blunt is fellow fan Mahovlic: "The funniest thing that happened around here was when Slider fell off the wall and broke his leg. Don't get me wrong, the kids love him. But, he's a distraction."

Both Adams and Mahovlic, after all, enjoyed the sanctuary of exile in the bleachers long before Jacobs Field was even an idea. Before them, a century's worth of fans, from misbehaving Victorian men in the bettor's pens to "Dem Bums" in Brooklyn, felt themselves free to speak out publicly against authority, to drum, yell, and in general to perform a range of behaviors unacceptable in most other public places. In other words, pleasure for many consumers of baseball has long been tied up with experiencing freedom, real or imagined, from institutional discipline. In the cozy confines of new retro ball parks, however, sanctioning too much of this kind of behavior would work against management's efforts to attract and reassure a new clientele.

Perhaps unintentionally, in order to provide abundant recompense, management packages and manages the symbols of outsider culture primarily for the new audience it has attracted. The Indians organization uses accents of race to simulate vernacular forms of urban freedom endangered during gentrification when the outside becomes in. They choreograph the return of blackness to a gentrifying urban space in order to help an almost exclusively white audience feel itself outside the tight grip of control that this very gentrification demands. By commemorating and compensating in this way, the architects and choreographers of the modern stadium movement attempt to give patrons a way to solve the problem presented by the catcher in the Rolaids commercial. However, instead of looking in vain for a way to *throw out* the threat of the black male body, today's spectators turn to love and their own form of theft. As white culture reclaims and recolonizes the physical space of downtown, baseball stadiums help a large segment of visitors imagine themselves as trustees to the cultural estate. Simulated forms of blackness available for consumption in new urban parks invest the space with the energy that a spectator might perceive as missing from suburban stadiums while providing convenient cover for a troubling new urban order pushing African Americans further to the margins.

Emphasizing this replacement is a portrait of the new face of welfare in Cleveland. In order to keep the ball club in the city, the local government has spent over $1 billion in tax revenue and/or abatements constructing, maintaining, and policing the new stadium in partnership with Indians ownership. In turn, this form of public largess benefits members of a relatively affluent audience, all of whom can afford $2,000 for season tickets. Meanwhile, residents of the nearby Kinsman neighborhood, which remains the largest African American section of town, struggle along, coping with cuts to social programs and watching their local schools continue to deteriorate. If indeed the fantasy of the catcher in the Henderson commercial is a desire to not only vanquish his African American counterpart but to *become* him, it seems clear that urban stadiums are enabling that fantasy in the most ironic of ways. Cleveland's new welfare kings and queens do not occupy the increasingly depressed slums of the inner city; instead, they sit in the box seats, luxury suites, and owner's boxes at Jacobs Field.[36]

CHAPTER SIX

RETRO PARKS IN THE CITY OF THE INSTANT

> This is what Technology does. It peels back the shadows
> and redeems the dazed and rambling past. It makes reality
> come true.
>
> —Marvin Lundy in Don DeLillo's *Underworld*

The provision of secondary diversions for spectators is a defining feature of new baseball parks constructed since Camden Yards. Most offer a range of standard items: food courts, speed-pitch machines, souvenir shops, and so on. Typically, each one also adds its own signature touch. In Arizona, for example, fans can enjoy the game while lounging in and around a swimming pool just beyond the outfield fence. In Texas, spectators can visit the Rangers Hall of Fame, and in Cleveland, visitors can lay down twenty dollars for the pleasure of recording an inning of play-by-play in the FanCast booth.

These activities, once considered secondary to the game itself, now play a primary role for professional baseball clubs. As Indians executive Bob Dibiasio puts it, "Gone are the days when you can give a guy a beer, a dog and a ball game and think it was enough." By this he implies that, in order to increase profits, the Indians must cultivate an expanded demographic and give them plenty to do. The die-hard fan, satisfied with simple culinary pleasures and a total immersion in the game, alone fails to satisfy the bottom line. There is not enough of this kind of spectator left (or at least not enough who can regularly afford to attend) to sell out the stadium. Additionally, this fan's particular mode of enjoying the ball park—an all-out identification with a team, a complete focus on the game itself— fails to generate sufficient secondary revenue.

After all, as most contemporary sports economists point out, baseball parks, rather than enlarging the overall pot of money spent on leisure in a community, simply compete with other local entertainment venues for a relatively fixed amount.[1] Dibiasio and his colleagues find themselves nightly in competition with managers of movie houses, video arcades, food courts, and water parks for the time and dollars of families and individuals choosing from a wide range of diversions. In short, their job is dependent in part on the club's ability to successfully expand the consumable activities at the park beyond the primary experience of the game. As the focus of ball-park entertainment has thus largely shifted away from absolute absorption in the game, the secondary diversions have taken on an increased cultural, as well as economic, role. These activities provide pleasure for an audience that has become, to a certain extent, collectors of the experience. Although in their own way Dibiasio's die-hard fans also collect the experience, absorbing memories of the game for their own recollection or for story-telling later, the new fans more than ever before seek to bring home authenticating objects of their trip to the stadium.[2]

This will to collect functions as one of the motivating principles behind much of the activity throughout Jacobs Field. In just about every section of the park, the Indians offer spectators the chance to purchase objects validating their experience by giving evidence of their attendance for posterity. The FanCast booth is most striking in this regard. Sitting in an authentic reproduction of a broadcast booth, the customer is able to imagine him or herself an indispensable part of the action. After all, in an age of mass media replication, the broadcast event (on television and on the radio) has become the primary means by which most fans are able to experience the game. Thus the fantasy of being an announcer, translating the game for a mass audience and becoming an active player in the production, holds undeniable appeal.

This dynamic, this ability to take part and influence the event rather than just to observe it, has always been a key component of baseball spectatorship. Since the era of the first enclosed stadium, side activities such as betting on outcomes during games have been commonplace in baseball parks. Today, however, during a time when the American president is able to announce without irony that, in response to dangers from terrorist attacks, citizens' primary patriotic duty is simply to consume more, the ability to play, or act, has perhaps taken on heretofore unmatched significance.[3] Producing something at an event that, on the surface, divides people into active players and passive spectators helps fans counter the enervating sense that they, valued by many primarily as consumers, are without meaningful influence. At the same time, the particular object they produce in the FanCast booth itself has undeniable cachet. Seamlessly weaving themselves in with the game in a techno-commemorative item, fans are able to take home irrefutable and long-lasting evidence of primary contact with the event. Pleasure in this regard is related to the timeless thrill privileged fans experience at transcendent but unexpected sporting moments. Like a lucky New York Mets fan who was at Shea Stadium in 1986 when the home team miraculously rallied to win game six of the World Series, the temporary broadcaster is able to claim "I was there when" and then back it up with technological evidence.[4] As such, the fan pays for the ability to make the ordinary extraordinary every time. Each ordinary inning of a midseason Indians game can be rendered extraordinary for a mere twenty dollars.

Of course, this tape of the game is just one of countless commemorative objects fans can purchase at Jacobs Field. At the team store, the hot sellers in the late 1990s were Jackie Robinson replica jerseys and "X" gear. Advertising a patron's attendance at the game as well as signifying a connection with iconic African American culture, many fans must have bought these items at least in part to project an identity based on access and hipness.[5] Just like the broadcast tape, these kinds of markers of the experience rely on the ability to go back to the future, connecting mementos from an earlier era with consumable authenticity. Like any form of commemorative historical item, these jerseys, hats, and tapes enact a logic of reduction. The gift shop goods reduce the complexities of race relations into a commodity intended to express solidarity with, or at least appreciation of, African American style. Similarly, the tape links consumers with the great voices of baseball's history—Russ Hodges, Harry Caray, and Vin Scully among others—whose folksy radio and television broadcasts brought the game to life for millions of listeners in the twentieth century. All of these items connect contemporary spectators to nostalgic sensations of a simplified, innocent, and idealized past, when baseball truly seemed to be the national pastime. They unite them with commodified notions of a less complex time, a time before JFK was assassinated and Bill Clinton was impeached for leaving a stain on an intern's blue dress, a time before terrorists knocked down the World Trade Center.

These objects also play a part in the attempt by fans to *keep it real,* an exceedingly slippery proposition in a ball park with more than six hundred television screens. In food court stalls and in luxury boxes, on scoreboards and along corridors, the game is reproduced televisually (and instantly) throughout the park. In the postmodern world, of course, television watching has become, in a sense, more real than the actual event. Instant replay accustoms the audience to witnessing the game from multiple perspectives. Seeing it only once, live and from a distance, therefore, can strike audience members as somehow unreal or dreamlike. So, ironically, the mediating technology of television is required to make the live event seem real to the spectator.[6] Thus in addition to its tendency to reduce meanings, the FanCast tape seeks to allow fans the ability to expand their connection to the event through virtual reality. In a world of simulacra, lived reality often seems less real, or at least less desirable, than technological enhancements of it.

In this sense, the broadcast tape souvenir has a synecdochical relationship to retro stadiums and their surroundings. The fantasy behind the back-to-the-future movement in stadium construction and the attendant city reorganization of which it is a central component is reliant on the same large-scale reduction and expansion of the referent. The logic of souvenirs is writ large on a space looking to produce for recreational tourists the ability to experience what is fantasized as a simpler, purer past. Meanwhile, stadium management employs the most up-to-date technology in order to keep the experience real for an audience whose impressions of reality are increasingly informed by televisual replications of the world. Spaces like Jacobs Field attempt to provide large-scale reconstructions of the "dazed and rambling past" for pleasant consumption. At the same time, they promise patrons entry into a post-urban space, a televisual city reproduced. So while retro stadiums are extremely successful in fulfilling a desire for multiple contemporary forms of pleasure, part of the experience at these parks is, for many fans, potentially tied up with loss—the temporal distance between original and replication.

Don DeLillo's 1997 epic novel *Underworld*, written during the heyday of retro ball-park construction, functions as an insightful meditation on the distance between original and replication in the world of both the baseball stadium and the new American city. In a savvy way, it describes the psycho-cultural forces informing the desire for retro authenticity at new urban ball parks. A close reading of it, therefore, functions as a jumping-off point for an examination of longing and loss at retro stadiums.

UNDERWORLD AND SIMULATION

The first section of *Underworld* takes the reader back to the Polo Grounds, the longtime home of the New York Giants, on its most famous day, October 3, 1951. This was the afternoon, of course, when Bobby Thomson, with a dramatic ninth-inning home run, struck the final blow erasing the Brooklyn Dodgers' three-run lead, inspiring Giants broadcaster Ross Hodges to issue perhaps the most famous call in broadcast sports history: "The Giants win the pennant! The Giants win the pennant!"

In classic DeLillo fashion, the writer allows readers to experience the moment *Rashomon* style, weaving in pages of fictional detail during the few moments in time that it takes Thomson to circle the bases and Hodges to make the call.[7] Readers see young Cotter Martin, a fourteen-year-old African American boy watching the ball travel in his direction in the outfield bleachers. They see J. Edgar Hoover in the VIP's box behind first base studying a *Life* magazine shot of the Brueghel painting *The Triumph of Death,* which has come floating down with other debris from the second deck. They see Jackie Gleason vomiting remnants of beer and hot dogs on Frank Sinatra's shoes in the same box. Throughout DeLillo's narration, all this detail is framed by the familiar raspy shouting of Hodges's "I do not believe it," a call which, as the narrator points out, has been immortalized because one man in Brooklyn happened to be taping the broadcast that day. In short, readers see the complexity of DeLillo's "historical metafiction," history as a combination of conjecture, documented fact, random chance, and, most important, the fantasy of the writer himself all working backward to supplement the indelible media image.[8] Like footage of the Kennedy assassination captured on the Zapruder film, which became the starting point for DeLillo's metafictional *Libra,* the Hodges call of the Thomson home run is ground zero for the writer's reconstruction of cold war America.

Of course, the fictional Hoover's presence at the game gives DeLillo space to comment throughout the novel on the curious and sometimes absurd way that historical events endure and become commodified. On the same day Thomson hit his "shot heard 'round the world," the Soviet Union exploded an atomic bomb inside its own borders, confirming its nuclear capabilities and heightening American postwar anxiety about threats to its sovereignty. The Russian blast was an opening salvo in the arms race that escalated into the cold war. On the front page of the next day's *New York Times,* the Thomson home run and the atomic blast ran side by side, partners in this highly charged historical moment. Yet the event in the Soviet Union has been virtually lost to the memory of a culture that has immortalized that afternoon's scene in the Polo Grounds.

This has happened, at least to a degree, because of the power of television. The game was broadcast live, allowing hundreds of thousands of people to become eternally caught in the aura of the moment. Television produced a kind of "city of the instant," linking people on rooftops, in pool halls, and in living rooms huddled around their sets, together yet apart, witnessing *history* as it unfolded.[9] Because footage of the home run then became iconic, highly representative of its period in American history through its use as an endless film loop during sportscasts and advertising spots promoting baseball on television, the charge of the experience of being there has become magnified in retrospect. The Soviet blast, meanwhile, had no such cachet. Its furtive nature allowed for no live broadcast and no visuals for posterity; in fact, most people were unaware of it until they picked up the paper the next morning.

THE AUTHENTICATING OBJECT

The more immediately recognizable of these dual historical events links two of DeLillo's main characters in a fascinating search for the moment's authenticating object: Thomson's home-run ball. Both Nick Shay and Marvin Lundy seek reassurance about their own end through the illusory search for a visible continuum with the past. Both, however, come to understand the quest as vexed, their acquisitive impulses ultimately laying bare what Jean Baudrillard calls the "precession of simulacra," a search for truth leading to the conclusion that there may be no truth at all.[10]

DeLillo's description of how history is replaced by an event commodified through technology speaks volumes about what Baudrillard calls the "terroristic hyperrealism of our world, a world where a 'real' event occurs in a vacuum, stripped of its context and visible only from afar, televisually" (*Transparency* 79–80). To Baudrillard, experience in contemporary America has only a fleeting relation to reality. It is largely a manifestation of its own pure simulacrum, producing a semiotic system of reality and perception based on the techno-capitalist logic of exchange. Within this system, the postmodern citizen can only traffic in commodified representations of the real. While of course Baudrillard's primary rhetorical mode is the polemic, exaggerating (sometimes smugly) the extent to which Americans are incapable of lifting the veil, he does contribute significantly to discussions about how meanings are generated and absorbed. The encroaching primacy of mediating technology has problematized attempts to engage in authentic experiences. At the same time, this primacy has largely created the conditions under which authenticity, or unmediated experience, has become such a cherished commodity.

DeLillo pitches both of his main characters into this world of the "hyperreal" by linking them in a search for a physical object that promises to keep alive the purity of the moment of Hodges's call. As such, the writer provides his own myth of origins, invoking a reverse big-bang theory pointing backward toward Thomson's original blast as representative of the inception of the primacy of simulacrum. For DeLillo's characters, the confluence of history, memory, and television during that one scintillating moment radically transformed the nature of how they were able to experience America in subsequent years. Because the event has been so thoroughly reified for them through more than four decades of film loops, it has become virtually indistinguishable from their experience of the game. In turn, rather than simply taking its place in the dust heap of past experience for them, the moment seems to promise abundant recompense, a more deeply felt connection with the past.

Of course, the past with which they look to connect is itself highly reified. The Thomson shot and the Hodges call have typically been employed in advertisements for either upcoming televised baseball games or commemorative items like encyclopedic histories of the twentieth century. Therefore, the grainy black-and-white image of jubilant Thomson hopping around the bases accompanied by the incredulous, raspy shouting of Hodges, have become important signifiers of the *authentic* nature of the products they are being used to sell. The standard usage of this footage has made the moment itself a recognizable collectors item, a metonymic stand in for an entire era, assimilable as black and white, heroic and strangely distant from the present. Yet its power as a commemorative item is found primarily in its promise that the moment might also have extreme relevance to the present. Every baseball game, its use as advertisement suggests, could potentially become historical, or worthy of continual filmic replication, a symbol of the current episteme for future consumption.

This way of using the footage to advertise televised baseball games suggests to viewers that they would be wise not to miss whatever game of the week is coming up. In order to assure his or her place in history (through the ability to claim "I was there" or, more precisely, "I was watching on television"), the prospective spectator must be certain not to miss the game. This dynamic thus places contemporary fans in the subject position of the collector. Like art, beer can, or stamp collectors, who regularly purchase objects without significant aura or value hoping that, over time, the brilliant randomness of history will augment the worth of these items, many fans long to witness sporting events that, for whatever reason, may become recognizable as special as their memory descends through time.

The use of historical footage to offer instant history is suggestive of one of the primary appeals of the retro stadium movement. The parks are themselves reifications of past eras, attempts to replicate the aura of the Thomson and Hodges Polo Grounds without having to wait for time to pass, for history to do its thing. On a large scale, they attempt to freeze the moment, to offer a tableau vivant of a time considered more gritty and real than the present. Yet of course the fantasy behind this attempt is ultimately somewhat irrational. Spectacular or memorable moments are frustratingly unpredictable and often only recognizable as exceptional over time; they tend to accumulate aura slowly, unreliably. To a certain extent, then, retro parks set up fans, or at least those fans eager to be part of a historically notable event, for a degree of disappointment. Not every game lives on as a classic, and young parks, despite being dressed up to look old, have not been around long enough to offer up years of history.[11]

THE LIMITS OF ACQUISITION

At the beginning of DeLillo's novel, Nick, mired in a midlife crisis, embarks on a quest stimulated by the same (perhaps fundamentally irrational) fantasy behind the old-time theming of retro parks. He begins his attempt to stockpile the past in plain view by telephoning Marvin to inquire about the Thomson home-run ball. Answering the phone, the retired dry cleaner, who himself had spent most of the last stages of his life tracing and authenticating the object's lineage, reacts with presumptuousness and skepticism:

> You're a loyal fan retired in Arizona with a heart valve they implanted
> with dacron cuffs and you developed a sweetness for the old days.
> You spent your career in mergers and what, acquisitions. Made
> millions but you're still dissatisfied. You want one last acquisition
> that's personal from the heart. (190)

During his own journey, Marvin has come to realize the folly in acquisition-as-soul-salve. A wealthy but admittedly dissatisfied retiree himself when he began this search, he too had fantasized about the ability of the collectible to rekindle the intense feeling (in this case, a kind of Keatsian "negative capability") he experienced as a Dodger fan, crushed when Thomson's ball cleared the fence.[12] This passage reveals his generic expectations of Nick. He assumes that DeLillo's protagonist is, like most collectors he has met, a hardened man who has submerged his spiritual and emotional life into thoughts of daily commerce until a late-in-life awareness of mortality forces him to conduct a double-time search for meaning. In fact, as Marvin recounts, he has already fielded dozens of such calls from "men with grainy voices . . . polymer packed in their gums . . . with quadruple bypass," men on their last legs searching for coherent meaning before it is too late. If, indeed, Nick is searching for cheap grace, Marvin lets him know emphatically that he has called the wrong number.

Yet Nick's response strikes Marvin as refreshing. "I'm not a fan anymore. . . . I'm not retired. And I haven't made millions," Nick tells him. "And I don't know exactly why I want to buy the ball." Marvin delights in the fact that Nick is not "palpitating in his mind for the old Giants or the old New York" (191). Wizened as he is by his own irrational search, the old man is content to let the city of the Polo Grounds, Cotter Martin, and the thousands of other details of the famous day rest in peace, part of an unrecoverable past. He recognizes that, just as part of his own innocence took flight the moment that Ralph Branca's fastball left Thomson's bat, and just as the Dodgers and the Giants had pulled up stakes six years after the blast for greener pastures in California, the spirit of old New York had somehow exploded outward as well: shards and fragments, former New Yorkers and their offspring, dispersed chaotically to what he considers late-twentieth-century mirages like Phoenix and Los Angeles.

It is clear, then, that Nick's evolving sanguine nature and Marvin's own connection to a disappearing old New York prompt the retired dry cleaner to sell the ball to his protégé. The old man has had plenty of offers, but now he finally has found the opportunity to pass the ball on to someone working toward a similar existential state, someone who will someday share his own "exact status" (191). Marvin has come to learn that "chasing down exhausted objects" was not ultimately about recovery, but about loss itself (191). Recovery of memorabilia brought little that was both tangible and worthwhile back to him. Instead, at its best, the quest merely placed him in the subject position of the historian, connecting the dots of history in order to produce a narrative, both related to and oddly independent of fact. In this sense, it sometimes allowed him to feel something, anything, at a time when much of his experience was numbing. Yet at its worst, the quest placed him, as owner of the object, in the position of an antiquarian, trying to live off the aura of "exhausted objects."[13] In this way, fulfillment of the quest could itself be anesthetizing insofar as it often reminded him of all the feelings of his past to which he no longer had access and of precious tactile sensations, like "the touch of his [late wife] Eleanor," which were fading from his memory (192).

The distinction between "antiquarian" and "historian" is a crucial one. Susan Stewart, in her book about memorabilia, *On Longing,* argues that "the social dis-ease of nostalgia," or the "antiquarian's" search for authenticating objects, is representative of the misguided action of the modern subject acculturated to an exchange economy. She argues that the attraction of the souvenir is that it promises, falsely, connection to a pre-commodified self, substituting a "context of perpetual consumption for its context of origin" (135). By this she implies that the object fallaciously advertises access to the "materiality" of an event which exists now only in narrative. In short, the souvenir is by definition always incomplete. Its operating principle is a metonymic provision of a mere sample of the original scene. In Nick's case, the ball is metonymic to the whole set of lost referents—the rooftop on which he listened to Giants' games, the thoughts of his clandestine romance with Klara Sax—which were part of the original experience. His investment in it is thus a frustrating, partial gesture toward recovery of all of the details of the original experience which DeLillo as novelist attempts to (re)create in his metafictional world. DeLillo, in this sense the "historian," is in the privileged position of being able to supplement the "impoverished and partial" souvenir with narrative, both "attaching onto" the ball's origins and creating its own independent myth of those origins (Stewart 135).

Seeing Nick's most futile sentimentality thus as the impossible longing of an antiquarian begins to explain his existential dilemma throughout the novel. As he sits alone in his Phoenix study fumbling with his trophy ball, he provides thoughts gesturing directly toward the crisis of the modern consumer Stewart identifies. "I long for the days of disorder," he says. "I want them back, the days when I was alive on the earth, rippling in the quick of my skin, heedless and real. I was dumb-muscled and angry and real" (810). The ball, merely a trace of the authentic experience, tortures middle-aged Nick with all that it is not. It is not a fountain of youth, able to bring back the libidinous desire of his teenage years; it is not a time machine, recreating the disordered streets of pre-suburban-flight Brooklyn; and, most important, it is not an object that can exist independent of narrative, collapsing the temporal space between signifier and signified. Despite its abundant promise, it ultimately fails to ease the pain of the contemporary consumer longing for a relationship to the world independent of exchange value.

Nick's contrast with the more resigned Marvin is instructive. Marvin, evolved as he has into a "narrator" rather than an "antiquarian," is at least able to see this form of consumption as a way to forget (or at least to invent) rather than a way to remember. In other words, Marvin's collection, its structure of organization and exegesis, is about Marvin himself. By assembling this body of collectibles—a miniaturized but proportionally accurate Polo Grounds scoreboard, an assemblage of gloves, bats, shirts, and so on—in his basement, Marvin produces a malleable semiotic system allowing him to recreate the world in his own image. Over time, with the help of Eleanor, he has come to realize that the only reason for collecting is to tell *his* story. By thus becoming the narrator, Marvin has been able to make every moment a point of origin, thrusting forward, whereas Nick gets stuck trying to diminish the temporal space separating him from the moment of lost innocence.

Marvin is thus similar to the Jacobs Field fan who spends an inning in the FanCast booth while Nick (prior to becoming jaded) is the die-hard, spending the same inning trying to imagine himself back in the "dazed and rambling past" of the Polo Grounds. In other words, the comparative sanguineness of Marvin and angst of the younger Nick provide clues to two of the diametrically opposed ways to seek pleasure at retro parks. This contrast suggests that patrons who bring a postmodern, or at least a detached, Generation X perspective to their experience will be more easily satisfied. Nostalgic practice, Marvin suggests, is not about recovery, not about authenticity, but about creation. This perspective trivializes the difference between revered subjects (African American baseball history) and kitsch objects (Jackie Robinson jerseys) and privileges the "been there, done that" ethos of tourism and collection.[14]

In truth, at Jacobs Field, many fans seem to either reject summarily or treat ironically the fundamental, "antiquarian" fantasy involved in the park's new old theme. Longtime supporters like bleacher drummer John Adams invariably see the theming of retro authenticity as phony: "The truth is, the guys running the show don't really know about Cleveland baseball," says Adams. "You gotta leave the real fan alone to do his thing." By this, Adams suggests that all the modern and commemorative accouterments of the new stadium, from the FanCast booth, to the nostalgic paintings of old ball parks, to the canned music between innings, serve as unwanted distractions, taking away from the pleasure of watching a ball game. He scoffs at the Indians' attempt to package "controlled spontaneity and authenticity" and says that he and his friends outright ignore most elements of old-time theming, dismissing them as mere marketing devices aimed at attracting a "different crowd." At the other extreme, many new fans, members of the "different crowd" that Adams and others say started showing up when the Indians moved to the Jake, seem to delight in consuming much of what is presented as authentic, albeit in an often colorful and tongue-in-cheek manner. For example, a group of flip teenagers with multicolored Mohawk haircuts was recently seen at the park sporting throwback Indian jerseys. This tableau, a juxtaposition of Mohawks and retro jerseys, suggests a clash of two competing cultures, the conservative, reverent culture of commemoration, idealizing how things were perceived to be, versus an in-your-face, contemporary reminder of how much things are subject to change. These young patrons seem to have brought a distinctly camp sensibility to the park, sending up its pretensions to retro authenticity precisely as they consumed the most earnest souvenirs paying homage to the old.

On the other hand, those visitors to the park who, like the young Nick, *want* to believe, those who admire the old city spaces that retro stadiums attempt to replicate, often find the experience alienating or at least cause for ambivalence.

"I'm jaded. I don't think they did the Gateway right," says John Zajc, the SABR executive director who works nearby. Although he likes the park tremendously, praising its site lines and amenities, he feels the Gateway, through the fault of no one in particular, is a manifestation of a "false promise" to bring genuine urban vitality to the area. "It [the Gateway] is about as good as it could be given the way Greater Clevelanders have been conditioned to think about parking," he says. "Suburbanites are used to going to a mall where they can park easily and for free." Zajc blames the combination of simple physics and the need for the ball club to accommodate the desire to enjoy suburban ease and comfort for the area's shortcomings. "The footprint is too large so the urban density can't be there," he says, noting that providing more comfortable seats and unobstructed views required the Indians to build a stadium with an extremely broad profile and that satisfying the need for quick and easy access for suburbanites ensured that the stadium would be surrounded by parking decks and thus cut off from the surrounding community.

Although Zajc understands that "beauty is in the eye of the beholder," that scores of fans who visit the area love its transformation and buy into the notion of Jacobs Field as an old-time baseball park, he feels that the city has perhaps lost a unique opportunity to create a more vibrant urban space by so thoroughly emphasizing large-scale recreation downtown. The Browns Stadium in particular "wasted valuable waterfront real estate," says Zajc, who as a passionate baseball fan points reverentially toward one of Jacobs Field's models, Wrigley Field in Chicago, as an example of a successful (albeit unintentional) integration of a ball park into the city: "Wrigley is in an actual neighborhood. It's so dense. Walking toward the park, everything feels so alive and real." Zajc understands, as does Nick, that many of the fundamental elements of an old city—density, diversity, clutter, and, at times, discomfort and danger—are incongruous with the desires of contemporary recreational tourists. One of the things that made the models for new retro stadium feel so authentic was their cozy, yet often tense relationship to the city around them. Zajc recognizes that this relationship cannot be commodified or encapsulated in either a souvenir or an experience that attempts to signify like one. Although he appreciates the fact that new restaurants, stadiums, and nightclubs in the area have brought with them increased foot traffic and a particular kind of liveliness, Zajc, like the fictional Nick, has come to see a certain illogicality in the endeavor of trying to "recreate the days of disorder" for modern consumption.

DISNEYLAND AND AMERICA

By forcing himself to compare his present status (middle-aged, middle-class, and a resident of hyperreal Phoenix) to that of his former self (young, working class, and a resident of Brooklyn), DeLillo's Nick loses faith in his own ability to live anything other than a simulation. "I know the ghosts are walking the halls," he says. "But not these halls and not this house. They're all back there in those rail-road rooms at the narrow end of the night and I stand helpless in this desert place looking at books" (810). His particular locution, "desert *place*," not a desert but like a desert, of course underscores the notion of Phoenix as a real-world Disneyland, a replacement of the desert with an air-conditioned, green-lawn simulacrum. His utter hopelessness, however, gestures toward something even more troubling to him: the notion that Disneyland might be all there is.

In *Simulacra and Simulation,* Baudrillard argues that the phenomenon of Disney originates from a need for what he calls "deterrence," or the presentation of a simulated world that "rejuvenates the fiction of the real in the opposite camp" (13). In other words, Disneyland and the other theme parks springing up in the second half of the twentieth century exist in order to advertise themselves as unreal and thus reaffirm belief that the cities they tend to appear in are real. However, to the French theorist, the actual Los Angeles, the very prototype for the sprawling late-century American city and the original home of Disney, provides merely a network of "incessant, unreal circulation." Like Nick Shay's Phoenix, the great southern California metropolis is, to Baudrillard, a city of "incredible pro-portions but without space, without dimension" (13). In this simulated world,

> people no longer look at each other, but there are institutes for that. They no longer touch each other, but there is contactotherapy. They no longer walk, but they go jogging, etc. . . . One reinvents penury, asceti-cism, vanished savage naturalness: natural food, health food, yoga. (14)

Of course, Baudrillard's perspective is one of ironic detachment. Himself blessed (or perhaps cursed) with the perspective of a tourist, he is able to judge Los Angeles from a distance, analyzing it as an intellectual idea rather than as a fact of his own being. Unlike a resident of the Venice district, who relies on "contac-totherapy" for his or her daily wellness, or a jogger from Compton whose "ascet-icism" is very real, Baudrillard's use of Los Angeles remains in the realm of metaphor. Nonetheless, it is a powerful metaphor, suggestive of what many people sense is missing from contemporary public spaces created in order to package authenticity for consumption.

Nick's Phoenix (like Baudrillard's Los Angeles and Zajc's downtown Cleve-land) might best be described as representative of a uniquely late-twentieth-century American paradigm, an aesthetic producing edge cities and downtown historical reproductions. Replacing elements of the vanquished land-scape and culture with consumable and commemorative forms, architects of edge cities and downtown revitalization projects attempt to synthesize the best of urban and rural living in a quasi-frontier setting.[15] In this sense, the edge city and restoration aesthetic is a utopian one, promising comfort, ease and (that great American ideal) private property, with connection to multicultural Amer-ican society and a heroic urban past.

A SKYWALK BETWEEN CLEVELAND'S GUND ARENA AND ITS ADJACENT PARKING GARAGE LIMITS BASKETBALL FANS' EXPOSURE TO PUBLIC SPACE.

Yet the realization of these kinds of commemorative city spaces also provides its fair share of dystopic qualities. Physically and economically, edge cities and historic restorations often create the conditions under which contemporary forms of social apartheid can develop. Many historians have lamented the social injustice wrought by the creation of these new urban spaces. Herbert Muschamp describes the emergent American city as a fortress, providing a strong security apparatus enabling visitors a chance to experience ersatz public space without fear of too much contact with the urban underclass. Similarly, Trevor Boddy decries the manifold ways that certain isolating design elements of edge cities have made their way downtown in recent projects of urban revitalization. According to Boddy, these design features—elaborate systems of pedestrian bridges and tunnels, glass walkways and isolated midways—proscribe a segregated physical space where poor people are often stuck on the open streets while middle-class and wealthy visitors travel safely above.[16] Sitting under just such a pedestrian bridge con necting a parking deck to the Gund Arena, Fred Brown, who has worked the Gateway's streets for seven years, panhandling and awaiting seemingly always-elusive job opportunities, is quick to agree with both Muschamp's and Boddy's fears about renewing city spaces. When asked what he thought about the transformation of the Gateway, he replies, "Ain't nothin' changed except there ain't no more black people. It's the white folks from the suburbs come down for baseball."

These social ills notwithstanding, the primary focus of DeLillo's criticism is the enervating experience of the new city for contemporary consumers themselves. In this sense, perhaps it is Sharon Zukin who best describes Nick's trauma when reflecting on his life in Phoenix as well as Zajc's sense of missed opportunity when discussing the Gateway. In *The Culture of Cities,* Zukin not only argues that the displacement of locals in an effort to (re)create privatized "historic" city cores is wrong but also that the act itself deprives these spaces of many of the very qualities making them desirable in the first place. Excessive comfort, regularization, and privatization often has the effect of rendering these new urban spaces sterile, devoid of the facts of city life—such as diversity and unpredictability—informing their original appeal.

Yet even though the Gateway is not exactly his idea of a satisfying urban space, Zajc understands its attraction. He describes a recent experience with a friend from out of town who, when touring the Gateway for the first time, kept remarking to him, "This is so great." His friend loved the new restaurant culture downtown and raved about the fact that the area was so clean and safe. Perhaps then, in coining the term "riskless risk," Russell Nye describes both the allure of the Gateway for this kind of visitor as well as Zajc's own ambivalence about it. In the seventh out of his "Eight Ways of Looking at an Amusement Park," Nye argues that one of the primary attractions of amusement parks, and by extension new urban spaces, is that they "provide a sense of imminent danger and the likelihood of disaster without the culmination of either" (71). Although the critic sees "riskless risk" (within the context of pleasure at amusement parks) to be a form of conspicuous joy "even if the risk is a sham," and although thousands of new visitors to the Gateway like Zajc's friend similarly delight in the combination of safety and energy, many greet recognition of the sham with mixed feelings (Zajc), anger (Brown), or outright depression (Nick).[17]

Ultimately unsatisfied with mere simulations of danger, Nick recoils at the lack of tactility and immediacy offered to him by the world of his riskless "desert place." As an adult, he has grown weary of the need for constant "reinvention" of experience defining his life in the suburbs. He recalls driving through the desert in search of former lover Klara and facing a sudden crisis as he came to notice the sterility of his experience inside his Lexus, "a car assembled in a work area that's completely free of human presence" (63). Insulated from nature in the luxury car, he suffered from a panic attack as he began to doubt his ability to reduce the buffers separating himself from all that he observed. He concludes that his life in suburban Phoenix is akin to being in "the Witness Protection Program," cut off from every past experience or connection that defines and locates one in life (66).

Clearly, Nick Shay's dilemma is more than just a garden-variety midlife crisis. It represents one of DeLillo's most forceful explorations yet of the relationship between the postmodern crisis of the gaze and emergent forms of American public space. If indeed the trophy baseball is, to Nick, "all about losing," what he has lost is belief in the physical space around him to make him feel real, and this is the hardest thing for him to accept. Nick's baseball and all its stored-up images— of Thomson circling the bases and of the slugger and Ralph Branca, the man who pitched the ball, appearing together in photographs with a succession of presidents—cannot give him a reflection of the reality of the moment. No matter how badly he wants back the "days of disarray" and the "real streets" of Brooklyn, the best Nick will be able to find is a simulation. His world is Disney. Yet he is a hero in DeLillo's novel for hungering for something more.

THE THING THAT HAPPENS IN THE SUN

Within DeLillo's fictional universe, the procession of simulacra that drives Nick to the brink utterly cannibalizes historical events. In *Libra,* the writer focuses on the legacy of the 6.9 seconds of film shot by Zapruder. The endless film loop and all the supplemental narratives—of TV news reporters, government officials, presidential historians, and conspiracy theorists—spin off from the event, constituting a hyperreal constellation of truth which is, in reality, largely just symbolic exchange of rhetoric and camera angles. In *Underworld,* DeLillo complicates matters further by making his fictional Hodges a conscious participant in a discussion about the implications of this kind of cannibalization.

Early in the broadcast, when the broadcaster's stat man tells him he looks "pensive," Hodges takes time to reflect on his odd mood (25). At first, he simply attributes his disquietude to the fact that, on this day of days, when the two local teams are culminating the most exciting pennant chase in baseball history, twenty thousand tickets remain unsold. At the outset, he is shocked that so many people would pass up the opportunity to be there. Yet as the game goes on, he seems to begin to understand why. "It's funny, you know . . . but I think it was Charlotte put the look on my face," he tells his colleague, referring to the job he once had in North Carolina doing re-creations of baseball games for radio broadcasts (25). During these re-creations (not coincidentally, a job held by a young Ronald Reagan, who perfected the art of presidency as telegenic simulacrum), he would take facts clacking in over the wires and invent all of the other color. He would make up the game's many details—from a young, carrot-topped boy in the grandstands catching a foul ball to a burly first baseman adjusting his grip before stepping into the batter's box. During DeLillo's fictional account of the Dodgers-Giants broadcast, Hodges comes to remember that in Charlotte he had dreamt of nothing else but broadcasting "real baseball from a booth in the Polo Grounds in New York" (25). But now, invested as he is with DeLillo's perspective of the world as simulacrum, the fictionalized version of the broadcaster begins to realize that the baseball game itself, the real referent, or, as he says, "the thing that happens in the sun," disappears into the very broadcast of it. It is natural that the stadium was half full, DeLillo seems to be saying through Hodges. The game—in this case not the actual event but "the game," postreferent, after Hodges's famous broadcast invested it with its particular aura—did not really happen until it ended. Being there thus meant listening to the call on the radio or on television as much or more than it meant being in the stadium.

To stress this point, DeLillo has Hodges engage in a minidrama about the fitness of his voice. "I hope I don't close down. My larynx feels like it is in a vice," he says between innings six and seven (26). Most readers recognize immediately that this drama is disingenuous. The balance of DeLillo's audience knows that having Hodges stop broadcasting is not really an option. Most of them are already familiar with the game's ending before even beginning the novel. From DeLillo's first line—"He speaks in your voice, American"—the inevitable telos becomes Hodges screaming of "The Giants win the Pennant!" Because this moment has become so thoroughly commodified, Hodges's wild, jubilant call endures tenaciously in American imaginary reconstruction of the 1950s. To write this out of his script, therefore, would force DeLillo to alienate the reader considerably, to change the course of history as it has descended in an era of hyperreality. The best he can do, he seems to be suggesting, is to invent hundreds of fictional details to fill in around the basic fact of Hodges's broadcast. In this sense, DeLillo himself is a stand-in for the young sportscaster in his Charlotte studio. The author takes historical facts and infuses them with color and meaning, interweaving Hodges's description of the game with a fantastical account of J. Edgar Hoover, Toots Shor, Frank Sinatra, and Jackie Gleason sharing a box behind the first-base dugout.

Yet despite willingly taking part in this kind of historical (re)creation, DeLillo uses Nick's unease to suggest perhaps his own discomfort at the atomizing tendency of broadcasting. He suggests that the primacy of the mediated event collapses lived urban space into broadcast time reducing the relevance of the stadium spectator toward a vanishing point. In *Pure War,* urban theorists Paul Virilio and Sylvere Lotringer discuss the disturbing nature of the "disappearing" live fan, arguing that, in an era of televised sports, the spectator is merely a body helping fill up the stadium so that it won't look empty. "Once the stadiums were full," they note. "It was a magnificent popular explosion. There were two hundred thousand people in the grandstands, singing and shouting. It was a vision from ancient society, from the agora, from paganism."[18]

If these theorists' ideas are valid, if the *real* event was indeed Hodges's broadcast of the game and not the game itself, being there meant being present in the city of technological time instead of geographic space. The fictional Russ Hodges, who has the privilege of DeLillo's advanced temporal position, can reject some of the theories about the empty seats offered by his broadcasting crew and instead focus on his own place in the construction of a global technological village. Instead of accepting his colleagues' speculation that overcast skies or lack of advanced ticket sales kept the crowd size down on this historic day, Hodges can focus on the incredible shift of which he is a major part. His call of the culminating moment allowed audience members such as Nick, listening from his rooftop, to experience the game in a way that even Cotter Martin, who snuck into the outfield bleachers that day and who came away with the home-run ball, could not. Yet whereas Baudrillard writes glibly about this threat to belief in the "causal and logical order of the real and its reproduction"—if anything he delights in its exposure of the folly of searching for the "original" in an age of simulacra—Virilio and Lotringer find it deeply disturbing. The accelerated culture of broadcasting is part of a matrix of forces threatening the existence of public life and hence democracy.

Social historians have argued in great detail how shady associations between American oil and car companies and the federal government paved the way for the construction of the ecologically and socially tenuous infrastructure of many of today's sprawling American cities. The replacement of public transportation with highways has produced a racially insular, suburban world of sprawl, smog, and solitude.[19] Virilio and Lotringer add to the critique by arguing that the ubiquity of television in daily lives, as much as the changed transportation infrastructure, enables suburbanization and sprawl. Psychically, television and other diffuse mediating technologies make the city obsolete. Nobody needs to live in Soho anymore, now that one can experience it vicariously through shows such as *Friends,* which relocates generic domestic situations, preoccupations, and energy into a simulated urban setting. Virilio and Lotringer, like Hodges, lament the fact that nobody needs to go to ball games or, by extension, to the city anymore. Nick's discomfort in the novel is largely attributable to this state of affairs, to the fact that the city and the ball park have become mere luxury items, curiosity pieces for pleasant consumption rather than threads in the fabric of everyday life. He has become post-urban, postfan. He no longer lives in Brooklyn, and he no longer attends games, yet his experience feels horribly incomplete. Any relationship he has with the urbanism of his youth takes place through the metonymic substitution of symbolic objects for experience.

Throughout the novel, DeLillo draws a straight narrative line between Nick's existential crisis at the end of the novel and his experience listening to the Giants-Dodgers game on the radio at the beginning. A consumer of broadcast reality on his rooftop, Nick learns early about the evolving immateriality of the city during the burgeoning era of the hyperreal. This unfortunate lesson prompts him to dislocate himself from his real streets and instead float around in the postrefer-ential universe of his adulthood. Understanding this trajectory, DeLillo seems to be arguing, is key to understanding America's (symbolic and real) shift from New York to Phoenix, from the Yankees to the Diamondbacks, the Brooklyn Dodgers to the Los Angeles Dodgers, from Cotter Martin's bleacher seat in the Polo Grounds to the luxury sky boxes in Dodger Stadium.[20] In short, Nick's trip through the hyperreal is one from community to solitude, from the public realm to the pri-vate, from "the thing that happens in the sun" to televised reproductions of it.

FROM BROOKLYN TO CHAVEZ RAVINE

It is crucial that DeLillo locates Nick's first discussion about the hollow meaning of his souvenir in the Stadium Club of the Los Angeles Dodgers' ball park. Constructed in 1962 with the help of $5 million of public money, Dodger Stadium serves as the prototype for modern sports arenas. Located on three hundred acres near downtown, on a parcel of land (the Chavez Ravine) that had originally been set aside to be affordable housing for low-income citizens, the stadium came equipped with amenities and security measures to attract and insulate a wealthier clientele than typically attended baseball games. Seating just fifty-three thousand people but providing parking for more than twenty-seven thousand cars, the stadium was one of the first to allow suburbanites quick, safe, and easy access to a semi-downtown event without forcing them to come into contact with downtown residents. Once inside the park, visitors to the Stadium Club, glassed in at their cloth-covered tables, were provided with separation, not just from the cheering masses but also from the game itself.

Nick enters this world skeptically. For years unwilling to even walk through the turnstiles of the new home of his old ball club, Nick is not surprised when he discovers for himself the kind of insulation one could purchase at the new stadium:

> We were set apart from the field, glassed in at press level, and even with a table by the window we heard only muffled sounds from the crowd. The radio announcer's voice shot in clearly, transmitted from the booth, but the crowd remained at an eerie distance, soul-moaning like some lost battalion. . . . [Nick's companion] Glassic looked at me and said, "We need video helmets and power gloves. Because this isn't reality. This is virtual reality. And we don't have the proper equipment." (91–92)

The ocular arrangement of the Stadium Club allows, or forces, Nick and his companions to experience the game (un)comfortably as television—images behind a glass screen with sound piped in on speakers. More ominously, it allows them to come across a gathering of a critical mass of people, one important sign of a city, televisually. Like images on television, the crowd is both alive and dead to its consumers. "Soul moaning like some lost battalion," the crowd exists only at a substantial remove and thus signifies, like a television show or movie, largely through metaphor and metonymy. Both dead and alive, "lost" in the unreal space of broadcasting, the modern crowd, refracted through a bombardment of images, can conjure up the feelings of solidarity and spontaneity Nick experienced as a youth in Brooklyn, but it cannot encircle and draw him in physically. So in this sense, what Nick's group is experiencing is, in fact, reality (or better yet, hyperreality) in a televisual age. They can watch the crowd, and perhaps even project themselves into it, much like viewers experiencing a particularly vivid and engaging movie. But they cannot take part.[21]

Although the experience troubles Nick on a profound level, he dismisses Glassic's notion as naïve. Instead of joining his friend in a denunciation of ball park "virtual reality," he simply orders another drink and resigns himself to the subject position of television viewer. Glassic meanwhile assumes that Nick's resignation has to do with abandonment issues. He offers his belief that, when the Giants and Dodgers moved west, they took Nick's "heart and soul with them." Yet once more the protagonist corrects him. "There was nothing left to take. I was already a nonfan by that time" (93). His words here are extremely important. Having a "heart and soul," being a "fan," would have required him to possess the ability to lose himself in the moment, to experience a team's loss as his own. However, even before his team pulled up stakes and abandoned his hometown, he had become accustomed to the cool reserve of a television viewer or radio consumer. Listening to the famous Giants-Dodgers game from his rooftop, being a part of the "city of the instant" connected by Hodges's home-run call, had changed him forever. It made him acutely aware of his distance from the event.

Nick's dismissal of Glassic mirrors Baudrillard's cynicism when the theorist discusses the video dimension of contemporary perception. "We don't need digital gloves or a digital suit," he writes, using words strikingly similar to DeLillo's. "As we are, we are moving around in a world as in a synthesized image."[22] Nick's melancholia at the end of the novel is thus wrapped up in a postmodern belief that contemporary spectators can never shed these gloves or suits. Broadcasts of sports have forever changed peoples' relationship to them; live games no longer seem real, nor should anyone expect them to.

FROM CHAVEZ RAVINE TO YOUR LIVING ROOM

In addition to its ontological basis, Nick's alienation (and resignation) at Dodger Stadium has a strong economic component. His low expectations at the Dodger game show him to be savvy to the ways in which the mediation, or perhaps the *media-tization,* of sports has informed a radically different role for the fan within the financial structure and attendant psychic economy of the modern stadium event. While it is true that gate receipts and income generated from secondary ball-park diversions augment the bottom line for baseball franchises and thus stimulate Dibiasio and his colleagues to pay careful attention to these elements of the stadium environment, the largest and most direct sources of a club's revenue today are television and radio contracts.

In 1998, international media mogul Rupert Murdoch went way outside the lines established by comparable purchases when he offered $1 billion for England's famous Manchester United soccer team and another $500 million for the Dodgers.[23] Though he appeared at the time to be overspending for these franchises (according to market standards), Murdoch was in reality acquiring relatively inexpensive *content* for his network of cable channels.[24] Never in his wildest dreams could he have expected to recoup that kind of money through ticket, hot dog, and souvenir sales. Instead, because sports keep down production costs for networks by providing ready-made television programming, and because advertisers recognize the sports market as their most knowable and lucrative demographic base, Murdoch was investing not in sports franchises per se but in high-yield programming and an attractive audience to deliver to advertisers.[25] From a purely theoretical perspective, an owner like Murdoch could see his team play in front of an empty stadium night after night and remain in the black.[26]

Yet despite the fact that sports franchise owners seem less dependent on huge stadium crowds, live sports fans continue to be anything but irrelevant. The basis of their relevance has simply shifted, rendering them important commodities for franchise owners/media companies. Because new financial realities have realigned the traditional ocular arrangement—replacing the stadium patron with the viewer at home as the primary spectator—a fan in the ball park has, to a great degree, become part of the content. A less-than-capacity crowd, like the one at the Polo Grounds on that day of days, diminishes the quality of the televised event, threatening to make it seem less important or intense.[27] DeLillo's continual reflection about the empty seats at the Polo Grounds points to his suggestion that the pennant-clinching game was a milepost signaling the inception of a postfandom era. In this new era, a spectator in the ball park finds him or herself to be, to an extent, a cinematic extra, part of the big picture beamed live to viewers at home.

Yet in modern parks, the spectators' role is even more complex than DeLillo suggests. Today, spectators gain relevance not just as content (or extras) but also as consumers. At Jacobs Field, for example, most patrons view the game simultaneously as live event and televised spectacle via the hundreds of television monitors located around the park. In bathrooms, underneath balconies, on scoreboards, next to concession stands, and in private luxury boxes, these televisions help mediate the experience for the customer. They allow management to instantly repackage the game, to provide bird's eye views of action, multiple perspectives, instant replay, and, most important, advertisements. In the parlance of Madison Avenue, the ubiquitous television monitors allow management to deliver a *captive audience* to advertisers. As part of the continual struggle between consumers who seek savvy ways to tune out the continual bombardment of advertisements interrupting their favorite television programs (mute buttons, channel surfing, recorders that automatically filter out commercials, etc.), the ability to deliver to advertisers an audience devoid of the means of tuning out has become increasingly important.[28] As a perfect synthesis of consumer and product, the Jacobs Field spectator thus inhabits an ideal subjectivity in an age of advertising.

Yet it is important that not all sections of Jacobs Field are equal in this regard. In the bleachers, patrons enjoy a spatial arrangement offering at least a partial rejection of the attempt to render them part of a captive audience. Bleacher dwellers, like concerned parents who attempt to insulate their children from a constant barrage of advertisement and frivolous entertainment by unplugging their TVs, are allowed literally to turn their backs to the giant JumboTron rising from the back of the section. Forming the familiar backdrop to the typical scene broadcast from Jacobs Field and framing the action for spectators throughout the bulk of the park, the screen features rotating and hologrammatic signs for beer companies and investment firms as well as slickly produced live-action advertisements. Television viewers and anyone watching the game from any position inside the stadium but outside the bleachers thus by necessity become part of the captive audience any time they glance toward the field of play or look up to see the pitch count. A viewer watching at home or from the box seats, like a client in a barber's chair who looks in the mirror at the mirror behind and sees an endless reflection of a reflection, subjects him or herself to similar overlapping layers of advertisements. She or he simply cannot witness a player catching a ball in front of the Budweiser sign on the scoreboard without also seeing an infinite repetition of the same sign televised on the JumboTron in the background. The bleacher patron, on the other hand, is allowed to face away from the visual onslaught. A bleacher seat affords the spectator, quite literally, the only perspective in the park from which the infinite display of the same advertisement is impossible. Thus one of his or her primary transgressions, and an important form of pleasure, is a refusal to be delivered to advertisers.

Nonetheless, if the bleacher fan is indeed less a part of the captive audience than the rest of the spectators, he or she is perhaps more integral a part of the content. Not bombarded by the scoreboard media images, bleacher fans seem freer to imagine a more immediate relationship with the game. Out of sight of the JumboTron's official calls to "Make Some Noise," "Stomp Your Feet" or "Fly Delta Airlines," they have been given the space to more actively create their own response to the game. As such, these creative fans attain significant relevance as

MOST PATRONS AT JACOBS FIELD VIEW THE GAME SIMULTANEOUSLY AS LIVE EVENT AND TELEVISED SPECTACLE VIA 660 MONITORS LOCATED AROUND THE PARK.

actors on a stage. They serve, in part, as Nick's "lost battalion," strategically located to perform for the cameras and for the other patrons in the park. Their actions (drumming, spontaneous cheering, starting waves), in addition to bringing them pleasure, upgrade the quality of the event for viewers at home and for spectators in the rest of the stadium.[29]

BOBBY THOMSON'S HOME RUN EVERY TIME

Ultimately, Nick Shay's perception of the modern baseball fan is a bit rigid and condescending. Seeing a crowd as a hermeneutical monolith overlooks the fact that each stadium patron brings his or her own capacity to interpret or create the experience in a manner that suits him or her. Clearly, the Mohawk-sporting teenage boy's ironic purchase and donning of a retro Indians jersey signifies differently than the same purchase and fashion choice made by an earnest fortysomething man. In addition to eliding differences among individual consumers, Nick's perspective suggests a kind of troubling middle-class presumption fetishizing the economic and social realities of poor people. From this point of view, realness, or the ability to experience raw emotions, is only accessible to those coming from marginalized cultures. Middle-class experience is constructed as somehow neutral, reinforcing a superstructure of adulation, admiration, and self-loathing. Nonetheless, DeLillo's novel-length exploration of his protagonist's obsessive relationship to baseball history, folklore, and memorabilia does suggest the powerful appeal of retro stadiums' promise to take patrons back to the future as well as some of the intellectual problems attendant with this kind of endeavor.

For most of the last century, baseball has enjoyed an almost mythic status as an emblem of a purer past. In the popular imagination, the game has a history of bringing Americans of disparate races, classes, and geography together in solidarity. The urban America of the Polo Grounds resonates in memory as a great mixing bowl, a rarefied place before gated communities, exurban starter castles, and extremes of economic polarization homogenized and regularized the lived experience of many Americans. The fantasy behind new old stadiums, the chance to experience a contemporary reenactment of the Polo Grounds without having to renounce the comfort and ease of modernity, thus has undeniable cachet. Yet because pleasure at retro parks is so enmeshed with selective memory, because most modern fans' imagination of the Polo Grounds is indebted to images of the stadium at its most electric moment (rather than at any of its countless hours of the mundane which have not been replicated over and again for contemporary consumption), these parks inevitably set fans up for a certain degree of disappointment.

In other words, a ticket to one of these venues seems to promise Bobby Thomson's home run every time to an audience used to immediate gratification. Yet, of course, because guaranteeing this type of pay-off is literally impossible, stadium management must turn to advanced forms of technology to fulfill fan desire. Throughout the game, stadium technicians edit and replay on the many televisions in the park the most thrilling moments of other games happening that night around the league. Thus a fan attending a game in Cleveland will catch on the telescreen the ending of the Red Sox game in Boston or the Mets game in Queens, if those games happen to produce thrilling late-game moments. During pauses in action throughout the evening, technicians will also cue up the most exciting replays of past Indians team, or even historical footage like that of Thomson circling the bases. If a fan is still not satiated by these videotaped supplements, he or she can then turn to some of the park's other secondary diversions. Batting cages, putt-putt golf courses, fast-pitch machines, and video games all, in their own way, attempt to guarantee to consumers immediate access to all the vicissitudes of sport. They offer spectators the vicarious thrill of winning and losing an infinite number of times throughout the game, regardless of what happens (or does not happen) on the field, and they provide fans the chance to imagine themselves as active participants rather than passive spectators.

Ironically, however, these substitutions themselves subtly threaten the park's ability to meet fans' expectations. For one thing, the mediating technology required to reproduce the thrills of Thomson's unexpected blast interrupts the primacy of the event, short-circuiting sensations of absolute engagement so much a part of retro parks' promise. Additionally, the provision of these substitutions feeds into a type of rampant impatience diminishing the possibility of a deep appreciation of, and surprise at, rarified moments. English football fan Paul Morley, when describing why he feels Americans have never really understood the appeal of soccer and consequently why the English are so threatened by an increase in participation by American firms in the production and marketing of their national sport, seems to be pointing accusatorily to this desire for immediate gratification. According to Morley, fandom in England requires a "miraculous stupidity," or the ability, in fact, the desire, to "suffer the 66 nil-nil draws, the pain, the horror, the misery, to get to that one moment when it all goes right and it's 4–1" (Redhead 35–36). Obviously, Morley's comments are rather nationalistic and fail to account for the many ways that the English Premier League Football stadium event has itself adapted to the desires of a postmodern, increasingly consumerist English culture even without significant American intervention.[30] Nonetheless, his words underline the extent to which modern sporting executives (in America and elsewhere) feel the need to manufacture highs and lows for many in their audience who expect absolutely to get them as part of the price of admission. As such, these executives run the risk of mitigating pleasure for future generations of fans in places such as Boston, where the beloved Red Sox, prior to 2004, have allowed their followers almost a century's worth of joyful suffering. The ill-fated Red Sox, coming tantalizingly close to a championship time and again before invariably breaking their fans' hearts, granted their devoted supporters the annual opportunity to utter the melancholy line, "Wait until next year."[31]

The irony of this process in a space devoted to a reenactment of what is commonly perceived to be a simpler time in baseball (and American urban) history is clear. The imagined, authentic past is partly one divorced from the vulgarities of consumerism and hyperreality. That is to say, many contemporary fans worship a time in baseball history before the era of multi-million-dollar contracts and franchise relocation, before the game was, they imagine, despoiled by technology and the capitalist logic of exchange run amok. However, the process of recovery, the will to collect, inspired by these parks, requires the ultimate commodification—that of history. The most nostalgic baseball fans are thus a bit like Nick in his more naïve and acquisitive moments, dreaming of access to a vanquished past yet certifying their distance from it through their pursuit.

THE GATEWAY AS POST URBAN SPACE

If the biggest drawback to the retro stadium movement was simply that it often fails to live up to its promise of pleasure for a certain type of middle-class consumer, it could be dismissed as largely just an attempt to package authenticity to an anxious segment of the population uncomfortable with its role as consumers of experience. However, this increasingly popular experiment takes place primarily in gentrifying areas frequently requiring a large-scale displacement of the erstwhile residents of urban America. A Disneyfied urban space like the Gateway surrounding Jacobs Field subsumes the city in its own aestheticization, making urban life quaint, a consumable relic of a purer, yet somehow improved-upon past. It allows modern visitors to the city an opportunity to seek a way out of hyperreality through the appropriation of the fading voices of the dispossessed or vanished. It gives them a chance to try on costumes, accents, and behaviors of people from other classes, other races, other time periods. Meanwhile, actual people—the "ghosts" of Nick Shay's dystopia, the folks whom DeLillo's protagonist experiences only as "some lost battalion . . . soul moaning . . . at an eerie distance" from his highly symbolic position in the Stadium Club—fade into oblivion.

As part of this transformation, the Gateway has become a post-urban location for many who experience it. Through technology, crowd control, and themed architecture, the designers and managers of its marquee attraction allow visitors to experience the urban without its sharpest edges. They then beam the whole picture live to the sprawling suburbs surrounding downtown, allowing them to create an urbanism of time and space. In doing so, they both replicate the atomized structure of the suburbs and enable it. Restoring a longed-for urbanism without destroying what is good about the imaginary or real urban past is, then, perhaps the most profound challenge facing planners and stadium designers today and in the future. One has to wonder if they will ever be able to (or indeed if it is even possible to) restore contact with utopian elements of an idealized past. Will these designers be able to plan for community, proximity, spontaneity, and racial and economic solidarity in a way that does not ultimately displace existing urbanites? Can they design spaces that generate culture inclusively rather than simply commemorating passing cultures?

Inevitably, one has to wonder about the half-life of these stadiums. Will they still have that sense of tantalizing incompleteness in, say, forty years, when no one alive has ever been to many of the older parks that they replicate? Or will they just seem *old,* and even suggest that the past they strive to reproduce is that of the 1990s? It might just be possible that modern baseball stadiums will have to be replaced with alarming frequency, like buildings in Las Vegas, a city of the eternal present, which every few years completely obliterates the past, razing decade-old themed palaces in favor of something completely new.[32] In this sense, it is clear that retro stadiums are destined to inspire complex feelings, sensations that they are at once immense architectural achievements and elaborate kitsch objects. Decades from now, retro ball parks might indeed be revered as enduring monuments (as Fenway Park, Wrigley Field, and Yankee Stadium are today). Of course, it is also plausible that they could be headed to the enormous waste pile of pre–cold war relics upon which DeLillo crafts his tome of memory and loss in an age of hyperreality.

EPILOGUE

455

It has been six years since Indians vice president Bob Dibiasio first prompted me to consider Jacobs Field and the surrounding Gateway as a "big picture." The metaphor allowed me to think about Cleveland's urban redevelopment project as, in part, an attempt to coherently portray the space according to a set of fascinating but sometimes disconcerting aesthetic and cultural idioms. Using warm materials like brick and faux wrought iron, presenting ubiquitous images of African Americans, and highlighting working-class inflected notions of the bleachers, the developers/marketers of the big picture attempted to render a sense of realness through worship of a projected and reified past. As such, they endeavored to smooth over many of the rougher edges of urban renewal.

Of course, in the intervening years, like Oscar Wilde's magical *Picture of Dorian Gray,* Dibiasio's portrait has continued to age and change.[1] One small but extremely significant new detail on the canvas is the number 455 enshrined on pillars rising above the Jake's center field. Painted next to the names of such Indians greats as Bob Feller and Larry Doby and representing the number of consecutive sellouts at the ball park from 1995 to 2001, a major league record, the three digits pay tribute to Cleveland fans during that period of unprecedented success. By 2003, as the rebuilding ball club struggled on the field and the park typically only filled to about a third of its capacity on game nights, the number hung there as a salient reminder of how quickly an era of perpetual championships and packed houses can fade into the realm of memory.

Nonetheless, despite representing the way that a building tends to change cosmetically and functionally over time, the number also suggests a fundamental equipoise revealing itself at the Jake and in Cleveland a decade after the park first opened. Inside the stadium, some longtime supporters consider the team's present gloomy situation reflective of the true spirit of Indians baseball. In fact, they seem almost relieved about the Tribe's less-illustrious new reality. "It was nice to have a winner for a while," says bleacher fan Darin Good, "but it did draw a lot of people because it was the *in* thing to do. Now it's back to how it was. Mostly just the true fans come out." Good and others now see the glory years of the late 1990s as almost a fugue state, kind of fun while it lasted, but invariably ephemeral and unreal, almost a dream. "It's settled back," says bleacher drummer John Adams. "Now that the place isn't full, you get people who are into the game . . . It's dead quiet when the pitcher sets and gets ready to throw. People are *following* it." Because he has attended almost all Indians home games for the past forty years, Adams can treat the present-day misfortune of his beloved club sanguinely. "Cleveland is still the same old good baseball town," he says. "At the old park, when there were twenty thousand [spectators] we cheered like there were seventy thousand." In fact, to Adams's delight, today's smaller crowds seem to provide more energy than did the full houses of the glory years. Even though empty seats typically outnumber spectators by 150 percent, the stadium often seems louder, more boisterous and "into the game" than it did a few years ago.

Perhaps part of this renewed energy can be attributed to the fact that, along with declining attendance and poor performances, a certain degree of oppositional sentiment toward the organization has returned among Indian followers. "Jacobs bought the team to spend money," says lifelong fan Dave Barta. "Larry Dolan [the Indians' more frugal new owner] seems to be in over his head." In truth, Barta's criticism has the ring of a mantra among those who continue to come to the ball park; just about everyone repeats it, almost dispassionately, as if it were self-evident. The belief behind this refrain seems to be both a product of a kind of instant commemoration of the past, celebrating former owner Richard Jacobs, whose free-spending ways and clever management brought the Tribe six consecutive division titles and a comfortable new stadium, and a revival of the standard criticism of Indians fans prior to the 1990s, when forty years of parsimonious ownership consigned the team, year after year, to the American League's second division. Dolan, like the fictional Rachel Phelps in *Major League,* once again provides an opportunity for solidarity among the team's die-hard fans. He gives them a target for their frustration, a convenient explanation for the team's woes that all can agree upon. In short, the experience of watching an Indians game at Jacobs Field has taken on many of the characteristics of an older order among fans like Good, Barta, and Adams, who supported the team for years at Cleveland Stadium.

Behind the scenes, the new script of the Jacobs Field tour guides similarly suggests that Cleveland baseball is in the process of settling back into its appropriate angle of repose. Whereas they used to recount the titanic exploits of star sluggers such as Albert Belle and Jim Thome, tour guides now emphasize player development, spending a good deal of the tour in the team's indoor batting cages behind the dugout detailing how Indians coaches help younger players work on their swings during games. Home once again to young, lovable losers, the Jake is promoted as a symbol of Cleveland's essential, underdog virtue; low-budget, mediocre baseball is packaged as a novelty item. Along the same lines, tour guides talk about the 1990s as if the decade were part of a distant past. In doing so, they conveniently elide certain economic truths about the relationship between big money, stadium construction, and championship baseball in order to commemorate (or mythologize) a time when the Indians, against all odds, regularly bested teams from bigger cities. Perhaps most revealing in this regard is how guides go to great lengths to downplay the cost of the park, even suggesting that a *modest* taxpayer subsidy is indicative of Cleveland's small-market, can-do spirit. "Think about it," said tour guide Marge Barner on a recent tour. "All of this was built for a mere $169 million investment, or less than the Yankees payroll."

Although it is unclear how she derives this particular number (in reality, Cleveland taxpayers contributed and continue to contribute much more than that), the meaning of the line seems fairly straightforward, revealing an attempt to restore an important part of Cleveland's psychological identity. The statement, which Barner repeated three times during the tour, portrays the Indians once again as a lovable runner-up, a club whose proud fans provide undying support for a team and a city even when forced to struggle through years of bad baseball and burning rivers. Perhaps the idea of this endearing, homey midwestern town as a national trendsetter, a magnet for global capital, a rival to New York and, gasp, a home to baseball champions, had simply been too much for the city to integrate. Perhaps Barner's new script also suggests certain inherent problems with the original (more confident and boastful) tour guide speech. During the glory years, Indians representatives were probably too eager to highlight the "new and improved" elements of the park given that, today, as the Jake ages and other cities build their own stadiums that both imitate and attempt to top it, many of the groundbreaking features seem less dramatic. Now that new Comerica Park in Detroit boasts the world's largest freestanding scoreboard, for example, the Jake's JumboTron, as only the second largest one, lacks a bit of its power to awe.

It may be that this is all just as well. As the stadium loses some of its initial luster, it really does seem to be gaining a degree of the authenticity imagined by its creators. It can now claim its own, real (ten-year) history rather than relying on the elevation of ersatz versions of the past from other stadiums. No longer a consistent draw for the "in" crowd, it leaves fans like Good, Adams, and Barta more or less alone to get "into the game." Perhaps most critical in this regard is the fact that since the sellout string has ended, some ticket prices have fallen by about 50 percent and game-day, walk-up seats have become readily available. This makes the park, as Cleveland Stadium had been before it, relatively accessible to the "real" fans mythologized by the first tour guide six years ago and praised by Adams and Barta today.

Outside the stadium, however, even as the experience of attending a game begins to be reminiscent of the good old, bad old days of Municipal Stadium, conversion of the area to a 24/7 work-and-play zone has continued to progress according to the realities of a new economic order. Even during a period of economic downturn, capital has continued to arrive in the form of new chain restaurants, hotels, and restored institutions like the many theaters in Playhouse Square a few blocks away. Not just baseball and basketball, but music, dance, lodging, and fine dining have begun to attract a consistent stream of visitors.

Along with this steady march of development, the culture of commemoration and replacement, with all of its attendant ironies, is gaining increasing traction. On East Fourth Street, another national fast food franchise, Wendy's Old-Fashioned Hamburgers has moved in. Upscale eating establishments such as the themed old-time Pickwick Restaurant have taken the place of check-cashing shops and discount shoe stores as workers apply the finishing touches to two more high-end condominium buildings next to and above the few remaining discount retail businesses clinging desperately to life.[2] Meanwhile, Bob Zimmer makes plans to convert his building to a multilayered symbol of the evolving Gateway. As he guts the top two floors to transform them into luxury condos, he continues to pack the second floor above his jewelry store with items commemorating "diversity in baseball." His Baseball Heritage Museum has become a big draw, playing host to conferences and attracting visitors from around the nation. "It's a funny thing though," muses his father Irv. "Almost all the collectors who come to see the Negro League items are white."

This kind of irony notwithstanding, many locals continue to be huge supporters of attempts to revitalize the area around an entertainment theme. Mike Marchese, who has operated a newsstand in the Caxton Building on Huron Road during the past ten years of Gateway redevelopment, sees the evolution of the area as an unequivocally good thing. "I don't understand the critics. Before, all you had was a rat-infested market and cold storage," he says. "Once you get some more restaurants and once the House of Blues opens up on Euclid, the Gateway will fill up." On the other hand, many of Marchese's neighbors, other local merchants with a stake in the economic future of the area find themselves increasingly disillusioned with the influx of large-scale entertainment attractions. "People used to come downtown to make money. Now they come just to spend," says Burt Kawkaby, who has served up burgers and fries in his small Huron Road diner for thirty years. "But nobody is going to come down and pay event parking rates to eat here. In the past two years, I've seen at least four to five hundred people who used to come here two to three times per day disappear." Kawkaby sees the current model for redevelopment as unsustainable. "All the small businesses are moving to the suburbs," he says. "So what do you have now? If you rip your pants, you can't even buy a pair to replace them down here anymore." Unlike Marchese, he sees the increased foot traffic around the stadium on game nights as an illu-

Anton Grdina Elementary school in Cleveland's Kinsman neighborhood.

sion, creating the appearance of vibrant city life but in reality serving as a kind of part-time playground. "It used to be that people came down here to shop and work. Now it's just baseball. But that doesn't help my business," he says. "The whole idea of downtown is mixed up. You build hotels and now they are all empty. You build big skyscrapers and they empty out too."[3]

Greg Smith, the superintendent of Marchese's Caxton Building, perhaps represents the majority of Gateway merchants, residents, and workers by walking a middle ground between the optimism of the newsstand owner and the frustration of Kawkaby. "Our building is 90 percent full, so that's good," he says. "But you couldn't pay me enough to live down here." He describes the process of revitalization as paradoxical in the extreme. The majority of apartment units constructed in the past few years sit empty, he says, because the area lacks both an infrastructure—no groceries or pharmacies—and a history as livable space. "There aren't enough people down here. When there is no game going on or you get a weekend when the Indians are on the road, it's dead." What he describes then is a large-scale game of chicken. Until enough people come to live downtown, it will continue to be difficult to attract people to live in the Gateway.

Farther out from downtown, the distant stadium and the surrounding Gateway revitalization continue to polarize along racial lines. Whereas many Greater Clevelanders (such as seventeen-year-old Matt Kyte from Parma, who considers the Gateway to be "awesome, a really great play to come to") see the stadium as a source of unadulterated civic pride, most residents of east-side inner-city neighborhoods remain resentful. The ball park is a place only for "people from the suburbs," says lifelong Kinsman resident Mitchell Green. "We don't really go to ball games, to tell you the truth." He adds that local residents categorically dismiss the notion that improved economic vitality downtown trickles into to his area. Recalling Mayor Michael White's promises of help for urban neighborhoods while lobbying for public subsidy of the ball park, he shakes his head and laughs. "They tried to fix things here, but it was just like patching up a few holes if you ask me," he says, referring to a couple of token projects in his area in the first couple of years after the construction of Jacobs Field. "You go down to Strongsville [just southwest of Parma] and look at their schools. They'd never have any conditions like you got here."

In short, most of the crucial tensions I noticed years ago remain: black-white, urban-suburban, entertainment-living, professional–working class, real-unreal, and so on. This book started out as an examination of the marketing/theming strategies attempting to soothe these binaries as the Gateway and other urban entertainment destinations across the country reinvent themselves. In the process of writing it, however, I became increasingly aware of the fact that, despite the desire to carefully script the experience of living, shopping, eating, and rooting in the Gateway, equally important is how it plays. Like Wilde's fantastical portrait, the evolution of the "big picture" is, to a large extent, out of the hands of its creators. The diverse lived experiences of bleacher drummer Adams (ignoring the commemorative features of the new park), the Mohawk-sporting teenagers (consuming them in an ironic fashion), and Kinsman resident Green (boycotting the park altogether) remind us of the variety of responses available to any such large-scale development. Ultimately, this multiplicity of consuming strategies will determine the texture of the area's history as much or more than the Gateway's elaborate retro authentic packaging.

NOTES

INTRODUCTION

1. Robert Rinehart, in *Players All,* writes about the relationship between spectator and sport in a way that is relevant here. He argues that one of the primary contributions of sports in postmodern culture is providing fans of particular teams "shards of their individuality" (17).

2. This sense of resurgence was aided by the fact that the club, fresh off the infamy of a 107-loss season (one in which it lost a staggering twenty-one games to open the 1988 campaign), had commenced rebuilding through youth, pitching, and enthusiasm. In 1989, the team shocked the league, contending for the American League East title until the final weekend of the season. Although it fell short, losing two out of three games of the pivotal culminating series to the high-priced Toronto Blue Jays (playing in their new, space-age SkyDome), the group of no-names and castoffs, rookies and hustling journeymen under the tutelage of Oriole legend Frank Robinson scrapped and clawed throughout, bringing the "magic" back to the old stadium on Thirty-third Street.

3. Riverfront Stadium in Cincinnati and Three Rivers Stadium in Pittsburgh, to the nondiscerning eye, were simply replications of Busch Stadium in St. Louis; Shea Stadium seemed too much of a piece with Robert F. Kennedy Stadium in Washington and Fulton County Stadium in Atlanta; and Memorial Stadium seemed largely indistinguishable from Cleveland's Municipal Stadium and Milwaukee's County Stadium.

4. Designed after the 1985 Robert Zemeckis film, Universal Studio's Back to the Future ride was one of the first to bring the technology of advanced flight simulation to a popular audience.

5. Jackson Lears argues that the possibility of this kind of encounter is one of the most important ways to distinguish between projects that revitalize and ones that gentrify. See "No There There," his review of both *Fortress America* by Edward Blakely and Mary Gail Snyder and *Changing Places* by Richard Moe and Carter Wilkie.

6. Perhaps no one embodied the rowdy spirit of old Memorial Stadium better than super fan "Wild" Bill Hagy. The hirsute Baltimore cab driver spent much of the 1970s in section 34, working fans into a frenzy by twisting and contorting his body to spell out O-R-I-O-L-E-S as the stadium erupted in laughter and cheers.

7. "Accidental" beer spilling from the upper deck to the lower one was a common occurrence at Memorial Stadium, particularly when the home team was not playing well.

8. Driving time from Washington to the stadium is now roughly equal to driving time from Baltimore's own northern communities. This contributes to fact that approximately 25 percent of the Orioles' spectators now come from suburbs surrounding D.C. For years, Orioles' owner Peter Angelos cited this figure as a reason why MLB owners should reject the relocation of an existing franchise to the greater Washington area. He claimed that drawing off this 25 percent would weaken his franchise and create two clubs that would struggle to compete financially with the Yankees, Dodgers, and other big-market teams.

9. Breaking the mold of suburban shopping centers, urban markets like Harborplace rejected big box stores in favor of mixes of specialty stores, which required an almost tenfold increase in the number of customers to produce the same amount of cash sales. Along the way, they also proved to be three to four times more expensive to build than standard suburban shopping centers. See Hannigan 55–59.

10. Hannigan points out that "between March 1995 and June 1996, the number of city-led initiatives in the urban entertainment development field rose from five to thirty-one, with an additional twenty-seven projects under active consideration" (63). See Robertson for a discussion of the psychological attraction of downtown destinations for suburban customers and tourists.

11. Many scholars have also criticized the cultural ramifications of festival marketplace development. For example, Ada Louis Huxtable, in *The Unreal America,* argues that these new city spaces elevate the unreal over the real, ersatz history over authentic history. Michael Sorkin suggests that "the gentrified architecture" of these developments is "an elaborate apparatus . . . at pains to assert its ties to the kind of city life it is in the process of obliterating" (xiv). Edward Soja laments the homogeneity of UEDs, arguing that monolithic financing, copycat architecture, and a reliance on national chain stores as tenants conspire to collapse the individual identities of downtowns. Trevor Boddy criticizes the construction of multileveled tunnels, bridges, and corridors carrying pedestrians from one private space to another, obviating the need to walk downtown streets, "the last preserve of something approaching a mixing of all sectors of society" (126). Similarly, Paul Goldberger calls these spaces "urbanoid environments," hermetic private areas masquerading as public space. Finally, Margaret Crawford argues that the new downtown of Harborplace is merely an extension of the shopping mall, bringing together customers searching for an authentic experience then rendering that authenticity as consumable by means of gifts for sale at boutiques.

12. See "Downtown Redevelopment."

13. In particular, see Baade and Noll.

14. Hannigan gives a couple of examples of this kind of argument. He quotes Toronto mayor Barbara Hall, who endorsed a large-scale downtown recreational development by saying it was "an important part of the next century of this city." Similarly, in Pittsburgh, the manager of the old Three Rivers Stadium spoke favorably of a public subsidy for a new UED because it demonstrated that "Pittsburgh is moving forward into the next century" (5).

15. Political trends in the late 1990s saw a backlash against direct public funding of stadiums for private profit. Places such as Minneapolis and San Francisco voted down bond

referendums that just a couple years earlier had been passing consistently in other cities. As such, what seems to be evolving is a reliance on other types of indirect financing products. Some municipalities grant franchises the right to sell naming rights to stadiums; others levy so-called sin taxes on tobacco and alcohol to foot the bill. Many others have discovered tax increment funding or increased property taxes in targeted areas—typically the business district surrounding the stadium. Tax increment funding, or TIF, usually does not require a public referendum and thus cannot typically be fought successfully by grass-roots organizations. For more on TIFs, see Hannigan 136–37.

16. Ironically, just as Baltimore lost its Colts, Cleveland lost its equally beloved Browns to Baltimore. The Ravens, attracted to Baltimore by a deal in which the state of Maryland issued bonds and dedicated lottery proceeds to help pay for a new home for them, play in Ravens (now M&T Bank) Stadium next to Oriole Park. In Seattle, the MLB Mariners play in retractable-roof Safeco Field while the NFL Seahawks play next door in Seahawks Stadium.

17. See Donovan.

18. In *The Culture of Cities,* Sharon Zukin warns against unquestioned acceptance of the typically uncontroversial images presented by newly privatized public urban spaces. She describes the impulse behind and the dangers of the creation of a more sanitized version of the city. Similarly, Christine Boyer, in "Cities for Sale," criticizes myriad cultural references at Manhattan's South Street Seaport that tend to paint a heroic picture of the history of trade while omitting any mention of the poverty and oppression characterizing the lives of most seamen.

19. Donovan points out that, ironically, the artifacts on display at the museum actually "predate the arrival of the Ruth Family and are thus misrepresented in the interest of perpetuating nostalgia" (233).

20. "The end of history" refers to Francis Fukuyama's controversial assertion in 1989 that the fall of the Berlin Wall suggested that humankind was approaching an "end point" in its "ideological evolution." In "The End of History," the deputy director for policy planning in the George H. W. Bush State Department argued that Western liberal democracy seemed to be triumphing, once and for all, over defective and irrational forms of governments such as fascism, hereditary monarchy, and communism. Of course, after September 11, 2001, during a period when America has been seen globally as embarking on a crusade (of "good vs. evil" according to George W. Bush or "imperialistic dynasty" according to critics), it seems more and more as if Fukuyama's declaration was premature.

21. *Pleasantville.* Dir. Gary Ross. Perf. Tobey Maguire, Reese Witherspoon, Joan Allen, William H. Macy. Miramax, 1998.

22. See Bartimole, "Who Really Governs?" Hannigan estimates the cost to be more like $395 million (138).

23. See Bartimole, "Who Really Governs?" and Rosentraub, *Major League Losers* 245–64.

24. The term "hyperreal" is most commonly associated with postmodern theorists Jean Baudrillard and Umberto Eco. Both Baudrillard and Eco explore the nature of cognition in a world increasingly mediated by technology. See Baudrillard, especially *The Transparency of Evil,* and Eco *Travels in Hyperreality.*

CHAPTER ONE

Understanding the Big Picture

1. See Gershman 142–43 for details about public financing of the construction of Cleveland Municipal Stadium.
2. The Indians set a major league record by selling out 455 straight home games from June 12, 1995, to April 2, 2001.
3. The term "Fordist" refers to the structures and strategies of American mass production popularized by automobile innovator Henry Ford.
4. "Renaissance City" is a term used frequently in tourist brochures and by newspaper reporters and politicians to describe the revitalized downtown.
5. Bartimole, "Who Really Governs?" 1.
6. Kucinich was elected mayor in 1977.
7. The local banks did offer to extend the loans, provided Kucinich agree to sell the municipally owned power plant to a privately owned utility in the city. Kucinich's refusal probably cost him the mayor's office the next year. Ultimately, however, his rejection of the proposal became the spark for his political comeback years later, when he won a seat in the Ohio Senate in 1994. His decision to keep the utility in public hands is believed to have saved customers millions of dollars by the 1990s.
8. The term "subject of history" comes from Frederick Jameson. Jameson describes International Telephone and Telegraph's (ITT) intervention on behalf of Augusto Pinochet's right-wing coup in 1973 as a significant moment in the formation of "multinational corporations." According to Jameson, as a result of America's failure in Vietnam and subsequent reluctance to intervene directly around the globe, corporations such as ITT discovered their power as de facto governments, learning to become "visible actor(s) on the world stage" (*Postmodernism* 205).
9. See Rosentraub's *Major League Losers.*
10. Voinovich has continued to be popular among Ohio's voters. In 1990 and 1994, he was elected governor. Then, in 1998, he won one of the state's U.S. Senate seats.
11. See Cagan and deMause for a description of the controversial record of funding for Cleveland schools during its recovery.
12. See Bartimole's *Point of View,* vol. 29, no. 12 for specific data on the economic condition of several downtown Cleveland neighborhoods.
13. Not coincidentally, free agency in baseball emerged in the 1970s during the post-Fordist era. Like their corporate counterparts, baseball players have become flexible and mobile labor, moving from city to city, leveraging one club's contract offer against another.
14. Critics point out that Major League Baseball franchises employ only about one hundred full-time workers, or no more than a department store. See Hannigan 148.
15. Bartimole, "Doing Gateway Up Right" 1.
16. For a description of public/private partnership tools, see Hannigan 129–48.
17. Although widely considered the last privately financed park, Dodger Stadium actually received about $5 million in direct public subsidy when it was built in 1962.

18. Pacific Bell Park opened for business in April 2000. The San Francisco city redevelopment agency contributed approximately $10 million in tax increment funding to help pay for the stadium's construction.

19. From the Baseball Heritage Museum Mission Statement.

20. See Huxtable 41–71 for a discussion of what she calls the "American tradition of invented places" (41).

21. Available at www.east4thstreet.com.

22. In the 1990s, this motif was exemplified by interest in the exploits of Cal Ripken Jr. and Mark McGwire. Chasing and shattering decades-old records, the two players almost completely monopolized the attention of baseball fans. Just seven years removed from the event, few fans outside of southern Florida can immediately recall that the Marlins won the 1997 World Series, but most of them will always remember McGwire's smash to left field shattering Roger Maris's forty-year-old single-season home-run record and Cal Ripken's victory lap around Camden Yards after he broke the record thought untouchable—Lou Gehrig's consecutive-game streak.

23. Cooperstown has become known as the birthplace of baseball largely because of a propaganda campaign initiated by Spalding. In need of a suitable myth of genesis, Spalding, as National League president in 1905, went to work rewriting history. As a young man, he had always bought into *Sporting Guide* editor Henry Chadwick's widely accepted theory that American baseball originated from the English game of Rounders. Yet by 1905, Spalding not only offered a different opinion—that baseball had evolved from a colonial American game called One Old Cat and had matured toward its present form thanks to the ingenuity and creativity of young Americans—but also appointed a bogus historical commission to "investigate" and draw a definitive solution. This commission—the National Board of Baseball Commissioners, comprising among others, Al Reach, Spalding's business partner, and three former presidents of the National League—relied primarily on evidence suggested by Spalding himself to settle the issue. See Peter Levine 112–15.

24. See White for an account of stadium construction between 1908 and 1923. See also Gershman's *Diamonds* and Phillip J. Lowry's *Green Cathedrals* for historical information on each ball park constructed in that era.

25. The New York Mets have proposed that the city of New York fund a ball park resembling Ebbets Field, but with a retractable roof, in the parking lot of Shea Stadium, their current Flushing Meadows home. The new park would incorporate many elements of Ebbets, including a rotunda at the entrance, an irregularly shaped right field, and a virtual replica of the original brick and sandstone facade. Unlike Ebbets, however, the new park would also include seventy-eight luxury boxes and five thousand club seats.

26. Most baseball fans who have followed the game during the past quarter century can describe perhaps the two most memorable home runs hit over the left-field fence in Fenway Park. Most Red Sox faithful will always fondly remember Carlton Fisk hopping down the first base line, dancing and imploring the blast he hit to remain fair and help the Sox beat the Reds in the sixth game of the 1976 World Series. Conversely these same Sox fans would probably like to forget weak-hitting Yankee shortstop Bucky Dent

lining a rope that cleared the Green Monster by only a few feet, helping the hated Bronx Bombers beat the Sox in a one-game playoff at the end of the 1978 season.

27. The new home of the NFL Ravens next to Oriole Park threatens this fantasy in Baltimore. Massive M&T Bank Stadium appears out of scale in its Camden Yards setting. Whereas the baseball park is virtually unseen from the highway, just another building on the edge of downtown, the football venue is taller than Camden Yards and not situated comfortably within the grid, largely undermining one of the central architectural feats of the earlier park—its understated simplicity.

28. Although parking decks provide a decent vantage point from which to watch the game, Indians policy dictates that security patrol the lots, expelling people attempting to watch from there.

29. See Boddy for a discussion of the social implications of privatized urban pathways.

30. Bob Uecker is the longtime Brewer announcer famous for self-deprecating television commercials promoting a national beer brand. In the most memorable of these ads, after being bumped from the box seats (before being sent to the "nose bleed section"), he hopefully offers the line, "I must be in the front row."

31. For a reaction against post-Fordist geographical mobility, see Sanders.

32. See Stallybrass and White for a description of the transformation of the Nice Carnival. In their essay, they describe attempts to repress and contain unauthorized, carnival economies at Bartholemew Fair and Donneybrooke.

33. See Willis, *Inside the Mouse* 52–53, for a description of the elaborate, yet hidden surveillance apparatus in Disney World. Also, see Kasson for a discussion of the psychological appeal of friendly technology in early versions of amusement parks.

34. See Foucault's *Discipline and Punish* for his theory about how the modern Western subject has internalized methods of control and surveillance first enacted by prison technology. According to Foucault's formulation, the "panopticon," an elaborate system of surveillance and sleight of hand, made prisoners feel as if they were being watched full time, even if they were not. The panopticon is Foucault's metaphor for the contemporary state tactic of implied control.

35. In spite of this level of surveillance, tension remains high at major league ball parks especially after September 11, 2001. Yet, despite increased efforts at crowd control, athletes and coaches have increasingly become targets of fan violence. Twice in a year (in September 2002 and April 2003), fans at Chicago's Comiskey Park inexplicably ran onto the field to attack players and/or coaches of the visiting Kansas City Royals.

36. Willis, *Inside the Mouse* 52–53.

37. In *Amusing the Million,* John Kasson suggests this appeal has been a part of the popularity of urban amusement locations since the beginning of industrialization. Discussing late-nineteenth-century Coney Island roller coasters, he speculates that, for workers who increasingly toiled at large machines, the thrill of using a big machine for frivolous enjoyment would have been tremendous (8).

38. See Rinehart for a discussion of how "spectator sport has become more than a simple observed game between two contestants or two teams" (x). Rinehart suggests that, at the beginning of a millennium, various degrees of "playing" sport have taken on increasing importance in the American psyche.

CHAPTER TWO

Baseball's "Beneficient" Revolution

1. Landecker first gives Spear's summary of the project: "They wanted a beautiful building, but not a 1928 retro ballpark." She then writes affirmatively: "What HOK Sport
gave Cleveland is not a knockoff but a whole new ballgame" (64).
2. See Starr et al. 56–57 for a discussion of these trends.
3. During the Indians' championship years in the late 1990s, Jacobs Field was the only ball
park in the majors to sell out every game shortly after tickets went on sale in the off
season. Although individuals managed to get tickets here and there, for the most part,
one had to either pay a hefty sum to a ticket broker or scalper or buy a full or partial
season-ticket plan in order to see a game. Bleacher tickets in 1998 cost $12 ($19 in
2002). When the 1998 price was multiplied by two (because most people bought tickets in pairs) and again by twenty (in a twenty game package), it came to $480. Add in
$10 to park per game, and $18 per game for two hot dogs ($4 each), two sodas ($4
each), and a program ($2), and the total amounted to over $1,000, or about 7 percent
of the median Cleveland income.
4. In the nineteenth century, and in some cases beyond, a hitter was described this way,
as opposed to the contemporary "at bat."
5. For more on this particular design, the Greensward Plan, see Rosenzweig and
Blackmar 248.
6. Later in the decade, the Central Park Board finally responded to pressure for more
space devoted to active sports by opening part of the North Meadow between 97th and
102d Streets to youth baseball. However, adult baseball games continued to be banned
in the park until the 1920s.
7. Pierre Bordieu in "How Can One Be a Sports Fan?" discusses this kind of change. He
argues that almost all sports originate as anticipatory endeavors before being appropriated and returned to a popular crowd in the form of spectacle. In essence, participants eventually become primarily consumers instead of players.
8. *Brooklyn Eagle,* May 16, 1862, qtd. in Gershman 12.
9. Ibid.
10. See Peiss for a description of the many cheaper amusements available to immigrants
and the working poor.
11. See Nasaw for a discussion of New York saloon culture.
12. See Peter Levine 22.
13. The response to the new affiliation was not all negative. Some players who made the
jump to the new league profited handsomely when well-capitalized owners ignored
previous agreements among NAPBBP teams and paid their stars theretofore-
unmatched salaries. Many fans also favored the new league because it consolidated
talent, producing a good brand of baseball.
14. For more on "neurasthenia" and baseball, see Peter Levine 98–100. See also Lears, "A
Psychic Crisis: Neurasthenia and the Emergence of a Therapeutic World View," in *No
Place of Grace* 47–58.

15. Spalding, qtd. in Peter Levine 24.

16. In the short term, the merger did not end competition. After the formation of the National League, many other comparable leagues continued to exist. Associations like the International League, for example, had teams with players equal in talent to major league clubs.

17. See Rader 118 for a description of how A. G. Spalding used this language to sway public opinion against fledgling player-run leagues,.

18. A few blacks did manage to participate surreptitiously during this sixty-year lockout. For an account of the handful of African Americans or natives of Caribbean islands who were able to pass as Native American or Hispanic, see Peterson 53–73.

19. For a description of PSALs and how they fit into the more widespread "organized play movement" (of which Theodore Roosevelt was the greatest proponent), see Peter Levine 109–12.

20. See Lears, *No Place of Grace* 108–17.

21. See Peterson 19–21.

22. During the week, most games started at around 3:30 P.M., long before day shifts ended. Thus most laborers could not have attended even if they had had sufficient money. Instead, crowds at National League games consisted primarily of clerks and professional men with flexible hours as well as members of the Victorian sporting community (e.g., show people and gamblers). For more on the class makeup of popular leisure pursuits, see Nasaw and Peiss.

23. Spalding 240.

24. Spalding does not give the exact citation for the Mills excerpt. Instead, he introduces the quote as follows: "Ex-President A. G. Mills, of the Washington Olympics, in an article on the subject of the national game, said:" (see 248).

25. Clearly, this kind of hubris was not restricted to the emergent American middle class. Writing about class in 1850s Victorian England, Charles Dickens in *Hard Times* captures this same sentiment in his portrayal of the odious Bounderby, whose constant refrain that he "wasn't raised on turtle soup and venison" echoes the pretensions of Spalding and Mills. Bounderby, like the American baseball owners, believes his status to be a form of election endowing him with inherent energy and vigor, distinguishing him and others like him from the other "peoples of the world."

26. Spalding qtd. in Rader 118.

27. See Peter Levine 58–65 for more on the "war effort."

28. The dynamics of this labor dispute mirror those of the 1998–99 National Basketball Association lockout. In order to force the players' association to renegotiate a more favorable contract, NBA owners locked out players and forced cancellation of about half the season. By all indications, the owners were prepared for (and in some cases even favored) cancellation of the entire season. Propped up by a long-term television contract that paid them even as games were canceled, league owners could have afforded to wait while the players, even though most made over $1 million a year, would have had a hard time recovering lost income.

29. Jackson Lears, discussing a variety of cultural pursuits in *No Place of Grace*, comes to a similar conclusion regarding the false promises of what he calls "the revolution in

spirit." He argues that "the twentieth century's 'revolution in manners and morals' was scarcely a revolution at all." Instead, "justifying the quest for intense experience as a therapeutic release, this 'revolution' eased adjustment to the emerging system of consumer capitalism and bureaucratic 'rationality'" (160).

30. Perhaps Spalding's most successful propaganda campaign in this regard was organized around an international tour of American baseball players in 1888–89. This tour was intended not only to create new markets for his sporting goods business but also to generate a kind of missionary fervor among American baseball fans. Even though he barely broke even on the tour, he and his ballplayers were feted as royalty when they arrived back in New York. In fact, Teddy Roosevelt and Mark Twain both enthusiastically spoke on their behalf at their reception dinner. At this banquet, the president famously claimed that sports "readied a man to do work that counts when the time arises." For more on the tour, see Peter Levine 97–98.

31. See Lears, *No Place of Grace* 108–9.

32. This language comes from chapter 14, descriptively titled "Statement of Causes that Lead to the Formation of the National League—Inability of Former Associations to Correct Demoralizing Abuses, 1875–80."

CHAPTER THREE

Equality versus Authenticity

1. Illustration from October 1865, reprinted in Gershman 15.

2. See Gershman 15. The use of barbed or razor wire was popularized at ball parks during this era. It was promoted as a low-cost way to ensure that only those who paid could watch the game.

3. Ed Doyle, qtd. in ibid.

4. See Gershman 22–23 and 60, and Lieb 18–19.

5. For drawings and photos of the various phases of Sportsman's Park, see Lowry 226–31.

6. The most famous illustration of Von der Ahe depicts him in a drunken stupor sprawled out in his coach, a woman on each knee waiting for him to wake up. See Lieb 6.

7. Spalding turned down this offer.

8. See Peter Levine 97–98.

9. This attack on Von der Ahe was published on February 29, 1896, shortly after the owner had installed some of his most elaborate rides and attractions. For more on Von der Ahe's relationship with Spink, see Lieb 3–26 and Burke 69.

10. See Burke 137 and Lieb 21–22. Interestingly, Burke's and Lieb's versions of the events differ significantly. Whereas Lieb, writing from the perspective of a fan, praises Von der Ahe as a lovable maverick, a father figure who presided over the glory years of the St. Louis franchise, Burke sees him as a demagogic opportunist, more a symbol of opportunistic ownership than true populism.

11. As soon as the league's hostile takeover of the Browns was arranged, the new owner quickly took drastic measures to cleanse Sportsman's Park of its past. The first act

carried out by Robison's administration at the park was the issuance of a sober proclamation: "No beer waiters, peanut vendors or score card boys will annoy patrons during games" (Lieb 24).

12. See Lears, *No Place of Grace* 101–17.

13. Indians vice president Dibiasio is sensitive about claims that Jacobs Field promotes inequality. His language in refuting charges of classism is similar to that of Landecker. "People like to criticize us because they think we only cater to the corporate suit and tie community," Dibiasio notes. "But they're wrong. Yes, we do have luxury suites, but baseball is for everyone."

14. This era is unique in American baseball history. It is perhaps the only time in which the sport attempted to reinvent itself primarily as a modern pursuit. A dramatic symbol of this short-lived break from the past is the trendiest feature to surface during this epoch: Astroturf. Synthetic grass allowed games to be played in space-age indoor domes, enabling baseball to overcome limitations imposed on it by natural forces.

15. Their size is also attributable to the fact that they served as homes to National Football League teams. Football stadiums have historically accommodated, and in fact privileged, size over intimacy.

16. The history of Cleveland Municipal Stadium is somewhat different than that of most other multipurpose parks. It was not built as part of suburban flight. Instead, it was constructed in 1930 by the city in hopes of attracting the 1932 Olympics (eventually awarded to Los Angeles).

17. This fictional office anticipates the new home of the real Indians' management in Jacobs Field built a few years after the film's release. See Bartimole, "Marble Tables" and "Gateway Dines" for descriptions of some of the publicly financed, private amenities of the ball park.

18. The stadium used for filming this movie was actually Milwaukee's County Stadium.

19. Loria's efforts did not gain traction. Montreal voters and government officials refused to commit sufficient public money to finance a ball park, prompting Loria to sell the club to the league, which currently operates the Expos. Loria meanwhile gained ownership of the Florida Marlins, a ball club also currently seeking a new, taxpayer-financed stadium. For years, the Washington, D.C., area was a useful pawn in the chess game that owners played with their respective municipalities. No fewer than six teams, the Padres, Brewers, Astros, Pirates, Twins, and Expos flirted with moving their teams to the nation's capital in order to gain sweetheart stadium deals with their own cities. All but the Twins and Expos were successful in these efforts. Meanwhile, baseball owners, cognizant of the absolute utility of having Washington without a team, held the nation's capital at bay. Rather than sell the Expos to one of the two groups that had lined up financing and tentative stadium deals in D.C. or northern Virginia, the league chose to hold onto the team and make it play about a quarter of its *home* schedule in Puerto Rico. In September 2004, after D.C. promised a taxpayer funded $440 million stadium, the league announced the Expos will move there in 2005.

20. In 1998, nine years after the movie's release, for example, four of the five best teams in baseball were also the wealthiest. The Yankees, who set a modern major league record for wins (both in the regular and post seasons), had the second highest payroll in baseball history.

21. The movie itself represents a last stand of sorts. Its sequel, *Major League II,* released in 1994, elides most of the class considerations that made the first one interesting. This time, the owner is not the embodiment of evil in the film. Instead, it is the players, spoiled by their success and seven-figure salaries, who have lost touch with the passion that enabled them to overachieve in the original. Mirroring the transformation of allegiances within the game itself, the movie pits heckling fans against pampered, spoiled ballplayers. Much like the scene at real stadiums, class resentment gets deflected from the owners to the players. As cynical as its own message, this sequel passes off Baltimore as Cleveland, Oriole Park at Camden Yards as Cleveland Stadium. This makes it much less effective than the original, which at least used another multi-purpose park (County Stadium) for filming. The best part of the first film was its examination of the dynamics of a place in transition—downtown Cleveland and the old stadium. The tension caused by the pressure of the new on the old captured an anxiety central to Cleveland's urban redevelopment. The sequel, on the other hand, is a much-less-complex comedy featuring a series of set pieces and one-liners highlighting the harmless quirkiness of its characters.

22. See White, particularly chapter 1, "The Ballparks," for a good description of the first generation of concrete-and-steel stadiums. See also Gershman and Lowry for facts related to the construction and use of the parks upon which retro stadiums are modeled.

CHAPTER FOUR

Bleachers

1. In *The System of Objects,* Jean Baudrillard discusses the sacredness of churches in ways that seem applicable to retro stadium bleachers. The tour guide's juxtaposition of technology with the old-time simplicity of the bleachers is reminiscent of what the French theorist identifies as two, intertwined, needs of the contemporary worshipper: "It is our fraught curiosity about our origins that prompts us to place such mythological objects, the signs of a previous order of things, alongside the functional objects which, for their part, are the signs of our current mastery. For we want at one and the same time to be entirely self-made and yet be descended from someone: to succeed the Father yet simultaneously to proceed from the Father" (83).

2. On nights when the Indians do not sell out (as has frequently been the case since 2001), the concourse underneath the bleachers is open to all. The JumboTron was surpassed in size by a scoreboard in Detroit's Comerica Park when it opened in 2000.

3. From 1996 to 2000, every ticket sold out prior to the season, requiring most fans to purchase a season ticket or a partial plan or pay a premium to a scalper or ticket broker to attend a game in Jacobs Field.

4. See "Steeling Home," as well as chapters 2 and 3 of this book.

5. See Rader 107–44 for a detailed description of the scene at nineteenth-century sporting events. Also see Nasaw 96–103 for a breakdown of the class and race dynamics of bleacher sections at the turn of the century.

6. *Dictionary of American Slang,* s.v. "bleacher."

7. See Fiske 49–68 for a discussion about the pleasure inherent when marginalized groups produce and share their own meanings. According to the cultural theorist, "popular pleasures arise from the social allegiances formed by subordinated people, they are bottom-up and thus must exist in some relationship of opposition to power (social, moral, textual, aesthetic, and so on) that attempts to discipline and control them" (49).

8. Ironically, the segregating gap between the grandstands and the bleachers at Polo Grounds #4 helped preserve the latter section when the rest of the park was destroyed by fire in 1911. See Lowry 192.

9. See White 10–46 for more on the cultural meaning of these parks.

10. See Golenbock for a commemorative account of the some of the antics of "Dem Bums."

11. Ted Giannoulas, the famous San Diego Chicken, got his start in 1974, when he was paid by KGB radio to don a chicken outfit and hand out eggs at the San Diego Zoo. Five years later, he was brought by motorcade to Jack Murphy Stadium, where he was "hatched" as the mascot of the San Diego Padres. In many respects, Giannoulas's act is the model for contemporary mascots at professional sports arenas around the country.

12. Importantly, Wheeler gives us insight into this form of longing at roughly the same time (1988) that the first retro park, Oriole Park at Camden Yards in Baltimore, was being designed. Clearly, the impulse to look to baseball for an answer to suburban blandness—the impulse which leads Wheeler to spend and entire summer in the Wrigley bleachers—was in the air at the dawn of this new era in stadium construction.

13. See Roland Barthes's famous critique of "The World of Wrestling" in *Mythologies* 15–25. In his essay, Barthes explores the semiotics of professional wrestling, ultimately suggesting that the sport's appeal can be linked to its promise of a completely knowable universe of signs and reference. One symptom of the postmodern condition for Barthes is the fantasy of pure signification, the reactionary nostalgia for a time of racial, class, and ethnic insularity, which seemed to produce absolutes of morality and identity.

14. In *The Way We Never Were,* Stephanie Koontz presents an alternative to Wheeler's nostalgia for the urbanism of the past. She argues that the housing boom of the late 1940s and early 1950s coincided with increased tension among the members of multigenerational American urban households. Oppression caused by the very type of shared cultural and linguistic assumptions romanticized by Wheeler, combined with the sudden abundance of affordable nuclear family housing and reliance on the automobile, generated the impulse toward suburbanization against which Wheeler reacts.

15. Dick Hebdige, in *Subcultures,* claims that the kind of group identification Murphy refuses is often a source of power for members of subcultures. In this respect, Murphy's group could be seen more as an "underworld" than a "subculture." Unlike the "punks" who were the main subjects of Hebdige's book, Murphy's group felt threatened by increased visibility.

16. See Fiske for a discussion of "some of the ways in which the body and its pleasures have been, and continue to be, the site of a struggle between power and evasion, discipline and liberation" (69–70).

17. See Rinehart 1–20 for a discussion of how a blurring of the distinction between playing and spectating is a primary aspect of contemporary sports' appeal.

18. Mantegna's dramatic account of this kind of solidarity based on shared misogynistic animus is echoed by Wheeler's description of the real Wrigley bleachers: "On Easter morning . . . there was a guy wearing a hat bearing the likeness of two female breasts in a bikini top. . . . Another wore a T-shirt with the letters DAMM, which stood for Drunks Against MADD (Mothers Against Drunk Drivers) Mothers" (31).

19. The term "imagineer" comes from Disney. It is what management calls its designers and the others who script the experience at its theme parks. See Huxtable 41–71 for a description of the social costs inherent when urban planners and architects are replaced by "imagineers."

20. Most patrons of Jacobs Field give the stadium a positive review. However, one consistent complaint is that these rings of luxury boxes forced the upper concourse to be constructed at a disconcertingly steep angle in order to provide comfort for Cleveland's corporate classes. For an evolving range of opinions on the experience of attending a game at Jacobs Field, see www.epinions.com.

21. See Morris and Nydahl for a discussion of the effects of instant replay on the sporting experience.

22. This is actually a point of some contention. In chat rooms rating the various ball parks, many fans lament the fact that Jacobs Field seems to suffer from a lack of energy. However, those who have attended marquee match-ups at Jacobs Field (the World Series, Reds games, etc.), contend that, at its best, Jacobs Field is among the loudest parks in the major leagues.

23. Of course, this (or any) attempt to reconstitute a site of what is perceived to be authentic experience is problematic from a purely economic perspective. During the first few years of the park, when the stadium sold out nightly, the actual class status of most bleacher dwellers dramatically limited their ability to exist outside the margins. The cost of attendance excluded many working-class and inner-city Clevelanders.

CHAPTER FIVE

Consuming Blackness

1. The "Now that Spells Relief" commercial for Rolaids antacid, 1990.
2. The character Marlow in Joseph Conrad's 1902 novella, *Heart of Darkness.*
3. For descriptions of racism in the early years of the National League, see Peterson 16–33 and Rader 95–97.
4. During Marshall's time, there were several failed attempts to organize black leagues. In 1887, for example, in an immediate response to the beginning of institutionalized segregation, the League of Colored Baseball Clubs was formed. It soon collapsed, however, falling victim to inadequate and/or undercapitalized management and to the same kinds of cultural barriers handicapping any African American–owned business just a few decades after Emancipation. The Negro Leagues as viable economic entities did not really emerge until the 1920s. For a description of the early years of Negro baseball, see Tygiel 3–180.

5. For more on Public School Athletic Leagues (PSALs) and fundamentals, see Peter Levine 109–12.

6. Robert Lipsyte in the introduction to C. L. R. James's *Beyond a Boundary,* xi.

7. Mackey 52, quoting from Leroi Jones [Amiri Baraka], *Black Music* 66.

8. "Sampling" in contemporary rap music represents a similar artistic strategy.

9. Former barnstormer Newt Allen quoted in Tygiel 21.

10. Stepin Fetchit, born Lincoln Theodore Monroe Andrew Perry, was the best-known and most successful black actor working in Hollywood in the 1930s. Considered the "arch coon" for his popular portrayal of "lazy, no-account, good-for-nothing, forever-in-hot-water," and loved-by-everyone servants, Fetchit draws inevitable comparison to Paige (Bogle 41). Both performers were known for their idiosyncratic body movements and antics. Both were also mythologized for their extravagances and sexual exploits off the field and off screen. Finally, both played to wildly enthusiastic white audiences and, against the odds, became wealthy as a result.

11. Tom Spink in the *Sporting News,* July 14, 1948. Reprinted in Tygiel 229.

12. Rickey interviewed Robinson on August 28, 1945, and offered him the chance to be part of the "noble experiment." That is, he promised him a chance to play provided the player vowed not to fight back in response to racial slurs and attacks.

13. ESPN, in its 1999 *SportsCentury* retrospective, chose Ali as the third greatest athlete of the twentieth century, behind Michael Jordan and Babe Ruth.

14. The snatch catch was similar in terms of its technical unorthodoxy to the way that longtime Giants center fielder Willie Mays caught pop flies using an underhanded basket catch. Mays is widely considered among the top three or four defensive center fielders in the history of the game.

15. See Verducci 76 for this quotation and others like it.

16. See Bogle 35–45 for a description of how African Americans in early Hollywood film made subtly subversive the roles of "coons" and "toms" (in effect, the only roles available at the time). In discussing Stepin Fetchit, Bogle argues that the actor cleverly opened up the possibility of more patently powerful roles for blacks.

17. After considering retirement at forty-four, Henderson made another successful run at the majors. In 2003, he first signed with the minor league Newark Bears before finishing the season with the Los Angeles Dodgers.

18. For further discussion of white ambivalence toward race, see Bhabha.

19. For a discussion of contemporary white youth consumption of black culture, see Jones. While his focus is on reggae in working-class and mixed-raced urban England, the writer is very clear about the role of black culture in the lives of young white Americans: "The cultural needs and aspirations of many young whites in the early 1950s had gone largely unfulfilled by a mainstream entertainment industry unequipped to register the changing patterns of leisure consumption in post-war American society. . . . Various social groups have championed and 'borrowed' [American black music's] oppositional meaning to signify their 'non-conformity' with the cultural mainstream" (xxi–xxiii).

20. Fisk set major league baseball's all-time record for most games caught with 2,226. He retired in 1993.

21. *SportsCenter* is the network's sporting news program and is shown several times daily.
22. Cameron Crowe directed *Jerry Maguire* (TriStar Pictures, 1996). Ron Shelton directed *White Men Can't Jump* (Twentieth Century Fox, 1992).
23. In the film, this treatise is provocatively titled "The Things We Think and Do Not Say."
24. The rap song on the stereo is "The Wrong Came Up," by L.V.
25. See Starr et al. 57.
26. In the five years immediately prior to the Dodgers' 1958 exodus, the move that shocked the nation, multiethnic Brooklyn had been home to the most prosperous franchise in the major leagues. Nonetheless, owner Walter O'Malley, wary of increasing ethnic and racial tension, cognizant of the rising importance of the automobile, and, quite simply, looking for a better deal, claimed that Ebbets Field was beyond repair. The home of "Dem Bums" seated only thirty-five thousand spectators, had parking spaces for only seven hundred cars, and, most important, was located in what O'Malley believed to be a decaying neighborhood.
27. Since 1987, the league's record has been more encouraging. In 1993, Bob Watson became the first black general manager in baseball, and shortly thereafter, four African Americans were hired as managers. Also in 1993, the league commissioned the Equal Opportunity Committee, which has since helped facilitate a significant number of minority hires in administrative positions. By 1997, nonplayer, off-the-field minority employment was at 22 percent. Nonetheless, at the highest levels of administration, the gains are relatively insignificant. By the end of the decade, Watson remained the only general manager of color in the league and qualified African Americans were being routinely passed over for managerial jobs. During the year preceding the Robinson dedication, nine managerial jobs changed hands. Yet each new position was filled by a non-Latino white. Additionally, no African Americans owned ballclubs and very few held organizational vice president positions. For more on race in contemporary baseball, see Starr et al. 56–57 and Weinstock 93–95.
28. Of course, numbers like this were not lost on management. In response to these alarming figures, the Braves immediately hired a "multi-cultural marketing manager" who, by pitching ticket deals to black churches and colleges and by including an occasional promotion targeting black patrons, was able to bring the number up to 8 percent. Yet while this percentage is better than the major league average, it is still paltry considering that the city is 60 percent African American.
29. At a recent midsummer series with the Anaheim Angels, an unofficial sample revealed that approximately 96 percent of spectators were white.
30. Berndt Ostendorf's ideas about the role of minority culture are relevant here. In *Black Literature in White America,* he writes, "Lower class folk in Western society and blacks among them, have served the dominant classes in two ways: first in setting up the material basis of high civilization, second in healing the injuries of that civilization by maintaining alternative life styles and cultures" (77–78).
31. Chief Wahoo, whose face still appears on Indians' caps, is an animated Indian, a trickster figure with a devilish grin, a cardinal red complexion, and a single feather in his cap. He is cousin to a hundred of years of racist Anglo depictions of Native Americans. In

fact, his visage is remarkable similar to that of Funnyface, George Tilyou's mascot from Coney Island's original Steeplechase Park. For a picture and criticism of Funnyface, see Kasson 60.

32. Slider's trick is reminiscent of Italian stripper-turned-parliamentarian Ciciolina's signature "doccia d'oro," or "golden shower." The climax of this famous erotic dance calls for Ciciolina to urinate on front-row audience members.

33. Tony Manero is the main character in the 1977 feature film *Saturday Night Fever,* which popularized the erstwhile underground disco craze. In *Hearts of Men,* Barbara Ehrenreich discusses Manero's panic about being seen as a "physically-striving man." The character, she argues, is a sign of the times insofar as he runs away from working-class identity in exactly the opposite way that men today, regardless of actual class status, run toward it. Barney is the purple dinosaur from children's television and video who looks a little like Slider. Lady Chablis is the African American transvestite who made a splash flirting with John Cusack in the 1997 film *Midnight in the Garden of Good and Evil.* Finally, Smalls was a popular "Gangsta" rapper prior to his shooting death in 1997.

34. Slider is so popular among young Indians fans that the ball club has had to hire two actors to portray him. When not performing at the stadium, he is routinely double-booked for children's birthday parties.

35. Most contemporary critics since Bahktin no longer discuss carnival as something that has been eliminated from modern life. Instead, like Stallybrass and White, they note the displacement of the "carnivalesque" onto bourgeois cultural forms like Slider. See "Bourgeois Hysteria and the Carnivalesque."

36. The term "welfare queen" was of course popularized by Ronald Reagan to suggest that black women, living easily off the largess of Aid to Families with Dependent Children, were responsible for the country's massive debt and economic downturn. Over approximately five years, the president told a largely unfactual story about a "Chicago Welfare Queen" who bilked the government out of over $150,000. For the most comprehensive description of corporate welfare for sports franchises, see Rosentraub, *Major League Losers.*

CHAPTER SIX

Retro Parks in the City of the Instant

1. For example, Robert Baade analyzed thirty-two metropolitan areas that had experienced a recent change in the number of professional sports teams and found that thirty of them had shown no significant relationship between the presence of teams and overall revenue growth.

2. See Rinehart 3–18 for a discussion of sports spectating and collection.

3. On September 20, 2001, George W. Bush addressed a joint session of Congress and the American people for the first time since the September 11 terrorist attacks. In his speech, he said, "Americans are asking, 'What is expected of us?'" His reply was simply, "I ask your continued participation and confidence in the American economy." In

response to this plea, entrepreneurs nationwide began to organize "freedom shopping sprees." Mitch Goldstone of Irvine, California, for example, arranged a five-thousand-shopper pilgrimage to New York City, calling it "a moral imperative, not to spend a little more but to spend *a lot* more" (MacDonald, 1).

4. In the tenth inning of game six of the World Series on October 25, 1986, Red Sox first baseman Bill Buckner let a routine ground ball slip between his legs, opening the door for one of the most memorable rallies in baseball history. The Mets went on to win the game and then the series in seven games.

5. "X" paraphernalia is commonly thought to refer simply to Malcolm X, whose image was popularized in the 1990s for a younger generation in part by Spike Lee's 1992 hit movie *Malcolm X*. In fact, nostalgic "X" baseball hats also immortalize the Cuban X Giants baseball team, an independent pre–Negro League team based in New Jersey from 1897 to 1907 and primarily composed of Cuban Giants defectors. One of the most successful early Negro teams, the X Giants won the 1903 Colored World Championships. The name resurfaced in the 1930s as a winter barnstorming club.

6. The preponderance of televisions of course also allows spectators to spend more time at the food court and in Wahoo World without having to miss any of the game.

7. *Rashomon* is director Akira Kurosawa's 1950 avant-garde film in which four different characters give competing narratives of a rape-murder in which they participated.

8. For a description of theorist Linda Hutcheons's use of the term "historical metafiction," see Duvall 287.

9. For more on the "city of the instant," see Virilio and Lotringer 87.

10. For Baudrillard's discussion of this precession of simulacra, see *Evil Demon* 13.

11. This need to offer "instant history" is taken to extreme levels on ESPN Classic. A spin-off of the popular ESPN sports network, ESPN Classic regularly offers viewers "instant classics." These games, remarkable for their well-played nature or thrilling finishes, are often repackaged and replayed as "classics" the same week they were contested.

12. British romantic poet John Keats coined the term "negative capability" in 1817 to describe his belief about the type of receptivity necessary to create great poetry. "Negative Capability," he wrote to his brothers in a letter dated December 22, 1817, "is when man is capable of being in uncertainties, Mysteries, doubts, without any irritable reaching after fact and reason." See Drabble 689.

13. Most discussions of "aura" begin of course with Benjamin. In "The Work of Art in the Age of Mechanical Reproduction," he discusses how the technology of mechanical reproduction has completely revolutionized the way viewers look at and judge artistic objects. Allowing for consumption without the presence of the original shifts the central ingredient of the experience from ritual to politics. "That which withers in the age of mechanical reproduction," he notes, "is the aura of the work of art" (220). See also Orvell for a discussion of the relationship between mediating technology in America and the early-twentieth-century cult of authenticity.

14. In *Players All*, Rinehart describes the "Been There, Did That" philosophy of tourism as a response to a "highly commoditized and standardized, mass-produced society." He argues that a tourist's proud display of the "Been There, Did That" slogan on a sweatshirt was "protestation that his attitude toward the best the world had to offer was

within his control; that as an individual, he could collect and classify experience, rather than having experience collect and classify him" (2).

15. For more on the phenomenon of edge cities, see Garreau.

16. See Muschamp, "Remodeling New York for the Bourgeoisie," and Boddy, "Underground and Overhead." See also Hannigan 189–200 for a discussion of the cultural ramifications of privatizing public space.

17. Hannigan sees Nye's description of "riskless risk" as the essence of Fantasy City, Hannigan's name for contemporary urban entertainment destinations appropriating "various foreign cultures and domestic subcultures" and rendering them sanitized and safe (71).

18. Virilio and Lotringer qtd. in Redhead 62.

19. Mike Davis is one of the most influential and critical voices in this regard. In both *City of Quartz* and *Ecology of Fear*, he suggests a relationship between social injustice and questionable planning practices in Los Angeles.

20. The Arizona Diamondbacks who began play in 1998 are one of major league baseball's two newest teams along with the Tampa Bay Devil Rays. They play their games in futuristic, retractable-roof Bank One Ballpark. This new stadium features a swimming pool in the outfield, scores of luxury boxes on its mezzanine, and an anachronistic dirt path from the pitcher's mound to home plate to remind visitors of nineteenth-century diamonds, which for largely unknown reasons included that characteristic.

21. To Baudrillard, Americans have the greatest access to mediating technology and are thus most responsible for making the world seem increasingly hyperreal. When, for example, he argues that the "Gulf War did not take place," he of course means for the bulk of its American spectatorship watching it at home on television in the United States. For those Iraqis and American soldiers who died during the conflict and in its horrible aftermath (when the surgical bombing stopped yet millions were left without clean water for years), the conflict was very real. In 2003, during the second Gulf War, "embedded" journalism, bringing selected images of the war live to American living rooms, reinforced the notion that television has been able to make the violence of contemporary life at once more intimate and remote.

22. From *The Virtual Illusion*, qtd. in Redhead 62–63.

23. After a prolonged battle that stirred up anticorporate passions among working-class followers of Manchester United, Murdoch's bid to buy the team was forbidden by England's Monopolies and Mergers Commission in April 1999. Ultimately, the Australian businessman had to settle for 9.9 percent of the team, which, as of 2003, was valued at approximately half a billion dollars.

24. Murdoch clearly started a trend among media giants. Several others followed and bought sports franchises during the late 1990s. However, in the slow economy of the early years of the new millennium, most of these companies are currently trying to unload them or have already done so. Disney sold off the 2002 world champion Anaheim Angels in April 2003, AOL Time Warner sold its NBA Hawks and NHL Thrashers in September 2003, and News Corp. sold the Dodgers in January 2004.

25. For more on how Murdoch's purchase of the Dodgers signaled a new era of corporate ownership, particularly by media conglomerates, see Bruck.

26. In "Why Baseball," Rosentraub makes this very argument. He suggests that, despite New York Yankee owner George Steinbrenner's insistence that the ball club would need to attract three million fans per season to remain profitable, the Yankees' large broadcast contracts ensure profitability even if the stadium remains empty night after night. He sees Steinbrenner's argument as a form of blackmail, attempting to either increase ticket sales or get the city of New York to finance a new ball park in downtown Manhattan.

27. Major League Soccer (founded in 1996) was quick to recognize this, almost immediately deciding to "downsize" stadiums during televised matches. MLS teams literally cover large sections of their stadiums with cloth murals, sacrificing some ticket sales in order to make the stadium look more full for its television audience and increase the commodity value of an individual ticket.

28. A few years ago, some minor league park managers even experimented with printing advertisements on hot dogs using nontoxic, colored dyes. Smacking of sacrilege, this effort at achieving a captive audience was not very well received by fans and was discontinued. Nonetheless, MLB continues to experiment with efforts to achieve a more captive audience. In the spring of 1999, for example, owners agreed in principle to change the bylaws of the league, allowing for advertisements on uniform sleeves.

29. In *Fever Pitch,* Nick Hornsby's memoir describing his lifelong obsession with London's Arsenal Football Club, the writer makes a similar argument. Describing the problems associated with rising ticket prices in English stadiums, he suggests that eliminating the working-class rowdies in the stands behind the goals would ultimately be a "parasitical" move in that it would extinguish the very "atmosphere" that wealthier patrons pay to experience: "These huge ends are as vital to the clubs as their players, not only because their inhabitants are vocal in their support, not just because they provide clubs with large sums of money (although these are not unimportant factors) *but because without them nobody else would bother coming*" (77).

30. For example, Chelsea's Stamford Bridge Stadium in southwest London, long one of the roughest parks in the English league, was remodeled in 2001 to incorporate two hotels, five restaurants, a fitness center, and a science museum.

31. At the time this book was going to press, the Red Sox finally overcame the curse of the Bambino by defeating their nemesis, the New York Yankees, in an unprecedented way. They came back from a three game deficit in the American League Championship series then swept the St. Louis Cardinals to win their first World Series since 1918.

32. For a discussion of the desire among advertisers to promote their products as "new and improved," see Vattimo 74.

EPILOGUE

1. In Wilde's novel, the titular character appears to remain young while his portrait ages.
2. US Hair, Rainbow, Lee's Beauty Supply, and Hair Plus are discount retailers remaining on the block.
3. Kawkaby notes that British Petroleum stayed in its forty-floor downtown building just a few years before moving to Chicago and taking hundred of hungry employees who used to patronize his restaurant with them.

BIBLIOGRAPHY

Angell, Roger. "Box Score." *New Yorker* 73, no. 4 (1997): 5–6.

Baade, Robert. *Heartland Policy Study No. 62*, "Stadiums, Professional Sports, and Economic Development: Assessing the Reality." Chicago: The Heartland Institute, Apr. 4, 1994.

Bale, John. "The Stadium as Theatre: A Metaphor for our Times." In *The Stadium and the City*, edited by John Bale and Olof Moen, 311–22. Staffordshire: Keele Univ. Press, 1995.

Bahktin, Mikhail. *The Dialogic Imagination: Four Essays*. Translated by Caryl Emerson and Michael Holquist. Austin: Univ. of Texas Press, 1981.

Barron, Kelly. "P.C. Nostalgia." *Forbes*, Oct. 20, 1997, 48.

Barthes, Roland. *Mythologies*. Translated by Annette Lavers. New York: Noonday Press, 1972.

Bartimole, Roldo. "Who Really Governs." *Point of View*, 25 Years of Cleveland Mayors special issue (1991):1–16.

——. "Jacobs: City's Welfare Burden." *Point of View* 20, no. 14 (1988):1–4.

——. "Stadium Campaign. Pee Dee Distorts." *Point of View* 22, no. 17 (1990) :1–4.

——. "Boyle, Hagan Dance." *Point of View* 24, no. 10 (1992) :1–4.

——. "The Cleveland Corporates." *Point of View* 26, no. 3 (1993) :1–4.

——. "County Faces $300-million Debt. Gateway Cost: $750,000,000." *Point of View* 26, no. 15 (1994) :1–4.

——. "Gateway Dines on Taxpayers." *Point of View* 26, no. 20 (1994) :1–4.

——. "$600,000 Gund Gateway Apartment." *Point of View* 28, no. 2:1–4.

——. "Pander!" 28, nos. 9 and 10 (1996) :1–8.

——. "Marble Tables at the Jake." *Point of View* 29, no. 12 (1997):1.

——. "Modell and the Stadium: A Brief, Instructive History." *Cleveland Free Times*, Feb. 15, 1995.

——. "A Selective Renaissance." *Cleveland Free Times,* Oct. 12, 1994.

——. "Cleveland Vultures." *Cleveland Free Times*, Oct. 2, 1996.

——. "Playing Rent Hardball." *Cleveland Free Times*, Nov. 20, 1996.

——. "Buying Opinions." *Cleveland Free Times*, Feb. 19, 1997.

——. "Gund Fighters." *Cleveland Free Times*, Mar. 12, 1997.

——. "Finally—Jacob Pays." *Cleveland Free Times*, Dec. 23, 1996.

——. "The Robber Baron Pays (Low) Rent." *Cleveland Free Times*, Nov. 6, 1996.

——. "Scary Figures." *Cleveland Free Times*, Oct. 18, 1995.

——. "Two Faces of Cleveland." *Cleveland Free Times*, June 15, 1994.

———. "Doing Gateway Up Right." *Cleveland Free Times*, July 21, 1993.

Basquiat. Dir. Julian Schnabel. Perf. Jeffrey Wright, David Bowie, Dennis Hopper, Gary Oldman, Christopher Walken, Willem Dafoe, Courtney Love. Miramax Films. 1996.

Baudrillard, Jean. *The Evil Demon of Images.* Sydney: Power Institute of Fine Arts, 1987.

———. *America.* London: Verso, 1988.

———. *The Transparency of Evil: Essays on Extreme Phenomena.* London: Verso, 1993.

———. *Simulacra and Simulation.* Univ. of Michigan. 1994.

———. *The Gulf War did not take place.* Translated by Paul Patton. Bloomington: Indiana Univ. Press, 1995.

———. *The System of Objects.* London: Verso, 1996.

———. "The Virtual Illusion: On the Automatic Writing of the World." In *Theory, Culture and Society* 12, no. 4 (1995):97–107.

Beard, George Miller. *American Nervousness. Its Causes and Consequences.* New York, 1881.

Benjamin, Walter. "The Work of Art in the Age of Mechanical Reproduction." In *Illuminations*, translated by Harry Zohn and edited by Hannah Arendt. New York: Schocken Books, 1976.

Berkman, Dave. "Long Before Arledge . . . Sports & TV: The Earliest Years: 1937–1947—as Seen by the Contemporary Press." *Journal of Popular Culture* 22, no. 2 (1988): 49–62.

Berlage, Gai Ingham. *Women and Baseball: The Forgotten History.* Westport, Conn.: Praeger-Greenwood Publishing Group, 1994.

Bhabha, Homi. "The Other Question: The Stereotype and Colonial Discourse." *Screen* 24, no. 6 (1983): 18–36.

"Big Mac All Alone with 62." *Daily Progress*, Sept. 9, 1998. p. C1.

Boddy, Trevor. "Underground and Overhead: Building the Analogous City." In *Variations on a Theme Park*, edited by Michael Sorkin, 123–53. New York: Hill and Wang, 1992.

Bogle, Donald. Toms, Coons, *Mulattoes, Mammies, and Bucks: An Interpretive History of Blacks in American Films.* New York: Viking, 1973.

Bordieu, Pierre. "How Can One Be a Sports Fan?" In *Cultural Studies Reader*, by Pierre Bordieu, 427–40. Routledge: New York, 1993.

Boswell, Thomas. "Nothing Accounts for Expense." *Washington Post*, Dec. 31, 1997, p. D1.

Boyer, Christine. "Cities for Sale: Merchandising History at South Street Seaport." In *Variations on a Theme Park: The New American City and the End of Public Space*, edited by Michael Sorkin, 181–203. New York: Hill and Wang, 1992.

Brady, James. "Great Day in Cleveland." *Advertising Age* 66, no. 23 (1995): 22.

Bruck, Connie. "The Big Hitter: R. Murdoch Seeks to Buy the Los Angeles Dodgers from P. O'Malley." *New Yorker*, Dec. 8, 1947, 82–93.

Burke, Robert F. *Never Just a Game: Players, Owners, and American Baseball to 1920.* Chapel Hill: Univ. of North Carolina Press, 1994.

Bull Durham. Dir. Ron Shelton. Perf. Kevin Costner, Susan Sarandon, Tim Robbins, Max Patkin. 1988.

Cagan, Joanna, and Neil deMause. "A Tale of Two Cities" *Nation*, Aug. 10, 1998, 24.

Caro, Robert A. *The Power Broker: Robert Moses and the Fall of New York.* New York: Vintage Books, 1974.

"Chris' Circus and Side Shows." Cartoon. *Sporting News*, Feb 29, 1896.

Clark, VéVé, and Cindy Patton. "Performing the Memory of Difference in Afro-Caribbean Dance: Katherine Dunham's Choreography, 1938–87." In *History and Memory in African-American Culture*, edited by Geneviéve Fabre and Robert O'Meally, 188–204. Oxford: Oxford Univ. Press, 1994.

Coontz, Stephanie. *The Way We Never Were: American Families and the Nostalgia Trap*. New York: BasicBooks-HarperCollins, 1992.

Crawford, Margaret. "The World in a Shopping Mall." In *Variations on a Theme Park*, edited by Michael Sorkin, 3–29. New York: Hill and Wang, 1992.

Davis, Mike. *Ecology of Fear: Los Angeles and the Imagination of Disaster*. New York: Metropolitan Books, Henry Holt, 1998.

———. *City of Quartz: Excavating the Future in Los Angeles*. London: New York: Verso, 1990.

Denby, David. "The Contender." *New Yorker*, Apr. 20, 1998, 60–71.

DeLillo, Don. *Libra*. New York: Penguin, 1988.

———. *Underworld*. New York: Scribner's, 1997.

Dickens, Charles. *Hard Times*. Penguin: New York, 1961.

Drabble, Margaret, ed. *The Oxford Companion to English Literature IV*. Oxford: Oxford Univ. Press, 1985.

Donovan, Erin. "Nostalgia and Tourism: Camden Yards in Baltimore." In *Myth, Memory and the Making of the American Landscape*, edited by Paul A. Shackel, 220–39. Gainesville: Univ. Press of Florida, 2000.

Dubbert, Joe L. *A Man's Place: Masculinity in Transition*. Englewood Cliffs, N.J.: Prentice-Hall, 1979.

Duvall, John N. "Baseball as Aesthetic Ideology: Cold War History, Race." *Modern Fiction Studies* 41 (1995): 285–314.

Early, Gerald. "Performance and Reality: Race, Sports, and the Modern World." *Nation*, Aug. 10, 1998, 11–20.

Eco, Umberto. *Travels in Hyperreality*. Orlando: Harcourt Brace and Company, 1986.

Edwards, Richard Henry. *Popular Amusements*. 1915. Reprint, New York: Arno Press, 1976.

Ehrenreich, Barbara. *The Hearts of Men: American Dreams and the Flight from Commitment*. New York: Doubleday, 1983.

Fiske, John. *Understanding Popular Culture*. London: Routledge, 1989.

Foucault, Michel. *Discipline and Punish: The Birth of the Prison*. Translated by Alan Sheridan. New York: Vintage, 1977.

Freud, Sigmund. "Beyond the Pleasure Principle." In *The Freud Reader*, edited by Peter Gay, 594–626. New York: W. W. Norton, 1989.

Fukuyama, Francis. "The End of History?" *National Interest* 16 (Summer 1989): 3–18.

Garreau, Joel. *Edge City: Life on the New Frontier*. New York: Doubleday, 1991.

Gershman, Michael. *Diamonds: The Evolution of the Ballpark*. Boston: Houghton Mifflin, 1993.

Gilmore, Al-Tony. "Black Athletes in an Historical Context: The Issue of Race." *Negro History Bulletin* 58, no. 3 (Oct–Dec. 1995): 7–14.

Gildea, William. "Power Propels Game to Glory: Homer Race Lured Folks Back and They Found a Lot to Like." *Washington Post*, Apr. 2, 1999, p. H3.

Goldberger, Paul. "The Rise of the Private City." In *Breaking Away: The Future of Cities: Essays in Memory of Robert F. Wagner Jr.*, edited by J. Vitullo Martin, 135–50. New York: Twentieth Century Fund, 1996.

Golenbock, Peter. *Bums: An Oral History of the Brooklyn Dodgers*. New York: G. P. Putman's Sons, 1984.

Goodwin, Doris Kearns. *Wait Till Next Year: A Memoir*. New York: Simon & Schuster, 1997.

Gore, Albert. *The Best Kept Secrets in Government: How the Clinton Administration Is Reinventing the Way Washington Works*. New York: Random House, 1996.

Hall, Stuart. "Brave New World." *Socialist Review* 21 (1991): 57–64.

Hannigan, John. *Fantasy City: Pleasure and Profit in the Postmodern Metropolis*. London: Routledge, 1998.

Harden, Blaine. "Yankees Find Cheer in the Cheap Seats. Run at Baseball History Intensifies Raucous Lobe Affair with Fans." *Washington Post*, Aug. 4, 1998, p. A1.

Harvey, David. "Flexibility: Threat or Opportunity?" *Socialist Review* 21 (1991): 65–78.

Heath, Thomas. "O's Raise Ticket Prices, Announce '98 Schedule." *Washington Post*, Dec. 20, 1997, p. F1.

———. "Lucky Fan Caters to McGwire, History." *Washington Post*, Sept. 8, 1998, p. D6.

Hebdige, Dick. *Subculture: The Meaning of Style*. Routledge: New York, 1979.

Hooks, Bell. "Representing Whiteness in the Black Imagination." In *Towards the Abolition of Whiteness: Essays on Race, Politics, and Working Class History*, edited by David R. Roediger, 338–46. New York: Verso, 1994.

Hornsby, Nick. *Fever Pitch*. New York: Riverhead Books, 1992.

Huxtable, Ada Louise. The *Unreal America: Architecture and Illusion*. New York: New Press, 1997.

James, C. L. R. *Beyond a Boundary*. New York: Pantheon Books, 1984.

Jameson, Frederic. *The Ideologies of Theory: Essays, 1971–1986*. Vol. 2, *The Syntax of History*. London: Routledge, 1988.

———. *Postmodernism: or the Cultural Logic of Late Capitalism*. Durham, N.C.: Duke Univ. Press, 1995.

Jerry Maguire. Dir. Cameron Crowe. Perf. Tom Cruise, Cuba Gooding Jr., Renee Zellweger, Kelly Preston. Tristar, 1996.

Johnson, Chuck. "City, Indians Combine Comebacks: New Ballpark at Heart of Downtown's Rebirth." *USA Today*, Oct. 21, 1997, p. 4C.

Jones, LeRoi. *Black Music*. New York: Wm Morrow, 1967.

Jones, Simon. *Black Culture, White Youth: The Reggae Tradition for JA to UK*. London: Macmillan Education, 1988.

Kasson, John. *Amusing the Million: Coney Island at the Turn of the Century*. New York: Hill and Wang, 1978.

Kauffman, L. A., Billy Robinson, and Michael Rosenthal. "Post-Fordism: Flexible Politics in the Age of Just-in-Time Production." *Socialist Review* 1 (1991): 53–56.

Koontz, Stephanie. *The Way We Never Were: American Families and the Nostalgia Trip*. New York: Basic Books, 1992.

Landecker, Heidi. "New Ballpark Opens in Cleveland." *Architecture: The AIA Journal* 83, no. 6 (1994): 35.

———. "Steeling Home." *Architecture: The AIA Journal* 84, no. 4 (1995): 64–69.

Lears, T. J. Jackson. *No Place of Grace: Antimodernism and the Transformation of American Culture, 1880–1920*. New York: Pantheon Books, 1981.

———. "No There There." *New York Times Book Review*, Dec. 28, 1997, pp. 9–10.

Levey, Bob. "Will Scalpers Spoil the New MCI Center? Not If There's a Scalp-Free Zone." *Washington Post*, July 18, 1997, p. E1.

Levine, Marc. "Downtown Redevelopment as an Urban Growth Strategy: A Critical Appraisal of the Baltimore Renaissance." *Journal of Urban Affairs* 9, no. 2 (1987): 103–23.

Levine, Peter. *A. G. Spalding and the Rise of Baseball: The Promise of American Sport*. New York: Oxford Univ. Press, 1985.

Lieb, Frederick G. *The St. Louis Cardinals: The Story of a Great Baseball Club*. New York: G. P. Putnam's Sons, 1944.

Lott, Eric. *Love and Theft: Blackface Minstrelsy and the American Working Class*. New York: Oxford Univ. Press, 1993.

———. "White Like Me: Racial Cross-Dressing and the Construction of American Whiteness." In *Cultures of United States Imperialism*, edited by A. Kaplan and D. Pease, 474–95. Durham, N.C.: Duke Univ. Press, 1993.

Lowry, Philip J. *Green Cathedrals: The Ultimate Celebration of All 271 Major League and Negro League Ballparks Past and Present*. Reading, Mass.: Addison-Wesley, 1992.

MacDonald, Jeffrey G. "This Christmas, Some See Virtue in Buying Sprees." *Christian Science Monitor*, Dec. 5, 2001, p. 1.

Macintosh, R. Scott. "Vine Street Rumblings." *Down Beat* 64, no. 12 (1997): 12–13.

Mackey, Nathaniel. "Other: From Noun to Verb." *Representations* 39 (1992): 51–70.

Mailer, Norman. *The Armies of the Night*. New York: New American Library, 1968.

Malcolm X. Dir. Spike Lee. Perf. Denzel Washington, Spike Lee, Al Freeman. United International Pictures, 1992.

Major League. Dir. David S. Ward. Perf. Tom Berenger, Charlie Sheen, Corbin Berenson, Rene Russo, Wesley Snipes. Morgan Creek Productions, 1989.

Major League II. Dir. David Ward. Perf. Tom Berenger, Randy Quaid, Corbin Berenson. Morgan Creek Productions, 1994.

Mantegna, Joe. *Bleacher Bums: A Nine-Inning Comedy*. New York: Samuel French, 1977.

Masters, Brooke A. "Taking Team Names to Court: Indians Logos Face Legal Challenges Across U.S." *Washington Post*, Apr. 7, 1999, p. B1.

Mayer, Margit. "Politics in the Post-Fordist City." *Socialist Review* 21 (1991): 105–24.

McGraw, Dan. "A Brand-new Blueprint for Baseball." *U.S. News & World Report*, June 3, 1996, 51.

"McGwire Ties Maris with 61st HR. St. Louis Slugger Needs Just One Homer to Set New Record." *Daily Progress*, Sept. 8, 1998, p. C1.

"McGwire Ties 37-Year Home Run Record." *Daily Progress*, Sept. 8, 1998, p. A1.

"McGwire Connects for 63rd Homer." *Daily Progress*, Sept. 18, 1998, p. C1.

"McGwire's Gear Already on Display." *Daily Progress*, Sept. 11, 1998, p. C3.

Melville, Herman. "Bartleby." *Billy Budd and Other Stories*. New York: Penguin, 1986.

Mitchel, S. Weir. *Wear and Tear; or, Hints for the Over Worked*. Philadelphia, 1887.

Morris, Barbara S., and Joel Nydahl. "Sports Spectacle as Drama: Image, Language and Technology." *Journal of Popular Culture* 18, no. 4 (1985): 101–10.

Muschamp, Herbert. "Remodeling New York for the Bourgeoisie." *New York Times*, Sept. 24, 1995, p. 2-1.

Nasaw, David. *Going Out: The Rise and Fall of Public Amusements*. New York: Basicbooks, 1993.

Naymik, Mark. "Spin City." *Cleveland Free Times*, Sept. 14, 1994.

Noll, Roger, ed. *Government and the Sports Business*. Washington, D.C.: Brookings Institution, 1974.

Nye, Russell. "Eight Ways of Looking at an Amusement Park." *Journal of Popular Culture* 15 (1981): 63–75.

Orvell, Miles. *The Real Thing: Imitation and Authenticity in American Culture, 1880–1940*. Chapel Hill: Univ. of North Carolina Press, 1989.

Ostendorf, Berndt. *Black Literature in White America*. New Jersey: Harvester, 1982.

Ozanian, Michael K. "Selective Accounting." *Forbes*, Dec. 14, 1998, pp. 124–34.

Patton, Cindy. "Embodying Subaltern Memory: Kinesthesia and the Problematics of Gender and Race." In *The Madonna Connection: Representational Politics, Subcultural Identities, and Cultural Theory*, edited by Cathy Schwichtenberg, 81–105. Boulder: Westview Press.

———. "White Racism/Black Signs: Censorship and Images of Race Relations." *Journal of Communication* 45, no. 2 (1995): 65–77.

Peiss, Kathy. *Cheap Amusements: Working Women and Leisure in Turn-of-the-Century New York*. Philadelphia: Temple Univ. Press, 1985.

Peterson, Robert. *Only the Ball Was White: A History of Legendary Black Players and All-Black Professional Teams*. New York: McGraw-Hill, 1970.

Pope, Steven P. "American Muscles and Minds: Public Discourse and the Shaping of National Identity During Early Olympiads, 1896–1920." *Journal of American Culture* 15, no. 4 (1992): 83–94.

Rader, Benjamin. *American Sports: From the Age of Folk Games to the Age of Spectators*. Englewood Cliffs, N.J.: Prentice-Hall, 1983.

Redhead, Steve. *Post-Fandom and the Millennial Blues: The Transformation of Soccer Culture*. London: Routledge, 1997.

Rinehart, Robert E. *Players All: Performances in Contemporary Sport*. Bloomington: Indiana Univ. Press, 1998.

Robertson, K. A. "Downtown Redevelopment Strategies in the United States: An End-of-the-Century Assessment." *Journal of the American Planning Association* 61, no. 4 (1997): 429–37.

Rogin, Michael. *Black Face, White Noise: Jewish Immigrants and the Hollywood Melting Pot*. Berkeley and Los Angeles: Univ. of California Press, 1996.

Rosenthal, Pam. "Jacked In: Fordism, Cyberpunk, Marxism." *Socialist Review* 21 (1991): 79–104.

Rosentraub, Mark. *Major League Losers: The Real Cost of Sports and Who's Paying for It*. New York: Basic Books, 1997.

————. "Why Baseball Needs New York to Just Say No." Nation, Aug. 10, 1998, 20–26.

Ross, Andrew. "Getting the Future We Deserve." *Socialist Review* 21 (1991): 125–50.

Rothberg, Peter. "Lockout!" *Nation*, Aug. 10, 1998, 32.

Rosenzweig, Roy. *Eight Hours for What We Will: Workers and Leisure in an Industrial City,* 1870–1920. Cambridge: Cambridge Univ. Press, 1983.

Rosenzweig, Roy, and Elizabeth Blackmar. *The Park and Its People: A History of Central Park*. Ithaca: Cornell Univ. Press, 1992.

Rushkoff, Douglass. *The GenX Reader*. New York: Ballantine Books, 1994.

"The Same Only Different." *Sports Illustrated*, Nov. 3, 1997, 22.

Sanders, Scott Russel. *Staying Put: Making a Home in a Restless World*. Boston: Beacon Press, 1993.

Scodellaro, Nadine M. "Get 'em While They're Hot (and Still Standing): Cherishing Baseball's National Treasures." *Discovery* 34, no. 2 (1994): 22–26.

Shapiro, Leonard. "A Lot of Green Helps Moss Grow Rapidly." *Washington Post*, Nov. 25, 1998, p. E4.

Sidro, A. *Le Carnaval de Nice et ses Fous*. Nice: Éditions Serre, 1979.

Smith, Claire. "Fewer Blacks Follow Robinson's Baseball Lead." *New York Times*, Mar. 30, 1997, sec. 1, p. 1.

Sorkin, Michael, ed. *Variations on a Theme Park: The New American City and the End of Public Space*. New York: Hill and Wang, 1992.

Soja, Edward. *Postmodern Geographies*. New York: Verso, 1989.

Spalding, Albert G. *America's National Game: Historic Facts Concerning the Beginning, Evolution, Development and Popularity of Base Ball*. 1911. Reprint with an introduction by Benjamin G. Rader. Lincoln: Univ. of Nebraska, 1992.

Stallybrass, Peter, and Allon White. "Bourgeois Hysteria and the Carnivalesque." In *A Cultural Studies Reader*, 382–90. New York: Routledge, 1993.

Starr, Mark, Todd Barrett, and Vern E. Smith. "Baseball's Black Problem." *Newsweek*, July 19, 1993, pp. 56–57.

Stewart, Susan. *On Longing: Narratives of the Miniature, the Gigantic, the Souvenir, the Collection*. Baltimore: Johns Hopkins Univ. Press, 1984.

Thoreau, Henry David. Walden. In *The Writings of Henry David Thoreau*, vol. 3. New York: Houghton Mifflin, 1906.

Tygiel, Jules. *Baseball's Great Experiment: Jackie Robinson and His Legacy*. Oxford: Oxford Univ. Press, 1983.

Vattimo, Gianni. *The End of Modernity: Nihilism and Hermeneutics in Postmodern Culture*. Translated by Jon R. Snyder. Baltimore: John Hopkins Univ. Press, 1988.

Verducci, Tom. "What Is Rickey Henderson Doing in Newark?" *Sports Illustrated*, June 23, 2003, 76.

Vick, Karl, and Thomas Heath. "After Bumpy Beginning, a Can't-Be-Beat Ending." *Washington Post*, Sept. 15, 1997, p. A1.

Virilio, Paul, and Sylvere Lotringer. *Pure War*. New York: Semiotext(e), 1983.

Voigt, David Q. *America Through Baseball*. Chicago: Nelson-Hall, 1976.

Walker, Alice. "Advancing Luna—and Ida B. Wells." In *You Can't Keep a Good Woman Down*, 85–104. New York: Harcourt Brace Jovanovich, 1983.

Weinstock, Jeff. "Blacked Out." *Sport* 83, no. 3 (1992): 93–95.

Wheeler, Lonnie. *Bleachers: A Summer in Wrigley Field*. Chicago: Contemporary Books, 1988.

White, G. Edward. *Creating the National Pastime: Baseball Transforms Itself, 1903–1953*. Princeton: Princeton Univ. Press, 1996.

White Men Can't Jump. Dir. Ron Shelton. Perf. Wesley Snipes, Woody Harrelson, Rosie Perez, Billy Hoyle. Tristar, 1992.

Wilbon, Michael. "With Class, Old-School Sosa Offers Lessons in Sportsmanship." *Washington Post*, Sept. 11, 1998, p. C1.

Wilde, Oscar. *The Picture of Dorian Gray*. In *The Complete Works of Oscar Wilde*, edited by J. B. Foreman, 17–167. New York: Harper and Row, 1989.

Williams, Raymond. *Culture and Society*, 1780–1950. New York: Columbia Univ. Press, 1983.

———. The Country and the City. Cambridge: Oxford Univ. Press, 1973.

Willis, Susan, ed. *Inside the Mouse: Work and Play at Disney World*. Durham, N.C.: Duke Univ. Press, 1995.

———. "I Want the Black One: Is There a Place for Afro-American Culture in Commodity Culture?" *A Primer for Daily Life (Studies in Culture and Communication)*. New York: Routledge, 1991.

Zukin, Sharon. *The Culture of Cities*. Cambridge, Mass.: Blackwell, 1995.

INDEX

Retro Ball Parks was designed and typeset on a Macintosh computer system using QuarkXPress software. The body text is set in 8.25/12.5 Leawood and display type is set in Memphis. This book was designed and typeset by Barbara Karwhite and manufactured by Thomson-Shore, Inc.

the political economy surrounding the
construction of downtown ball parks,
which have emerged as key components
of urban entertainment-based development. Blending economic and cultural
analysis, he considers the intersection of
race and class in these new venues. For
example, he shows that African American
consumers in the commercial district
around Jacobs Field have largely been
replaced by symbolic representations of
African American culture, such as piped-in
rap music and Jackie Robinson replica
jerseys. He concludes that the question
of authenticity, the question of what it
means to simultaneously commemorate
and commodify the past in retro ball
parks, mirrors larger cultural issues
regarding the nature and implications of
urban redevelopment and gentrification.

THE AUTHOR:

Daniel Rosensweig is a professor in
the Bachelor of Inter-disciplinary Studies
Program at the University of Virginia.
Visit www.retroballparks.com for more
information.

Jacket design: Barbara Karwhite
Jacket illustration: Jacobs Field and downtown
Cleveland from the upper deck. Photograph
by the author.